T0327657

Precious
Metals
Trading

Founded in 1807, John Wiley & Sons is the oldest independent publishing company in the United States. With offices in North America, Europe, Australia, and Asia, Wiley is globally committed to developing and marketing print and electronic products and services for our customers' professional and personal knowledge and understanding.

The Wiley Trading series features books by traders who have survived the market's ever changing temperament and have prospered—some by reinventing systems, others by getting back to basics. Whether a novice trader, professional, or somewhere in-between, these books will provide the advice and strategies needed to prosper today and well into the future.

For a list of available titles, visit our web site at www.WileyFinance.com.

Precious Metals Trading

How to Profit from Major Market Moves

PHILIP GOTTHELF

WILEY

John Wiley & Sons, Inc.

First Edition, *The New Precious Metals Market*, McGraw-Hill, 1998, 0786308400.

Library of Congress Cataloging-in-Publication Data:

ISBN-13 978-0-471-71151-3
ISBN-10 0-471-71151-9

10 9 8 7 6 5 4 3 2 1

*Dedicated to the memory of my late father,
Edward B. Gotthelf, who has inspired
countless investors with his unique
perspectives on the markets*

Contents

Introduction

Not long ago, gold and silver played primary monetary roles in the world's economies. From about the mid-nineteenth century through 1975, these metals regulated global money supplies. Humanity has placed faith and trust in noble metals for thousands of years. Through the ages, we have exchanged goods and services for pieces of silver and judged the wealth of kings in terms of gold. Even when we became sophisticated enough to realize paper was easier to handle than coin, we continued to back paper currency with metal. Yet, after years of loyal service as our means of exchange, gold and silver fell from grace within a decade. From 1975, when gold ownership by U.S. citizens became legal again, through 1985, when prices failed to recover from a spectacular rise and fall, precious metals generally lost their investment luster.

By the 1990s, venerable newspapers dropped gold as an economic indicator. Silver was reduced to being just a commodity. The degree to which the world turned its back on these metals astounded those who lived through the first half of the twentieth century. At the same time, paper assets created unprecedented wealth. From surging fixed-income returns occurring during the 1980s to a raging bull equities market in the 1990s, paper truly became king while traditional stores of value like hard assets and real estate proved unworthy of consideration.

On August 3, 1995, I signed a contract to produce a book about the precious metals markets (*The New Precious Metals Market*; McGraw-Hill, 1998). At that time, gold and silver were languishing after long periods of unimpressive investment performance. Having tracked gold since it was legalized in 1975, and silver well before that, I was intrigued by the growing consensus that precious metals were fading as investment assets. I had a strange sense that gold, silver, platinum, and palladium retained unique qualities as trading vehicles. I was astonished that investors were not recognizing that changes in dynamics between currency and monetary metals like silver and gold held enormous profit potentials. Investors simply needed a new perspective.

A friend asked, "Why write about precious metals if their investment role is lost? What purpose is a review if new financial vehicles and strategies have taken over?" When I wrote the Introduction to that book, my answer was that we needed a well-founded explanation for silver and gold's lack of investment performance from 1980 through 2001. I maintained that facts were clouded by emotional interpretations and self-serving reports. I wanted investors to consider that during the gold and silver price declines of the 1980s, "gold bugs" insisted a new bull market was just around the corner. Little negative news came from industry groups. In the face of static performance, gold and silver received constant advocacy to the point of crying wolf. Despite a steady rise in production, we heard the world constantly faced a shortage—exactly what die-hard bulls wanted us to believe.

Reality painted a different picture. In the aftermath of the 1980 peaks, metals yielded to surging interest rates and a massive anti-inflation effort. Suddenly, interest rates offered returns well in excess of inflation. Passive strategies like buying and holding bonds proved surprisingly profitable. At the same time, mining capacity was building rather than shrinking. Demand for base metals translated into secondary silver and gold production. Platinum recovery and refinement etched away at a rising demand curve. Effectively, supply was meeting demand. The move away from precious metals was a wise decision. The paper chase was on.

Yet, interwoven within this negative reality, I pointed out that tremendous profit opportunities still existed. For example, palladium supply and demand were precariously close from 1986 through 1996. This balancing act set the stage for major bull and bear trends. Indeed, the fortification of demand with any new application such as debunked cold-fusion energy production or the disruption of demand by either Russia or South Africa could easily send palladium soaring above $1,000 per ounce. I recall critiques of the earlier book chuckling over such a high price forecast in light of palladium's price range from only $150 down to a paltry $115 in 1996. (See Figure I.1.)

Sure enough, demand fundamentals were firming because the palladium-to-platinum price ratio favored using palladium over platinum. Europe was rapidly adopting more stringent auto emission standards. Palladium prices rallied from below $200 in 1998 to around $320 in 1999's last quarter. Then, Russia began limiting palladium exports in 2000. As the limitation of Russian supplies became an export suspension, prices exploded from approximately $320 per ounce to a walloping $1,080 from July 1999 to January 2001. So, the "impossible" became a reality and I was vindicated. Assuming a ride from bottom to top, the gross move was worth $76,000 per contract with average brokerage house margins under $1,500 per position.

I must confess that my personal interaction with this price event was unexpected and unprecedented. In 1989, a friend and business associate

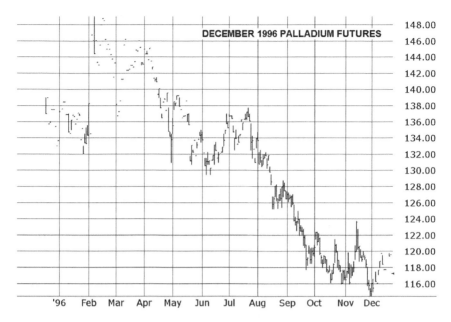

FIGURE I.1 The 1996 price range for palladium gave no evidence that a major bull move could take place. Prices dropped from $150 per ounce to less than $115. (*Source:* eSignal Futuresource workstation)

of mine, Robert P. Regan, joined me in a venture to mint one-ounce and half-ounce palladium medallions based on the speculative prospects of cold fusion. Our logic was simple. If cold fusion became a reality, the medallions would become the most valuable of all precious metals. Alternatively, the palladium would always retain some value, albeit greater or less than the original purchase price.

Initially, sales were modestly brisk. Unknown to us, newspapers were selective and restrictive about coin dealer advertisements because of the possibility of fraudulent schemes. We were barred from widespread advertising just when the palladium debate was heating up. Alas, we found ourselves sitting atop of hundreds of medallions with no marketing channels or advertising means. Making matters worse, cold fusion was rejected as junk science and palladium prices plunged. Ouch!

Regardless, our initial sales provided us with a breakeven. Hence, we were not horrifically upset about being stymied in our continuing sales efforts. With palladium distributed throughout my house, Bob and I decided we would wait for another selling opportunity. You can imagine that when palladium moved above $400 per ounce, it caught our attention.

I called Bob to suggest that we might sell the medallions and simply make a profit on the metal as opposed to the collector's item. He agreed and I investigated channels for selling. Since we had stamped the palladium into medallions, it needed to be reconstituted as bullion. Fortunately, the mint we used was recognized and our certification of .9995 pure palladium content was acceptable to dealers. By the time my initial investigation was completed, palladium prices had risen to $600 per ounce—how nice.

Our best offer came from a Delaware company called FideliTrade Incorporated. One of its representatives informed us that we would need to open an account to sell the physical metal. By that time, prices exceeded $700. It seemed timing could not have been better. In fact, Bob and I wondered whether we should hold on to our inventory until the market showed signs of a break. Prudence ruled over emotion and we fell back on our conviction to sell while the selling was good. Once the account was opened, I gathered our inventory, packaged it, and shipped it to FideliTrade via registered and insured mail. (See Figure I.2.)

By the time the metal arrived, palladium had climbed above $800. Wow! But it gets better. Days later, I discovered that I had not placed a sell order for the metal. By the time I placed the order and it was executed, Palladium reached $1,050 an ounce. The top was $1,075. I would like to boast that I was responsible for catching the top of palladium, but the execution was circumstantial. Still, it was a remarkable experience and worthy of publication.

In addition to my actual palladium experience, I predicted that platinum was vulnerable to the same supply dislocation. Like palladium, platinum production and consumption were delicately balanced. In 2003, platinum was subjected to a supply squeeze just as it was being exchanged for the formerly expensive palladium. By April 19, 2004, platinum futures prices reached an impressive $954 per ounce. (See Figure I.3.)

Delightfully, other predictions made in the original book came to fruition. These included the price ranges for silver and gold as well as the circumstances under which each would rally outside of predicted ranges. Options strategies detailed in this text were used in actual trading before and after the original publication date and I am proud to say that the results have been consistently outstanding.

In 1988, I appeared on the *Today Show* with Jane Pauley to explain that silver was facing hard times. Chile and Peru were increasing production while filmless photography posed a threat to the number one industrial application for the white metal. I predicted that silver could easily fall below $5 per ounce. It did.

When the first book was printed, filmless photography was renamed digital photography and the first mainstream still-shot digital cameras

FIGURE I.2   Once the balance between supply and demand was tipped by restricted Russian sales, palladium soared above $1,000 per ounce as originally predicted. (*Source:* eSignal Futuresource workstation)

were making their way into the market. The book predicted an eventual demise of silver-based photography and an associated decrease in silver demand. As most of us have seen, digital pictures have achieved the quality and advantages necessary to displace conventional photography.

My forecasts for consolidation among mining companies also came true as economies of scale created incentives to expand through acquisitions. Names were, indeed, consolidated, and the trend is likely to continue into the future.

In all, the original book was actually bid up beyond its original retail price when the first printing ran out just as precious metals markets were heating up in 2003–2004. Even with renewed enthusiasm for precious metals and significant developments like 9/11 and the war on terror, the original premise remains the same. Precious metals markets are evolving, and traditional perspectives will not necessarily apply to future situations and developments. The fact that digital photography has made progress and will continue to advance exemplifies the evolutionary process and proves the need to consistently reevaluate investment potentials for precious metals as a group and individually.

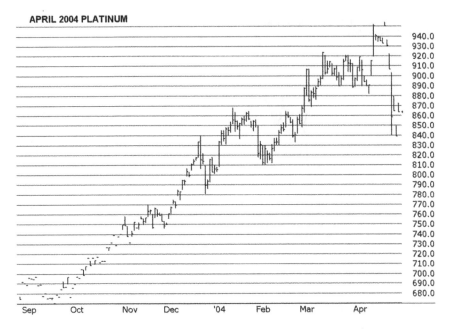

FIGURE I.3 With deficit supplies versus demand, platinum staged an interim rally similar to palladium beginning in 2003 and extending through 2004. (*Source:* eSignal Futuresource workstation)

WHY DID PRECIOUS METALS TARNISH?

It is important to explore fundamental supply and demand changes that drove the dynamic duo of gold and silver to unthinkable lows in the face of continuing inflation through the 1980s and 1990s. As mentioned, gold and silver are vulnerable to technological progress and changing investment moods. Therefore, gold and silver are not always the most appropriate investment vehicles. In fact, precious metals may not offer the best hedges against inflation nor do they necessarily reflect deflation. The monetary delinking of gold and silver dulled their luster, and it is not likely we will see polish from any relinkage in the near future. So this book addresses these issues as objectively as possible.

With such a perspective, a new age of precious metals investing in a new market has emerged that also requires explanation. Technology is changing the way we mine and use precious metals. In fact, the entire precious metals market structure has been changing. Fundamentals related to supply and demand are different. Monetary systems are different. Political systems have changed. There are new investment vehicles that include derivatives, currency futures and options, interest rate futures and options, and more. Strategies must be redefined. These are reasons for a book about modern precious metals investing. The chapters ahead explore traditional roles of silver, gold, and industrial precious metals like platinum and palladium. The book takes a broad and comprehensive view of supply and demand, answering the critical questions, Should you invest and/or speculate in precious metals? If so, what are the best ways?

From 1980 through the first half of the 1990s, I was an outspoken precious metals bear. On CNBC, NBC, and the CNN television networks, I predicted silver would fall from $6.50 an ounce in 1988 to less than $4.00 over the next several years. In the face of one inflation prediction after another, I held fast to my belief that silver would not regain its footing and gold would not manage a long-awaited rally. The reasons were simple. An objective look at supply patterns revealed increasing production with static consumption. This reality did not stand alone. In addition to expanding supplies, gold and silver truly decoupled with currency parity as the world became increasingly comfortable with floating exchange rates. In other words, currency was no longer compared with gold or silver to derive a relative value against other currencies. The global monetary system had confidence in a floating exchange that could be easily traded like commodities in the foreign exchange or "Forex" market.

The original book was released prior to the introduction of the euro currency. The consolidation of major European currencies into a single currency unit further diminished the assumed relationship between gold and currencies because the treaty under which the euro was established foreclosed using gold as a "reserve asset." Thus, gold could no longer act as a store of wealth for Europe's participants in the euro. Of course, currency consolidation could eventually lead to some reintroduction of metallic valuation, as we discuss in Chapter 12.

When viewed as commodities, currencies fluctuate in accordance with their own supply and demand forces. If the euro were to gain strength against the U.S. dollar, traders can move from dollars into euros. Where is gold? Who needs gold? Periods of inflation seem to be selective and regional, illustrated by the U.S. Federal Reserve's removal of food and energy from its inflation assessments. Now, investors can maneuver from an inflating currency into another more stable currency. In the old days, gold and silver were used to offset effects of rising and falling interest rates. In the early 1980s, new markets like Ginnie Mae futures, Treasury-bond futures, interest rate options, and a host of other derivative vehicles diminish requirements for hard asset hedges. The list has expanded to include the London Interbank Offered Rate (LIBOR), two-year and five-year notes, and even municipal bonds. In a rising interest rate environment, traders can sell interest rate derivatives like futures and options. As rates retreat, futures and options can be purchased. Simply put, the roles of gold and silver were displaced through financial invention.

The Information Age

In the wings, rapid information dissemination and processing also took a toll on gold and silver. Prior to the information age, convention dictated moving into precious metals when uncertainty needed to be sorted out. While investors waited for facts and interpretations, gold and silver were comfortable places to store wealth. When the information age arrived, the uncertainty hedge dissipated. We had facts faster. We could analyze impact more easily. If there are any doubts about the influence of information processing on investment markets, correlate the decline in silver and gold with the rise of the personal computer. Consider that new derivative financial vehicles would not be possible if computers were not available to rapidly and accurately calculate values and extrapolate relationships.

In an earlier book, *Techno Fundamental Trading*, I touched on "synthetic investing." That book was published in 1995. Within a year, synthetic investing had expanded into "cyber investing." Investments could be created from information. An index could become a contract. A contract could be exchanged. It could all take place on the Internet in cyber markets—paid for with cyber money in cyber transactions. It seemed the status of gold and silver would continue to deteriorate. After all, you could bring up a pretty good picture of precious metals on a web site. Perhaps we can even have the sensation of touching, holding, or wearing gold in "virtual reality." Who needs the real thing?

Responding to this move into cyberspace, I now caution that instability is inherent in the system. A data glitch or program failure can bring cyber markets crashing down. It is certain that gold and silver are real; virtual reality isn't. As we move away from reality, will we need reality? At what point will we question the validity of cyber cash or even dollar bills? As technology races forward, it will be easier to produce $100 bills complete with embedded coding strips on a high-resolution color printer. Forged holograph imprints will be no problem. What's real? Who will know for sure? Your credit cards, voice, fingerprints—everything used for transactions—will be vulnerable to technological tampering in the wrong hands. Where will we place our trust as technology advances? Perhaps we will be forced to return to our old standards. As one Generation Xer said, "Gold's cool."

PRECIOUS METALS BASICS

Although examining new market developments is intriguing, a text on precious metals investing is not complete without reviewing basics. Yes, cyberspace is fascinating, but what are gold, silver, platinum, and palladium, and where do these metals come from? How are they used? Why are they valuable? Do we consume silver, platinum, and palladium as opposed to gold? What technologies will expand or contract precious metal consumption? How might computers replace platinum as a means for cleaning engine emissions? Will new engines eliminate the need for catalytic converters? How much platinum do we use each year for these catalytic converters? The basics are important if we are to profit from precious metals in the years ahead.

As rapidly as technology is advancing, so is political change. Again, we can thank information technology for much of the globalization process that has torn down barriers and constructed new political incentives that can drive precious metals. Consider that the majority of the gold and silver hoard is stored in central bank vaults. These metals remain political assets. If there has truly been a divorce between money and the sibling metals, the message has not been fully accepted by central banks. Even today, treasuries are not too keen on the idea of selling precious metal inventories, a process referred to as *divestment*. What is the significance of global gold reserves? What are the important influences gold reserves have upon investment strategies? Alone, explorations of silver and gold politics can fill several books.

To appreciate the big picture, this book briefly explores geology, mining, refining, and applications of these metals. How do copper prices affect silver, gold, platinum, and palladium? What about other base metals like nickel, tin, zinc, lead, and iron? Can fusion and fission technology dictate precious metal prices? What about religion, population, demographics, and education? Can we be conditioned to abandon gold and silver? Can we be taught that these are simply metals like all others? Is there a master plan?

Finally, this book considers strategies. How can you invest in precious metals? Why should you invest? When should you invest? Are stocks better than physical metal? What about futures and options? Should you consider rare coins, medallions, and coin of the realm? What is the significance of face value?

Does it all sound interesting and exciting? Let's get started!

CHAPTER 1

What's All the Fuss About?

THE LURE OF PRECIOUS METALS

"Good as gold," "silver lining," "platinum record"—these familiar expressions are all references to supreme value. It is not a coincidence that precious metals are interwoven into concepts of value, good fortune, and accomplishment. Examine each metal, one by one.

Gold

See it. Hold it. Move it from hand to hand and bring it up to the light. If you have ever seen and held an ingot of pure 24-karat gold you know it is not just a commodity. There is something fascinating about this metal. I believe it truly has mystical powers over human emotions. When I was 12 years old, I visited the Federal Reserve vault in New York City to see the so-called backing for the U.S. currency. Gold and silver were still linked to the money supply. It was illegal for private U.S. citizens to own bulk quantities of gold. There it was. Bricks of gold lay before me in absolute glowing splendor. I was excited. I was moved! After all, I was being raised on stories of pirates and treasure rather than *Bevis and Butthead* or *South Park*. My father told me about spending gold. He gave me a $5 gold piece just before my visit to the vault. Gosh, it was fun. I'll never forget it. Perhaps that is why gold has held a unique place in the hearts and minds of men and women. It is the world's most beautiful metal by any standard.

Years after my visit to the New York Federal Reserve, I was invited into the vault of a private bullion dealer. It was just after the U.S. gold prohibition had been lifted in 1975. Although the quantity I saw there was not as impressive as that in the New York Federal Reserve, I was invited to lift the pure ingots. Some readers will understand when I say the weight-to-size ratio is astounding. We all may know gold is one of earth's heaviest elements. Yet, to lift a gold brick with a grunt or feel a hand-sized ingot that weighs a more than two pounds is totally unexpected, enlightening, and exhilarating. There is simply nothing like it. No matter how unemotional you may want to be toward this metal, a personal encounter with gold in bulk is a profound experience for most of us.

Virtually every society holds gold as a symbol of value. Whether it has been demonetized by governments and central banks or is remonetized, gold maintains a parity relationship with all the world's currencies. Simply put, gold is a fact of human existence and I doubt we will ever mature to the point where we all consider it just a commodity.

From the time I had my personal encounter to the hours I spent writing this book, I have always enjoyed my gold craving. This is not to say that I am a "gold bug." In fact, from 1980 through the turn of the millennium/century, I was more of a bear than a bull. Still, the craving persisted like a sugar junkie trying to give up chocolate. I love to see and feel pure gold ingots. It's delightful. It's fascinating. It is awe-inspiring. The effect gold has on people is its very salvation. Reality suggests that gold has limited usefulness beyond its perceived value. Industrial demand, although extremely important, is fractional in relation to investment demand. It is said that most of the gold mined throughout history is accounted for today. Very little gold is totally consumed. Most is stored and sometimes worshiped.

Silver

Turn your attention to silver. Although silver may be less mouthwatering to some, you need only see a proof-struck coin to understand how silver rose to reverence. With its mirror complexion and white sparkle, silver represents the perfect complement to gold. Together, silver and gold form a complete picture. If you don't believe me, make an effort to view polished gold and silver side by side. I doubt you could honestly say you had absolutely no urge to own a bit of each.

From my first birthday through my teens, I had an uncle who sent me one silver dollar each year—one for my first year, two for my second, and so on. Every so often, I would go into my closet and take out the thick cotton bag with a reddish brown drawstring that safely held my silver stash. Although it was hardly appropriate treatment for the venerable coins, I enjoyed clinking them into a small pile. (I admit that I polished one even after being told it would adversely affect its value.) Like gold, silver has an

Silver dollars surround U.S. $10 and $20 gold pieces.

innate appeal. Maybe this is because of its reflective properties. Perhaps it is the ring when a silver coin is dropped just right. It is a lustrous metal that beautifully applies to eating and serving utensils, jewelry, mirrors, and ornaments.

At dawn, the sky lights up with a fiery golden hue. In the evening, the moon reflects a silvery pattern on an ocean, a lake, or a bay. Gold and silver are the most inspiring colors in nature. If you disagree, examine our literature. Study the history. Nothing on earth short of life itself has been more revered than gold or silver. That's what the fuss is about.

Platinum

Of course, the family is not really complete. Platinum joins silver and gold with its appealing bright and deep silvery shine. The weight and uncanny hardness add to the attraction. This is a difficult metal to refine. It is relatively new in our history, yet it has made remarkable inroads as a supreme value. Platinum has character all to itself. As we will examine, this metal along with its sisters palladium and rhodium can claim unique chemical properties. Unlike gold, with its stability and noble physical properties, the platinum group is reactive. Platinum's tight molecular lattice provides catalytic capabilities for small-molecule compounds like hydrocarbons. Platinum is a valuable industrial commodity with vast applications and irreplaceable functions.

Platinum's unique color and resistance to oxidation have elevated it to the highest standard for jewelry. Most importantly, platinum's hue blends more attractively against pronounced skin color, which makes it desirable in Asian countries and the Indian subcontinent. Platinum jewelry demand in China and Japan as well as India have created an important price influence that rivals jewelry demand for gold.

Given the current rarity of platinum group metals in combination with increasing uses in industry and personal ornamentation, there is an important role for platinum in any precious metals investment strategy.

Palladium

The trio of gold, silver, and platinum represented the precious metals group for most of the twentieth century. Yet palladium is an important member of the platinum group and enjoys expanding popularity. Until 1989, palladium remained relatively obscure. Its first real public appearance came with the announcement of cold fusion by two University of Utah professors in March of that year. Palladium was hailed as the potential source of clean, cheap, limitless energy. Prices surged from less than $100 to more than $180 per ounce. When cold fusion was condemned as fraud and folly by the scientific community, palladium prices promptly plunged to a low under $78 per ounce. However, an impression was made.

Very modest interest in cold fusion continues and may eventually result in a commercially feasible process using palladium. Later chapters review this potential in greater detail. In the aftermath of the initial cold fusion fiasco, palladium gained other respectability as a substitute for platinum in automotive and truck catalytic converters. This is not to say that cold fusion was the reason palladium was used for catalytic applications. It is to say that the news gave rise to more palladium awareness.

Palladium also gathered momentum with the explosive growth in electronic components, dental alloys, and chemical processes. As we will review, technology trends and environmental concerns are a driving force behind demand for this metal.

Rhodium

Are you familiar with rhodium? With the exception of exotic and forbidden metals like purified uranium and plutonium, rhodium has held some of the most spectacular values per ounce of any precious metal. Rhodium saw prices above $7,000 per ounce in the 1980s. It is vital for certain processing technologies and is essential in the three-way catalytic converter. When you consider a metal that can vary more than $4,000 an ounce, you are looking at the ultimate speculative precious metal—for now.

Unfortunately, as of this writing, rhodium can be traded only as a cash commodity. There are no futures contracts or exchange-traded options for rhodium. This dearth means investors cannot use leverage to participate in rhodium trading. In addition, it is difficult to buy rhodium if you are not a dealer or user. In short, rhodium is not an easy investment.

ORIGINS OF PRECIOUS METALS

In addition to examining precious metals investing, it is helpful to understand the metals themselves. What is gold? Where did it come from? Is there some cosmic reason why it is so rare and intriguing? Similar questions apply to silver, platinum, and palladium. To appreciate their place in our universe, we must go back in time to the very beginning of matter. Most of us are aware of the big bang theory. It postulates that our universe and all within it formed in a huge cosmic explosion billions of years ago. Obviously, this massive event involved enormous heat and energy that we are just beginning to comprehend through advanced nuclear physics. In reality, we have very little understanding about the origins of matter. The world's greatest minds are still pondering the forces that bind the universe together. Scientists continue searching for a universal theory that explains how and why the cosmos in its entirety functions. You may hear about new unified field theories and perfect symmetry. Eventually, someone will get it right. However, this book focuses on the formation of the elemental chain or periodic table, which is reasonably established through observation.

The first element was hydrogen, the building block of all elements and first on the periodic table with an atomic weight of 1.008. Hydrogen is the primary fuel of the galaxies. It is believed that huge hydrogen clouds condensed under gravity in the early universe. As these massive clouds contracted, enormous pressures began building until hydrogen fused into helium. This process powers most visible stars.

Stellar fusion does not end there. Throughout billions of years, all of a star's hydrogen is eventually fused into helium. Because helium is a denser element, greater forces build up, causing helium to fuse into lithium. As elemental fusion climbs up the periodic table, a star implodes to the point where forces cause an explosion or a black hole. If a star explodes into a nova or supernova, there is a chance it will be reborn.

This is believed to be the process that formed our own sun. The debris or stardust is thought to be the origin of planets. In effect, everything in our physical world is stardust. It stands to reason that the higher the element is on the periodic table, the later its evolution in the fusion process. In addition, it seems logical that the fusion process in higher elements did not last as long as primary reactions. Thus, many higher elements on the table are also more rare. As a percentage of matter in the universe, gold and the platinum group are among the smallest. Not only are these metals rare on earth, it is reasonable to assume they are rare throughout existence. Having established this fact, we might conclude that precious metals truly have a universal appeal if scarcity is a primordial determinant of value. Not only would humankind value these metals, so might any other civilizations sprinkled throughout the universe.

WHY PRECIOUS METALS ARE PRECIOUS

Of course, the positions of precious metals on the periodic table are not their only basis for value. Virtually all precious metals exhibit extraordinary properties that establish value based on function. Moreover, from an earthly viewpoint, gold, silver, and the platinum group are uniquely deposited throughout the globe. Mining and refining processes are difficult. Discovery is tedious. Recovery is expensive. All of this adds to the allure of precious metals. As later chapters explain, each metal has a vital industrial or monetary role.

Eventually, technology or invention can displace usage. By the same token, technology or invention can create new roles and applications. There are strong indications that precious metals may account for political and monetary power at some point in the future. Control over these metals may represent control over government and society. I can assure even the most skeptical reader that my personal love affair with precious metals is shared by most of the world's populations. The psychological attraction binding us to precious metals defines their primary role. Ownership is a sign of power. Power is a means to dominate. For now, humans are an aggressive species. This implies that power and dominance will continue as our motivation throughout the twenty-first century and beyond. If gold, silver, and platinum group metals gain monetary or industrial significance, those who own will be those who lead. This is what the fuss is about.

If you are a citizen of the industrialized West, your perspective is probably much different from that of a citizen of the Far East, Middle East, or India. Throughout most cultures, gold is as much a symbol as a monetary standard. Consider the simple wedding band: a symbol of love, dedication, and a contract between husband and wife. The ring may weigh only a few grams and have a purity of less than 14 karats. Yet when multiplied by the number of married couples, these small items can amount to robust annual demand that expands with the overall population. More importantly, from 1972 forward, liquidity and wealth began more rapid expansion in regions where a wedding can call for as much as a kilo of gold among even lower classes.

As later chapters detail, liquidity, population, and tradition are likely to dictate the next major gold trends. This will be extremely important as investors decide which precious metals offer speculative opportunities. Only gold carries the extensive ritualistic significance that can define demand.

To a lesser extent, silver can perk up as weddings increase. We are all familiar with Grandma's silver service. Unfortunately, convenience and the fast pace of modern living have tarnished the tradition of "bringing out the silver." Few within the general population have the time or inclination to set a proper table, let alone polish the silver. It is possible for tradition to come full circle. At some point, we may return to elegant and formal dining with appropriate sterling silver settings. However, the current trend points to a declining number of brides registering for silver services. Thus, it is unlikely silver can count on an increase among global populations to the same extent as gold. Some may argue that silver's future lies in its primary industrial application: photography. As global populations become more sophisticated and wealthy, demand for photographic records will grow. More importantly, we should see a steady rise in demand for professional photography, X-ray, and photolithographic printing. Travel, a new baby boom, emerging newspapers and magazines, upgraded health care— the list of positive factors for silver goes on and on.

Of course, not every cloud has its silver lining. Technology, which gave silver its industrial life, could soon take a toll on the so-called white metal. Computer imaging and digital photography loom on the horizon as the greatest threat to as much as 30 percent of all annual silver production. As decreasing photographic demand for silver accelerates, can new technologies absorb the slack? Applications that include silver biostatic properties and electrical conductivity may eventually dwarf photography as the primary industrial application for silver. For investors, the question is, "When?"

It is interesting that precious metals are among the least understood investments. Perhaps this is because few people are aware of historical roles for these elements. Even the most sophisticated investors may harbor distorted views of how gold and silver have been used over the centuries. Essentially, the view of precious metals may be clouded by all the fuss. Is it surprising to learn that gold and silver have played very brief roles as global monetary instruments? Is it shocking to find that precious metals have not performed well as long-term investments? Is it unimaginable to discover that precious metals are among the weakest hard-asset performers?

Understand that much of the modern-day fuss about precious metals was spawned by only two events. First was the gold rush that began in the western United States in 1849. This was the first inspiration for a dramatic increase in gold supply since the discovery and early exploration of the New World. Although many Americans narrowly believe the gold rush was limited to the United States, those with a more general knowledge are aware that the event circled the globe and lasted through 1920. (In fact, there is a gold rush today.)

The second great event was the post–energy crisis inflation of the 1970s that pushed precious metals to unthinkable heights and threatened to unravel our trust in the global monetary system. Silver approached $50 an ounce (See Figure 1.1). Gold reached levels above $800 (See Figure 1.2). Platinum soared to $1,000 an ounce, and palladium blasted beyond $400.

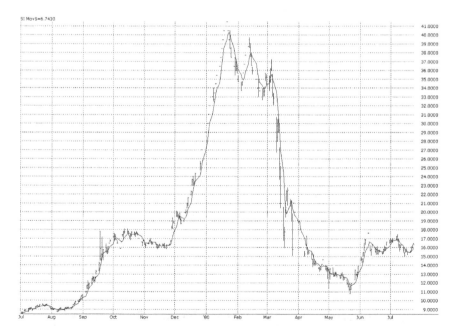

FIGURE 1.1 Silver made its most memorable move of the twentieth century during 1979–1980. Inflation fears and a speculative scheme by the Hunt brothers drove prices to spectacular levels. (*Source:* eSignal.com)

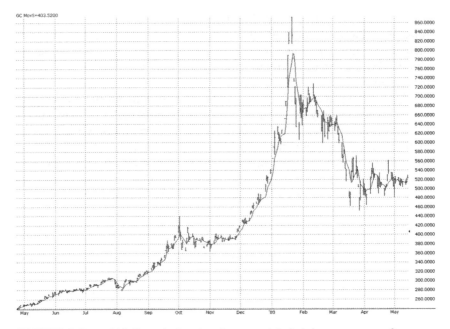

FIGURE 1.2 Gold followed silver in what were labeled the go-go years for precious metals (1978–1980). (*Source:* eSignal.com)

These were truly spectacular price movements that occurred from 1978 through 1980. As speculative vehicles, precious metals had no match. It seems this single event left an indelible impression among investors and converted gold, silver, platinum, and palladium into would-be investments.

Many may argue that this book should emphasize major events like the use of metal to back currency. They might claim that it should consider the gold realignment of the U.S. dollar by President Franklin Delano Roosevelt. What about the confiscation of gold from U.S. citizens? American history features the Bretton Woods Agreement and President Richard Nixon's closing of the U.S. gold window. Obviously, there are many important developments in the history of precious metals. Although the book may touch on these events, a complete historical perspective is beyond its scope and goal.

HOW PRECIOUS METALS WILL REMAIN PRECIOUS

Rather than simply recap history, it is essential to understand traditional roles and traditional market structures. Obviously, gold and silver have played significant monetary and political roles. Platinum and palladium have not. The key to understanding the new nature of precious metals markets is to evaluate whether traditional roles can return or if new roles will emerge. Will people ever carry gold or silver coins again? Will central banks ever return to a monetary standard based on silver or gold values? Is the real opportunity in industrial applications like platinum fuel cells, silver-based computer memory cards, gold plasma "sono-luminescence" reactors, or superconductive alloys? In other words, it may be time to turn our attention away from tradition toward the new and different. The future of these markets and associated speculative opportunities depends on such an altered perspective.

Perhaps a historical overview tells us we will always have a special interest in precious metals. That may be the extent of what we can learn from the past. Our history in its entirety has been brief. Consider that if four generations span each century, recorded history covers fewer than 400 generations. People may be surprised to discover that much of what they believe about silver and gold is myth. Yes, gold has been worshiped for centuries but infrequently used as money. Copper and silver have been vehicles for exchange. Patterns and trends suggest this may continue to be true in the future. Major events can cause a revolution in precious metals as well as an evolution.

CHAPTER 2

Monetary Roles

M etals have been directly used as money. Certainly, we are familiar with copper, silver, and gold coins. This has been the most basic use as monetary instruments. As economic systems evolved in the nineteenth century, silver and gold were linked as monetary standards and coupled with currency. These actions established two-tiered monetary systems and were responsible for rapid economic expansion during the industrial revolution. This evolution of world economies was the direct result of several gold discoveries, including the U.S. Gold Rush beginning in 1849. As mentioned before, a gold rush continues today.

LINKING MONEY WITH METALS

Prior to the huge expansion in gold production, monetary linkage primarily focused on more plentiful silver and other coinage. This is an important consideration because effective monetary linkage depends on plentiful supplies. The lack of sufficient gold from the 1960s through 1975 and a lack of ownership diversity were the most significant reasons gold was abandoned as a global monetary standard.

Limitations of Using Gold Reserves

The period following World War I mobilized industries. The expansion that followed came to an abrupt end with the stock market crash of 1929. Although excessive speculation was a catalyst for the meltdown, a liquidity crisis plunged the United States and companion nations into depression. The ultimate solution was to increase the U.S. money supply by raising the official price of gold from $20.67 to $35 an ounce in 1934. To promote monetary stability among industrialized nations, the U.S. Treasury agreed to buy and sell gold for monetary purposes at the official price. Thus, the dollar was linked to gold while other currencies could be linked to the dollar. This in turn led to the Bretton Woods Agreement that allowed member currencies to be narrowly adjusted around the gold/dollar standard. The international monetary system based on Bretton Woods existed from 1946 to 1971. However, the limitations of using gold as the official "reserve asset" became apparent as countries developed trade dislocations with deficits and surpluses.

In particular, postwar Germany took advantage of its ability to focus on consumer industries without the need for extensive military expenditures. Having lost the war, Germany was denied an internal military-industrial complex for its own use. This freed economic resources (capital and labor) to build strong export industries. The result was an inflow of dollars and an outflow of goods. Germany took advantage of the U.S. gold window, which permitted the exchange of dollars for gold at the official price, by turning in dollars for gold. Other nations took similar action on a lesser scale. By 1960, the United States faced a run on its gold reserves. The London gold fix jumped to $40 and there was an automatic incentive to convert dollars at $35 per ounce into gold at $40. (Gold "fix" is a name for the setting of a daily gold price in London.) Although countries wanted to place their faith in a gold-backed U.S. dollar, it appeared obvious that holding the metal was preferable.

This brings up an important consideration. When precious metals are freely traded, there is an automatic arbitrage created by official pricing or assigning face value. For example, if silver is selling for $1 an ounce on the free market, the government can buy it at $1 and coin the metal at $5. There is an automatic gain of $4 on the transaction. However, if silver moves to $10, an investor can buy the coin from the government at $5 and sell in the free market for a profit. Further, if production is in private hands and unrestricted, there is no incentive to sell to the government unless payment is at the market price. Official pricing has a similar effect when the system has convertibility.

This process is not limited to precious metals. Copper pennies have been hoarded and even melted down from time to time when the value per pound exceeded the face value. Governments have been forced to consider alternatives to metals that can have significant variability after years of inflation and expanded consumption. This is why several countries have considered manufacturing metalized plastic coinage. Such coins have the conductive properties of metal so that they can be used in vending machines. However, the metal content is insignificant and the manufacturing costs are a fraction of the cost of minting solid coins.

Investments versus Monetary Vehicles

From the 1980s forward, governments have issued coin of the realm. The $5 silver Maple Leaf of Canada and the silver U.S. dollar are examples of investment coinage. Because these coins have face value, the presumption is that buyers have a floor under which the parity value cannot decline. Traditionally, governments have not marked up values to earn profits based on face value. When silver moved below $5 an ounce in the 1990s, collectors had the comfort of knowing they could use their coins as money. In effect, face value *did* preserve a portion of their investment.

Often, we fail to realize that when metals are used as monetary vehicles, investment value approaches zero. This is because relative value is established by caveat rather than market forces. Consider that a potential consequence of moving to a gold or silver standard can be the official confiscation of metals from private owners. Assuredly, the owner would not receive the ultimate value for gold or silver if such an event were to take place. There is no growth potential because value is fixed. Thus, if the United States were to return to a gold standard, it is unlikely that physical gold would hold any appreciation potential. This does not mean that gold cannot provide safety during a monetary crisis. In the long run, anytime there is monetary linkage speculation becomes difficult or impossible. In the short run, owning gold or silver can offset the possibility of suffering from a so-called monetary realignment.

In a single-tier system, commodities are directly related to a single form of money. For silver, the unit may be the troy ounce. Economic forces determine how much parity an ounce of silver will have with various goods and services. A pound of grain might be associated with an ounce of silver. If a pound of grain were considered half as valuable as a pound of beef, then two ounces of silver would be required to buy a pound of beef. All values for goods and services evolve from cross parity against the standard like an ounce of silver. Parity is simply a ratio between commodities and money.

The alternative is barter, whereby two pounds of grain would be exchanged for one pound of beef. Obviously, using cross parity against a monetary standard is more effective. The purpose of moving from barter to money was to allow the easy exchange of diverse goods and services. Because silver was far more plentiful than gold, it was the common precious metal used for money. By comparison, gold was so rare that it was mostly used for ornaments rather than as money. Gold coins minted be-

Coins of ancient Israel dating back to the first and second Temple struck in bronze, silver and gold. Gold coins were very rare in comparison to bronze and silver. Gold was not a popular coinage since few in the secular population were wealthy enough to justify using gold.

fore the Common Era were more commemorative than monetary. This is because it was impractical to create units of gold small enough for everyday transactions. A monetary standard needs certain long-range characteristics to survive. Quantity is a primary consideration.

Linking Metals with Economic Systems

Generally, survival in a single-tier system requires the money supply to grow at the same pace as the economy. As the population increases, so will demand for goods and services. If the money supply remains constant, goods and services will deflate relative to the standard. At some stage, the money supply may dwindle to the point where the system no longer functions. Scarce money often results in economic depressions. When the general population or governments cannot obtain enough of the existing money, a new form is likely to emerge.

Two developments significantly changed the global pace of economic expansion. First was the age of mercantilism, which converted economic systems from feudalism and localized structure to more global and trade-based economies. The wealth of nations was not simply based upon internal resources, but also the ability to trade. Mercantilism greatly enhanced the availability of goods and the need for monetary standards. International trade required international monetary standards. Gold and silver satisfied the requirement.

Following the age of mercantilism the world entered the industrial revolution, which in turn led to the new age of transportation. In some respects, the age of transportation began with mercantilism because it flowed from shipping. Once railroads were developed, the world had a truly complementary trade system. However, the real significance of the industrial age was its impact on economic growth and technological innovation. Entirely new industries were born that demanded more money to support more wages, raw material purchases, plant and equipment investment, and expanding trade. As if to answer economic prayers, gold was discovered at Sutter's Mill in California and ushered in the 1849 Gold Rush. It has been estimated that more gold was mined and processed between 1800 and 1900 than in the previous 50 centuries. Industrialization was fueled by this rapid expansion of an internationally recognized monetary standard.

It is interesting that gold was a significant monetary standard for only two centuries. In the beginning of the eighteenth century, Sir Isaac Newton fixed the price of gold to the pound when he was master of the mint. However, more formal currency linkages were not established until the middle of the nineteenth century. In effect, gold's reign as primary standard was limited to the approximately 80 years extending from 1850 through 1930, excluding the suspension during World War I. The Great Depression proved the limitation of a fixed standard when the world's post–World War I economy ran into a monetary wall. Consider that the solution to the Depression was a revaluation of gold, which allowed the United States to expand its money supply. This was the first hint that gold could no longer sustain its role as the international monetary standard in the modern era.

When a two-tiered system was developed, silver and gold coins circulated along with redeemable certificates. In the United States, individual bank scrip, redeemable in gold, gave way to federal notes that could also be exchanged for gold. Franklin D. Roosevelt foreclosed gold redemption and ownership, and the basic U.S. economy returned to silver coinage. Great Britain had taken such a step two years earlier. International debts were still settled in gold; however, the public carried silver in their pockets and only silver certificates were honored in the United States. Even silver gave way to "full faith and credit" in the 1950s as supply pressures limited the ability to freely circulate silver as money. During the two-tiered system of exchange, paper assumed its value from its gold and silver parity. Gold's value was fixed to silver, which was fixed to a unit of exchange like the U.S. dollar or the British pound.

This is not to be confused with bimetallic systems, which can be either single-tier or two-tier. Understand that the first tier is the metal whereas the second tier is the paper. Using two metals like gold and silver allows more paper or more coin to be issued. The restriction comes when one metal outstrips the other by becoming disproportionately more valuable.

Money is a means for transacting business. Money represents value. Money drives economies. Some economists believe money should be stable. Usually, money is earned. Sometimes, money is found. Circumstances surrounding the Gold Rush promoted a get-rich-quick mentality. Thousands of prospectors flocked to alleged goldfields seeking the mother lode. Some were lucky; most were not. Yet gold fever left an almost indelible feeling that gold was the universal key to wealth. If you could find gold, you would be rich. This logic holds even as we move through the twenty-first century. Despite the divorce between gold and money, there is still a huge effort to discover new ore deposits.

Silver glistened almost as much as gold following the inflationary 1970s. Early in that decade, a series of shortages ignited a global price spiral. First, weather patterns caused a crop failure in the Soviet Union that followed on the heels of a devastating 1971 corn blight in the United States. Back-to-back with these events, a warming of Pacific Ocean currents off the west coast of South America destroyed the Peruvian fish meal harvest. This important source of animal feed placed significant pressure on grain prices. The famous Russian wheat deal of 1972–1973 drove world prices for wheat, corn, and soybeans to record highs. Food prices significantly inflated. Thereafter, Middle Eastern oil producers banded together to embargo oil exports to the United States in retaliation for U.S. support for Israel. Energy prices skyrocketed. These events culminated in an upward price spiral that challenged the public's confidence in money by the end of that decade.

One extremely powerful oil family in the United States, the Hunts, attempted to resurrect a silver monetary standard while cornering the silver market. They almost succeeded. In the wake of a fantastic upward price trend, investors flocked to silver. Everything from silver bullion to bags of old silver coins became popular investments. People sold grandma's silverware. Silver futures became the hottest game in town. But, as quickly as the silver bonanza exploded, it fizzled. A concerted effort to break the Hunts' investment play pushed them out of the market. Middle Eastern oil producers were persuaded to abandon plans requiring payment in silver or gold. From the brink of monetary disaster, industrial nations were able to take control of their money supplies and rein in prices. The massive move in precious metals in 1979 and 1980 instilled a dream in the hearts and minds of investors. Even today, there are those who long for a return to the go-go years for precious metals.

WHAT A METALS-BASED SYSTEM WOULD MEAN TODAY

If the world returns to a metals-based system, gold and silver investors could receive an unpleasant shock. Consider the circumstances that might cause a return to silver and gold. Surely, such a move would follow a confidence crisis. Governments would move to secure supplies. Confiscation is not beyond probability. If citizens were allowed to keep gold and silver, the value of gold and silver might be aligned to new paper, which could actually devalue holdings. In other words, any return to precious metals for monetary backing will not automatically favor investing. Despite this, a monetary panic is exactly the time to move into precious metals. While currencies are being redesigned, gold and silver may be the only assets maintaining value. During any transition from panic to calm, precious metals offer an insurance policy that has been reasonably tested throughout history.

Absent a monetary crisis, it is doubtful whether there is any immediate incentive for the world to return to metals-backed currency. Yet the potential for a global monetary meltdown should not be taken lightly. Not long ago, a group of intellectuals predicted the world would run out of fuel and food by the year 2100: Based on the most sophisticated computer models and available information, the world is on a collision course with raw material shortages and disaster. Memories are short. At the height of the post–energy crisis trauma of 1973, world leaders braced for a continued trend of increasing scarcity and associated economic woes. However, the predicted economic pall never came to be. The patient was miraculously cured. So far, the medicine has been a combination of increasing efficiency, new energy technology, more fossil fuel discoveries, and emerging energy policy. Yet people are not assured technology will keep pace with global demand.

In addition, the global monetary system survived a series of illnesses that included the Third World debt crisis, the U.S. savings and loan crisis, West Germany's absorption of East Germany, the dissolution of the Soviet Union and formation of the Commonwealth of Independent States, the Eastern bloc economic crisis, the Japanese real estate and banking crisis, the $7.5 trillion U.S. stock market meltdown from 2000 through 2003, the transition back to a hot war against global terrorism, and the list goes on. Any of these attacks on global financial stability could have triggered panic. Interestingly, the investing and consuming public has refused to join in any mass hysteria despite the magnitude of these various problems. It seems the one potent elixir against chaos has been information.

When well informed, people are less inclined to panic. Today's communication is more rapid, presumably more accurate, and more available than ever before. Television spans borders, and the Internet allows free communication with few restrictions. As long as we know a solution to a problem is under consideration, we can wait for an outcome. Although communication has given us a new lease on economic stability, it does not eliminate all potential for an ultimate crisis. The possibility remains for governments to lose control over a delicately balanced system of global confidence. A potent example that was never evaluated for its full devastating potential was the close U.S. 2000 presidential election, which was resolved by a U.S. Supreme Court decision. The probabilistically unimaginable occurred, during which time the only remaining world superpower was thrown into a near civil war between Republicans and Democrats, conservatives and liberals. The repercussions extended through to the 2004 election, where issues took a backseat to the simple hatred of the incumbent president who was viewed as having "stolen the White House." Fortunately, the recession did not extend through the George W. Bush presidency. Had severe economic woes developed in the aftermath of 9/11, economic panic could easily have been a consequence.

Another important factor in the new world order is the treatment of money as a commodity. Silver and gold are not the only vehicles placed within the commodity category. Most of us are aware that currencies can be traded—bought and sold—in the same manner as are gold, silver, wheat, pork bellies, and crude oil. The value of a currency is essentially a function of the country's risk, productivity, interest rates, and trade balance. It is this very speculation in currency that some believe will sow the seeds of economic ruin. Intercurrency volatility during the past 30 years has grown several hundred percent. In 1995–1996, 10 percent swings in intercurrency parities were common. By the turn of the century, the newly introduced euro varied by more than 30 percent against the U.S. dollar in less than a year. More impressively, some double-digit swings could take place in less than a quarter year. Figure 2.1 illustrates how the U.S. dollar performed on an indexed basis against a basket of foreign currencies in 1994–1995, and Figure 2.2 shows U.S. dollar volatility from 2000 to 2004.

11.25%

FIGURE 2.1 The U.S. Dollar Index futures from 1994 to 1995 experienced an 11.25 percent decline against a basket of foreign currencies in just four months. (*Source:* eSignal.com)

CHANGES IN CURRENCY MARKETS

Although necessity is the mother of invention, hedge and risk-aversion strategies may become hard-pressed to deal with excessive volatility. At some point, currency parity can wipe out import and export profit margins. There may come a time when international trade requires a more constant means for exchanging goods and services across borders. Is there hope for silver and gold?

Today's economic environment is unique. There are no rules to follow and no historical perspectives for comfort. During the 1970s, currency traders operated on the principle that any government that was forced to raise interest rates was in economic trouble. Higher interest rates were used to curb spending and fight inflation. Rising interest rates were a warning to exit one currency in favor of another whose issuing country had more stability. Thus, rising interest rates adversely affected currency parity. If the United Kingdom increased interest rates relative to the United States, it was likely the pound would fall against the dollar. This logic encountered a 180-degree reversal during the 1980s. From approxi-

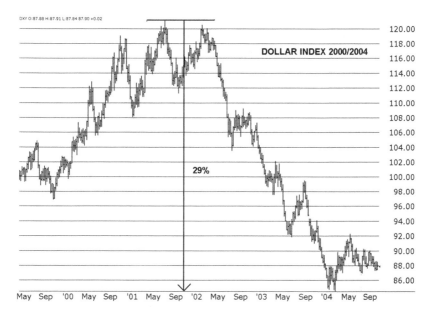

DXY O:87.88 H:87.91 L:87.84 87.90 +0.02

DOLLAR INDEX 2000/2004

29%

FIGURE 2.2 From October 2000 through December 2004, the U.S. Dollar Index futures contract completed a 29 percent cycle from trough to peak and back down. Interim swings accounted for as much as 10 percent in both directions. (*Source:* eSignal.com)

mately 1982 through 1989, currency traders began seeking interest rate differentials for arbitrage opportunities. Countries with the highest interest rates provided the best yields and, consequently, commanded the highest parity. Suddenly, economic risk previously associated with fighting inflation was no longer a consideration. What changed?

New strategies incorporating currency futures and options began enabling traders to offset parity risk. At the same time, interest rate fluctuations could be accommodated using associated interest rate futures and options. The invention and implementation of these new trading vehicles structurally changed currency markets as well as fixed income vehicles. The change was so profound that an entire trading philosophy was reversed. Thus, if the European Union's interest rates became more favorable than U.S. rates, a trader could buy European bonds denominated in euros. At the same time, any currency risk could be hedged with a sale of futures or the purchase of euro put options. Coincidentally, this is not the strategy professional traders use. Obviously, if there is a strong correlation between rising interest rates and rising currency parity, the hedge would be sure to lose. The important point to recognize is that the transaction works because hedge tools are available.

Now billions of U.S. dollars, euros, British pounds, Japanese yen, Swiss francs, Australian dollars, Canadian dollars, Mexican pesos, Brazilian reals, Russian rubles, Chinese yuan, and dozens of other currencies change hands every day at different parities. Currency trading is a multi-trillion-dollar business. Parity changes are the lifeblood of traders in some of the largest financial institutions. The entire currency trading arena was born out of structural changes in the 1970s that allowed world currencies to float.

Many believe that as quickly as the world of bullion-backed currencies evaporated into floating exchange rates, the scene can revert to its metals-backed tradition. For example, the European Common Market that evolved into the European Community (EC) (now the European Union) began designing a cooperative central banking system to create a common currency during the 1980s. An essential step was the Maastricht Treaty, which attempted to hold member currencies within limited parity ranges while setting goals for inflation, government debt, and an agreement to join in a common currency unit. Thus was born the concept of the European Currency Unit (ECU). Although the currency unit is reflected by a basket of member currencies, the plan merged into a common currency called the euro. This implies the possible dissolution of individual currency markets. As of 1997, a single European currency was still a concept more than reality, and the debate over a real ECU or parity ECU continued. Could an actual euro bill go into circulation, or would individual currencies be valued against the euro? Understand that a single European currency foreclosed some cross-parity speculation. Thus, the multibillion-dollar European currency trade was destined for extinction.

The euro was officially established as a monetary standard in 1998, and was used for book entries among the European Union members up to the launch of actual euro bills and coinage in 2000. This was one of the most monumental monetary developments in modern times. In the blink of an eye, the bulk of Europe switched from local currencies to a single unified currency. Naysayers were convinced the entire process would deteriorate into a monetary disaster. There were forecasts for widespread panic or, at the very least, Europe-wide discontent.

No doubt, widespread uncertainty was reflected in the enormous price volatility experienced from October 1998 through February 2004. (See Figure 2.3.) From an almost par position against the dollar, the so-called book euro quickly gained momentum, reaching approximately 1.23. This meant that $1.23 was required to buy a single euro. By October 2000, only 82.45 cents was needed to buy a euro. The total move from top to bottom represented a one-third decline in value. However, when the euro

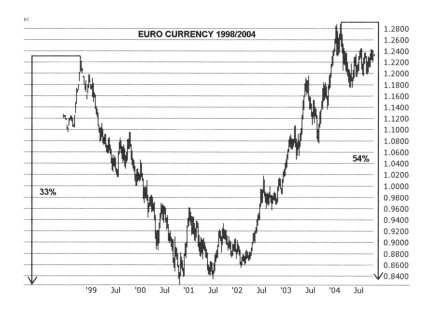

FIGURE 2.3 The euro began trading as a book entry in 1998 and as actual currency in 2000. Dollar parity declined 33 percent from the euro's initial high and rose 54 percent from its bottom. (*Source:* eSignal.com)

recovered from July 2001 into March 2004, it appreciated by more than 50 percent! The magnitude of these moves should not be underestimated.

As an illustration, imagine that you are manufacturing glassware in Germany for export to the United States. You receive an order in July 2001 for $10,000 worth of merchandise. You calculate a 25 percent profit margin in euros based on the dollar exchange rate at that time. The goods are manufactured over the next several months, and by the time they are shipped, the euro has moved up against the dollar by 25 percent. However, you priced your goods in dollars! Thus, your entire profit margin has been offset by the euro's appreciation against the dollar. Now, imagine you are manufacturing capital equipment or jetliners that can take more than a year to complete and deliver. As we see from the charts, currencies can experience cross-parity swings exceeding 50 percent.

What was gold doing from September 1999 through May 2000? Figure 2.4 reveals a significant spike higher that was attributed to European gold auctions and the possibility some planned distributions would not take place. Once discounted, gold (top chart) drifted lower from the end of October 1999 through May 2001. Notice that gold does not track the dollar

FIGURE 2.4 The top chart of gold shows some disassociation from the bottom chart of the U.S. Dollar index. (*Source:* eSignal.com)

index very well through the period. The assumption that gold will decline in dollar parity when the dollar rises and will rise on a falling dollar becomes very dangerous as demonstrated by this period. However, we do see a correlation that confirms the relativity of gold/dollar parity.

The positive correlation between gold and the dollar represents the commonsense assessment that a reciprocal relationship exists. Thus, gold advocates insist their favorite metal remains a de facto monetary standard. As we see, gold moved up along with the dollar during 2001 and 2002. This departure from a direct relationship suggests that gold is, indeed, a commodity that is sufficiently independent from currency linkage to contradict a monetary argument.

For example, the price of gold can increase in dollars while decreasing in Swiss francs. Under such a scenario, the Swiss franc would be increasing against the dollar, too. But the key point is that a Swiss investor would see a negative return on gold at the same time a U.S. investor enjoyed a positive return. In both instances we presume singular markets. This is to say that both the U.S. and the Swiss markets are islands unto themselves.

A currency trader would argue that there are no islands. Everything converges into one huge market representing all the currencies. Of course, a currency trader seeks differentials between currencies to make a profit. The precious metals investor looks for long-term appreciation. The speculator wants to identify interim instability for a quick profit.

This brings up the concept of three-way arbitrage among gold, the dollar, and foreign currencies. At any moment, the price of gold in London or Hong Kong can change based on intramarket supply and demand. At that moment, gold might lie static in the United States because the same intramarket forces are not at work. The nimble trader can immediately buy gold in U.S. dollars while selling at a higher price in British pounds or Japanese yen. The result is a three-way arbitrage profit.

To be fair, the same three-way arbitrage can exist among any commodities that are traded in different global markets. Sugar and coffee are traded in the United Kingdom as well as the United States. This sets up a three-way arbitrage among these commodities, the dollar, and the pound. In fact, there was considerable excitement among currency traders when the Organization of Petroleum Exporting Countries (OPEC) appeared to be contemplating pricing oil in euros as well as dollars. As one of the largest commodity markets in the world, crude oil could yield exceptional currency arbitrage. This is particularly true when considering that oil is traded around the clock.

As oil reached record highs in 2004, as much as 25 percent of the price in U.S. dollars could be attributed to the decline in the dollar relative to the euro and other currencies. Oil prices did rise globally, but the dollar move was accentuated by the decline of the greenback against other currencies. The same logic held for gold. As prices vacillated around $400 per ounce, the media was quick to draw the conclusion that gold was tracking the U.S. dollar. As is usually the case, media attention focuses on current developments with little, if any, long-range analysis. Although missing from newscasts and newspaper business sections, the correlation between crude oil and gold became conspicuous from January 2002 forward.

As Figure 2.5 demonstrates, prices action prior to 2002 may have been reasonably correlated, but the deviations were sufficient to discourage any short-term pattern recognition. Even an interim position in gold relative to crude oil represented a rough ride. In comparison, 2002 galvanized the gold/dollar/crude parity into strikingly similar ascents and descents. Needless to say, enthusiasm for gold was building at the very moment the metal was slandered as a nonperforming asset. As quickly as gold had been removed as an economic indicator, the resurgence of demand coupled with new monetary apprehension brought gold back to the forefront of investor attention.

It should be easy to see why investors can be inspired to embrace gold when examining the cycle of falling into and out of love with this venerable metal. It is precisely this new love/hate relationship that defines a

FIGURE 2.5 From 2002 forward, gold (on top) reestablished its correlation with rising oil prices (on bottom), suggesting a monetary link could reemerge. (*Source:* eSignal.com)

"new market" for gold. In the prior chapter we answered the question, "What's all the fuss about?" The premise is that human beings fuss over gold because they are fascinated by its properties and awed by its beauty and rarity. So, how is it possible to fall out of love with gold? The answer may be that gold is like the average marriage. Every so often, a husband and wife can argue. As with all good relationships, we eventually kiss and make up.

Will gold kiss and make up with the international currency markets? This pressing question is likely to intensify under a variety of circumstances. Most notably, any long-term correlation between gold and currency parities can create monetary linkage. If one can extrapolate Figure 2.5 forward, gold can, once again, be a monetary measure. One could argue that all commodities can be monetary measures. However, gold has always been uniquely positioned as a standard for currency.

The distinction between a currency and a monetary measure should be made clear. Currency is the actual means for exchange. As currency, gold would be coinage or certificated depository notes issued by a sovereign treasury. As a monetary standard, gold becomes a value against which currencies can be pegged. There are similarities as in the case of a gold standard whereby a unit of currency, like the dollar, was fixed to a quantity of gold. This required the actual gold to be on deposit and exchangeable with gold certificates or international drafts. In contrast to a fixed value for the dollar as a quantity of gold, the dollar might be linked or pegged to a variable quantity of gold. This is a convoluted way of saying the gold can float as a monetary measure. Of course, currencies already float against one another. Gold already floats against currencies. What is the distinction?

As a monetary measure, the amount of movement is regulated, and policy determines value among all currencies measured against gold. It is an intermediate position between a fixed standard and totally floating exchange rates. Why might such a measure be implemented? After all, hasn't the U.S. dollar been successfully used as a standard? Currencies have had fixed ratios to the U.S. dollar. Gold is fixed in dollars. Oil is priced in dollars. The primary reason given for a gold-based monetary measure is that it establishes stability through a single nonpolitical monetary medium. At the same time, gold offers a measure of confidence. Herein is the current and persistent argument for using gold as a monetary instrument.

Some economists postulate that measuring monetary value through gold will calm the huge swings in currency parities. The example is drawn from the era of a fixed international gold standard. The modern version of golden monetarism acknowledges the need for moderate flexibility within a limited framework. Perhaps this theory is the basis for a continuing central bank gold hoard, despite calls for governments to divest themselves of nonperforming assets like gold.

Any argument for asset-based monetary systems invariably includes silver. Unlike gold, silver is more of a consumable. Most of us are familiar with silver halide film that is used for conventional photography, photolithographic printing, industrial X-ray, and medical imaging. Silver is also used in high-efficiency batteries and a host of other applications we will cover in greater detail. These applications consume a greater percentage of annual silver output than we would see for consumable gold. However, silver is more plentiful than gold, as is reflected in its average price and the ratio maintained between the two metals.

Like gold, silver has been used to represent money and to back currency. In fact, silver was the preferred metal because of its abundance relative to gold and, consequently, its price. Though gold may appear to reflect oil prices from time to time, silver was actually considered a means for exchange when the dollar inflated during the oil crisis of the early 1970s. This culminated with the famous Hunt brothers' silver manipulation in 1979 when silver almost reached $50 per ounce. The plan was to accept silver in lieu of currency. The reasoning was the same as for gold.

FIGURE 2.6   Silver shows stability relative to crude oil. The price was limited to a narrow range as oil moved from $12 to almost $50 per barrel between March 1999 and July 2004. (*Source:* eSignal.com)

When comparing silver to oil at the turn of the twenty-first century, we notice a relatively stable price, despite oil's movement from approximately $12 per barrel to almost $50. (See Figure 2.6.) This stability is actually a desirable monetary feature because it displays a tendency to remain fixed relative to changing commodity prices and, in particular, oil. The analogy can be drawn to the fixed values of gold and silver when they were, in fact, monetary standards.

SUPPLY AND DEMAND

The evolution of the euro along with the massive multitrillion-dollar foreign exchange market brings up an interesting question. If organizations can merge billions of Deutsche marks, French francs, Italian lire, and other European currencies into a single unit, why not return to gold and silver monetary standards? At present the answer remains, "Limited supplies." If the value of all the world's currencies were divided into the world's entire gold inventory, an ounce of gold could have a book value exceeding $400,000! If economists created parity only with U.S. dollars, gold would still have a value in excess of $150,000 per ounce.

Some economists believe such values are feasible for international transactions. In other words, an ounce of gold would be the same as a $.25 million bill. But, as common money, this metal won't fit that bill—or the bill won't fit the money. Silver is a significantly better candidate. Unfortunately, today's industrial demand for silver consumes too much to allow any accumulation of free stocks for a monetary standard. Free stocks are supplies that are not needed for particular applications like photography, solar panels, water purification, and more. As later chapters show, technology may rapidly change the situation for silver and gold such that supplies become more abundant.

Symbolic parity is not beyond reality. It may be possible to link silver and gold to a single Global Currency Unit (GCU). There is nothing that says accounting cannot be done on a fractional basis to accommodate a GCU. Investors might trade in 1/400,000th of an ounce. This scenario would raise other issues. First, some believe economies could see tremendous dislocation whereby gold- and silver-producing nations would have a significant advantage over nonproducers. This theory has already been tested false. Under such an assumption, South Africa should be one of the world's wealthiest nations. It wasn't during the Golden Era and it is not today. Japan, with virtually no gold production and the lowest central bank reserves, flourished. In fact, Japan became an economic superpower with very few natural resources, period!

Certainly, there may be a windfall on the initial sale of gold and silver production. Thereafter, economic strength would move supplies between nations. Most importantly, who would own the mines? Knowledgeable investors would want stock in every gold and silver mine they could get their hands on for the first 10 transitional years. Could you imagine the profit margins? Realistically, production would probably come under some governmental control.

It should not be difficult to understand why the world was forced off a two-tiered, metals-based monetary system. Economic progress was to blame. There may always be individuals who believe economies should return to gold and silver money. However, to understand the new precious metals markets, investors must accept the reality that precious metals don't make good money—for now.

Although gold and silver may not be appropriate monetary instruments in today's economic systems, they still represent a value of last resort. In countries with unstable economies, the person who owns gold will be protected against currency devaluations and economic disaster. Gold is a portable, tangible asset. Further, there is an implied gold standard because anyone can easily convert this metal into any currency. In some respects, nothing else is "as good as gold."

Finally, consider that central banks continue holding millions of ounces of gold as reserves. If, indeed, the world has abandoned gold as a monetary standard, why is it still hoarded as a nonreserve asset? In fact, countries like Taiwan, Spain, United Kingdom, Japan, India, and Switzerland have actually expanded gold reserves since 1975. The answer is obvious. If all else fails, gold will retain its monetary value. The fact that huge gold reserves exist plays heavily on the day-to-day market. Rumors of possible divestiture supported by some central bank sales like Belgium, Australia, Portugal, the United Kingdom, and the United States have had a depressing effect on prices. Certainly, any joint move to sell gold reserves will flood the market. However, in the aftermath of such an event, citizens would be wise to accumulate their own personal reserves.

As later chapters show, gold and silver production is accelerating. The speed with which technology and discovery increase production could determine whether it will be feasible to return to some remonetization of precious metals. Because reserve balances already fluctuate with changing currency parities, economists have a basis for accepting that gold and silver can be used as reserve assets. Much will depend on a new generation of world leaders who are assuming power as you read this book. Certainly, baby boomers are familiar with events like the Great Depression from stories their parents or grandparents told. Those born between 1945 and 1975 lived through the legalization of possessing bulk gold in 1975, but may not have fully appreciated the significance of that event. Anyone born after 1965 can hardly remember the energy crisis of the early 1970s.

As the new generation takes power, there may be reluctance to return to past standards. In particular, individuals in the investment industry watched paper assets soar while precious metals have had lackluster performance. Only in the aftermath of the terrorist attacks of September 11, 2001, and the subsequent market uncertainty did we see a potential reuniting of gold with currency parities. Still, if new leaders believe more can be made trading paper than holding gold reserves, we can see a move toward selling nonperforming assets in favor of government participation in financial markets. After all, many a projection of the U.S. Social Security system has been made assuming simple dollar-averaging investing in the Dow Jones Industrial Average or Standard & Poor's 500 stocks. Indeed, arguments exist that the Social Security system would be more than fully funded had the U.S. government been able to make such commitments.

What if central banks did divest gold and silver holdings? Would we really see a massive decline in prices? In 1991 and 1992 Belgium liquidated approximately 200 tons of gold while the Netherlands sold 400 tons. Within the same period, sales by Russia and the Middle East added another 300 tons to the market. The purpose was to bring gold reserves in line with other EC member nations—and to raise cash. Figure 2.7 charts the gold price through these two years in comparison with a spanning 10-year period. Notice that there was no moderate sell-off from $500 per ounce in 1988 to about $330 per ounce by 1993. The downtrend was already in place well before these sales, and the market remained reasonably stable through the sell-off. The rebound from 1993 through 1996 took place while the Clinton administration was boasting economic prosperity with high employment and low inflation. Not only was the free market able to comfortably absorb the additional supplies, there was a large private accumulation that managed to overcome the forces of central bank sales. It is true that 600 tons is far less than an estimated 40,000 held by governments at that time. However, there is absolutely no indication that all government reserves will ever be simultaneously dumped.

In research paper after paper and argument after argument the question is still, "What does the future hold for gold and silver as monetary instruments?" Since the move toward European unification, world leaders have conspicuously avoided specific references to gold as a reserve asset.

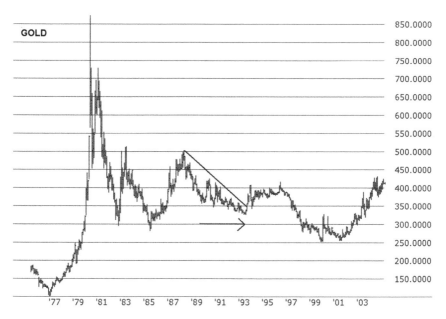

FIGURE 2.7 Monthly gold futures prices on a continuation basis from 1976 through 2004 illustrating a period of gold divestiture by central banks of Belgium, Netherlands, Russia, and Middle East nations. (*Source:* eSignal.com)

Gold is neither an official reserve nor a nonreserve asset. It is simply there, held in central bank vaults. According to the International Monetary Fund, World Gold Council, and reserve estimates by country, central banks held an estimated 35,000 to 45,000 tons of gold as of 2004. Each ton represents 32,150 troy ounces. Assuming the higher 45,000-ton estimate with a price of $400 per ounce, 2004 bank reserves had a value of $578.7 billion. The U.S. gross domestic product alone was several trillions of dollars. The enormous economic expansion from 1900 through the present time has required an equally large increase in our global monetary base. Gold supplies have not kept pace with this growth. As seen in Figure 2.8, official world gold reserves rose from 1948 through the 1965 peak. Thereafter, the central banks' hoard decreased dramatically from 1965 through 1979, when divesting flattened out.

Figure 2.9 illustrates approximate world gold production from 1850 through 2000. We can see the rise in production following the gold discovery at Sutter's Mill and the Gold Rush through the global gold accumulation from 1900 forward. Notice how the slope appears relatively constant with a modest increase after 1975. Those who would espouse a return to a gold standard point to the healthy uninterrupted acceleration in output. Those who would oppose a gold standard rely on the disproportionate increase in money supplies in relation to gold's modest growth.

As mentioned, a transition took place in the mid-1980s that moved in-

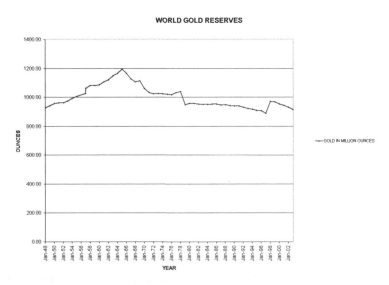

FIGURE 2.8 Official world gold reserves from 1948 through 2002.
(*Sources:* World Gold Institute, International Monetary Fund, World Gold Council)

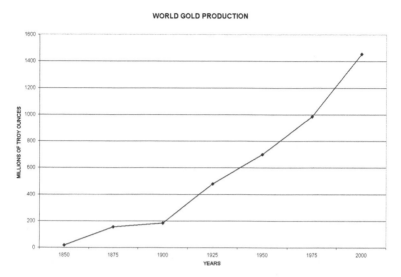

FIGURE 2.9 Post-1849 estimated world gold production through 2000. (*Sources:* GFMS, Ltd., U.S. Department of the Interior, World Gold Council, Gold Institute)

dustrialized nations from net accumulators to net distributors. A small example was the attempt to profit from coinage. Conceivably, official sales depressed prices from the mid-1980s forward. This has been a major argument presented by gold advocates. They claim the real gold price is obscured by official sales that artificially distort supply. As long as official inventories hang over the market, gold's performance will not properly reflect value based on the current supply and demand balance.

This was a powerful argument into the 1990s. By smoothing the sales from 1986 through 1995, a discernible trend can be noted toward increasing official gold divestiture. The further central banks move away from gold, the more difficult it will be to return to any gold standard. What is interesting about the equation is the degree to which private gold hoarding has kept pace with official liquidations. Over the same time period from 1986 through 1995, gold bars were steadily accumulated. Strangely, the pace of central bank sales slowed from 1997 through 1999 into nonevents and, in fact, some nations became net accumulators. These include Japan, France, Germany, Italy, the Netherlands, Spain, and the United Kingdom, to name a few.

As governments sell gold, private bar hoarding is an important barometer of investment demand. Total net official sales distributed 1,284 tons of gold from 1986 through 1995, whereas bar hoarding absorbed 2,733 tons. Therefore, net investment accumulation was more than twice as much as official distribution. This accumulation occurred even as official world mine production has been steadily adding to supplies, as is apparent in Figure 2.9. Approximately 25 to 30 percent of current gold production appears to be hoarded. This is impressive, but even at this rate, total accumulation will remain too slow to appreciably increase the hoard to levels required for monetary use within any reasonable time. Consider that even if official holdings doubled to 80,000 tons, they would tally to slightly more than $1 trillion in value at $400 an ounce. The trend in gold discoveries and mining technology should lead to increasing output that can double every 5 to 10 years. At that rate, it would take 10 to 20 years to produce the amount held in official hands as of 1995.

The only circumstance that could provide an environment conducive to a return to a gold standard seems to be a deflationary spiral. Nations would need a massive contraction in the global monetary base that could allow gold realignment at reasonable levels. Such a deflation was predicted by popular analysts to occur by the mid-1990s. Robert R. Prechter Jr., the man credited with reviving the Elliott Wave Theory, predicts the end of the economic boom and the coming of a huge economic implosion. If you believe in the Grand Cycle, gold might return as money by the year 2020. At that point, the global economic cycle should have bottomed out.

If governments take the implosion theory seriously, we could see a change in net accumulation patterns moving through the first few decades of our new millennium. What should you do if you are interested in riding the next gold wave? My instincts tell me that the first signs of an investment boom will be some form of commodity linkage such as was seen with oil and gold from 2002 forward as illustrated in Figure 2.5. This is only a hint of monetary correlation and does not represent a true remonetizing. The fact that oil was on a steady trek higher in the midst of political uncertainty, along with the Westernization of China and India, can explain why a high oil/gold correlation took hold. For real potential, official accumulation and distribution patterns will be critical. At the first sign of a monetary meltdown, you can be sure central banks will move to protect themselves with something more than intergovernmental promises. Gold will be the cornerstone for stability. But don't be surprised if the official price is far less than the market price if any monetary decision is made to bring back the yellow metal.

Given restricted gold supplies, it is equally likely the central banks will seek a bimetallic monetary standard. Therefore, we should keep a watchful eye on official silver inventories that might be accumulated quickly to supplement gold reserves. The price ratio has been favorable, and if the amount of silver relinquished by a move away from photographic film accelerates, there might be more of an incentive to use a gold/silver parity rather than a single metal. At $5 per ounce, a metric ton of silver is valued at $160,750. At 20,000 metric tons of production, the value of one year's output at $5 is $3.215 billion.

Unfortunately, this amount remains fractional compared with the world monetary base. Even if the world's annual silver production tripled, nations would hardly have sufficient metal to accommodate current economies without regard for economic growth. Further, official silver reserves are not sufficient as monetary assets. Government accumulations would need to be large indeed before nations could comfortably go into a bimetallic system. When the United States dissolved silver convertibility, there were approximately 1.7 billion ounces held by the U.S. Treasury. This amounts to only $8.5 billion at $5 per ounce.

The debate over metal as money will rage and simmer for years to come. The only positive conclusion is that huge adjustments in global economic systems and thinking would be required to inspire economic leaders to adopt a metallic standard. Either an exceedingly fine fractional system using substantial values would need to be in place ($400,000 per ounce of gold and some silver-to-gold ratio) or the world would have to undergo a massive monetary contraction. As of this writing, the prospects for metal as money remain remote, even in an age of terror-based instability.

CHAPTER 3

Are Precious Metals Investments?

There are many different views on the definition of an investment. In general, an investment is a sacrifice of present utility or effort in return for future gain. You can invest your time in a project because you anticipate some form of reward. A person invests money in financial vehicles to achieve an increased future value. Some invest in art for both the pleasure of its beauty and potential monetary appreciation. However, financially specific investing deals with a process that encompasses a monetary commitment related to an expected value. Expected value is commonly called the *return*. The degree to which the investor's expectations are realized is associated with risk. The amount placed at risk is called *exposure*.

A simple illustration is the flip of a coin. We know that fair coins have heads and tails with equal probabilities of appearing face up on an unbiased flip. Thus, the probability of either heads or tails is 50 percent or 50/50. Probability is associated with risk. We can say that the risk of a loss from betting on heads is 50 percent for each independent flip. Would you bet 10 cents on a coin flip? Why not—the exposure is only a dime. However, what if I raised the bet to $1 million? Understand that the risk remains the same at 50 percent. All that has changed is the exposure.

These are important terms and concepts because they are often misunderstood and misused. For example, options have become popular. An option is the right, but not the obligation, to buy or sell something at a predetermined price, called the *strike*. An option remains active during a specified time period, called the *duration*. The cost of this privilege is called the *premium*.

A common sales practice is to represent options as "limited risk." A salesperson may explain that a silver option being offered has a $6 strike, costs only $500 in premium, and expires in December. He or she may tell you that your risk is limited because the most you can lose is the $500 in premium. Is this true? If the chance silver can achieve a price exceeding $6 an ounce between when you buy your option and its expiration is zero, your so-called risk is actually 100 percent. In addition, silver must move above $6 by more than your $500 premium before you can make money as of the expiration. Thus, the only limit in the transaction is on your exposure. It is true that the most you can lose is $500. However, the entire concept of "limited risk" is highly misleading since it is rare to see it presented as a combination of risk and exposure. In precious metals markets, this is a particular concern. Countless scams have been designed around high-premium options having little or no chance of ever appreciating in value. As this chapter shows, there are correct strategies and wrong strategies for using options on precious metals.

Traditional portfolio theory proposes balancing three investment concepts—risk, exposure, and return. As mentioned, an investment sacrifices present value in anticipation of an expected return. The expected return is a function of risk, exposure, and return. In simple terms, you might consider investing in either Microsoft at $30 per share or a penny stock like Advanced Viral at 10 cents per share. You have $10,000 to invest. Advanced Viral has one drug in phase II testing with a stretched balance sheet. Microsoft is . . . well . . . Microsoft. The probability that Microsoft will achieve $40 within 12 months might be about 30 percent. The chance Advanced Viral will hit 30 cents might be about 40 percent. The chance Microsoft will retreat to $20 might be 15 percent. The chance Advanced Viral will go bust might be 30 percent. Keep in mind that this is *absolutely hypothetical*. There is no intent to cast aspersions on either company.

The expected value over 12 months would be the respective percentages multiplied by the associated appreciation. This is taken within the context of the amount invested. We see that there is a 30 percent chance all $10,000 could be lost in Advanced Viral against a 40 percent opportunity to make $20,000. For Microsoft, there is a 30 percent chance to make $3,333 and a 15 percent chance of losing $3,333. The criteria are personal and subjective. You might like the thrill of Advanced Viral. Someone else might not want to risk the entire $10,000 even if the probability of loss is only 30 percent.

Missing from the example is the potential dividend paid by either stock. This provides the yield as well as the appreciation potential.

INCOME POTENTIAL AND UNDERLYING VALUE

With these thoughts in mind, are precious metals investments? Certainly there are periods when buying silver, gold, platinum, and palladium can provide speculative gain. In addition, historical price data and fundamental analysis may provide a foundation for measuring risk and exposure. Yet historically, metals have not performed well as investments. First, metals have no intrinsic yield. Most stocks, bonds, and real estate have associated cash flows or income potential. Stocks yield dividends. Bonds return interest. Real estate generates rent. In addition to cash flow, the underlying value of income-generating investments can increase. In fact, increasing value is correlated with cash flow potential. This is why a stock's price-to-earnings (P/E) ratio is considered so important. Because physical precious metals have no yield, their value is solely based on supply and demand. The exception might be large institutions that lend gold at an interest rate. However, we are dealing from an individual investor's perspective.

In approaching the new precious metals markets, it is important to avoid old clichés. The most notable tradition remains the link between gold and monetary value. There is a popular correlation between an ounce of gold and the price of a fine men's suit, which demonstrates that gold has maintained a stable purchasing power despite inflation. This parallel confuses a good store of value with a good appreciating investment. Yes, gold may seem to keep pace with inflation, but the purpose of investing is to move appreciably *ahead* of inflation to accumulate wealth. There is also the story of the man who had 2,000 ounces of gold and sold just two ounces per month. Plotting the sale against gold prices, he was able to live a comfortable life for the past 1,000 months (83 years). Compare this gentleman with Warren Buffett, who went from having virtually nothing to being worth more than $30 billion by the turn of the twenty-first century. I believe the point is made. The first gentleman would have been better off selling his gold and investing in Berkshire Hathaway.

Precious Metals as Commodities Rather Than Investments

Since the mid-1980s there has been a growing consensus that precious metals are *not investments*. They are commodities. As with any other commodity, the value of silver, gold, and the platinum group will be determined by the amount mined, global demand, and sales from public and private hoards. This thinking implies that metals can only provide speculative opportunity rather than investment potential. The difference between speculation and investing is subtle. Speculation is associated with short-term gains. Speculative financial vehicles are traded rather than held. Certainly, you can make money buying low and selling high. This is true of stocks, bonds, and real estate as well as commodities. Yet, if you compare the purchase of the Dow Jones Industrial Average stocks against a comparable amount of gold or silver over any 10-year period, you will find that equities have outperformed metals as investments. This is apparent in Figure 3.1. Equities experience an overall appreciation known as the *secular trend*. Although corrections can be related to recessions or inflation, stocks and bonds continue as more stable investments.

Before decoupling from monetary roles, gold and silver established international currency parities. The U.S. dollar derived its intrinsic value from its gold parity of $35 per ounce. If parity cannot change, gold will inflate along with the dollar or any other linked currency if the commodity price index or consumer price index is rising. Compare the progress of gold against the Dow Jones Industrial Average since ownership of gold by U.S. citizens was reestablished in 1975. A historical overview reveals that the energy crisis during the early 1970s precipitated the Nixon-era stagflation. Americans experienced a recession and inflation, reflected by poor

FIGURE 3.1 Gold's performance over 20 years, from 1984 through 2004 remained in a trading range between approximately $275 and $530 per ounce while the Dow Jones Industrial Average had a steady positive secular trend. (*Source:* eSignal.com)

stock market performance and subsequent soaring precious metals prices. Thereafter, the world began adjusting for a purely paper system that pushed equity and bond values higher, while removing incentives for owning precious metals. The essential difference between paper assets and physical metals is the earning potential. Companies earn money, which translates into dividends. Bonds provide a steady stream of interest revenue. Real estate has rental income and property appreciation. Precious metals can make money for the average investor only if the metals' value appreciates and holdings are liquidated. When interest rates move as high as 18 percent to 21 percent, the temptation to move from hard assets to debt instruments becomes overwhelming. Such was the case by the mid-80s.

The nineteenth-century gold and silver boom generated income for producers, as well as those selling picks, shovels, mules, covered wagons, and train tickets. As previously mentioned, the gold rush continues today. Not surprisingly, moneymakers are still producers. Likewise, the best precious metals investments have been exploration and mining stocks. The fantastic performance of mining stocks during the 1980s and 1990s can be directly correlated with technological advancements and strong product demand. The costs of extraction and processing steadily declined while the prices remained reasonably stable. Profit margins grew along with volume. Huge price advances of 1979–1980 presented enormous speculative opportunities. Gold prices rocketed from $150 an ounce to just under $1,000, as shown in Figure 3.2, which plots June 1980 gold futures prices during that famous run-up. The profit potential was enormous, if one had the foresight to divest just after the $916 peak on January 21, 1980. Without such insight, gold failed miserably as an investment. In contrast, several mining stocks and mining-oriented mutual funds benefited greatly from the repositioning of gold and silver as speculative commodities. These companies were not limited to precious metals mines. Nickel, copper, lead, tin, zinc, and other base metals contributed, increasing ancillary income from by-product production of precious metals from base metal tailings.

We see that silver's performance was even more spectacular than that of gold, as illustrated by the price chart for the same period seen in Figure 3.3. On a proportional basis, silver topped all the metals, with futures prices reaching an amazing $41.50, before instantly reversing. In less than a year, silver managed to move from $7.59 in March 1979 to its $41.50 high for a 546.6 percent increase. Gold moved from approximately $260 to $916 for a 35.2 percent gain.

At that time, the only comparable moves took place in other physical commodity markets like grains, sugar, and coffee. Because of the incredi-

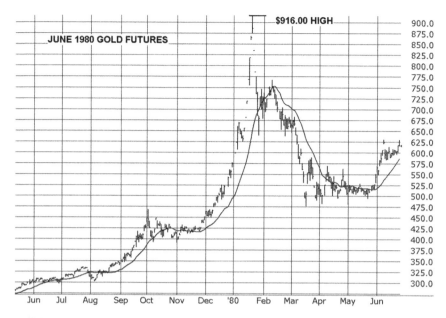

FIGURE 3.2 Gold prices soared to more than $900 per ounce during the go-go years from 1979 through January 21, 1980, when bullish sentiment suddenly evaporated. (*Source:* eSignal.com)

ble speculative opportunities realized in commodities, economists actually entertained concepts of commodity-based investment strategies. Gold and silver were touted as the alternatives to underperforming paper assets. Make no mistake—*this could easily happen again!*

In comparison, there is no doubt that high-tech stocks represented by the Nasdaq-100 Index demonstrated a similar chart pattern into 1999's last quarter. Notice the pattern in the March 2000 Nasdaq-100 futures chart shown as Figure 3.4. The value moved up 834.6 percent from July 1996 through March 24, 2000. Although the time frame is extended to four years as opposed to 11 months, the net gain exceeds silver's by almost 300 percent.

Perhaps these examples only confirm that a speculative frenzy can occur in paper assets as well as hard assets. When it comes to "irrational exuberance," all investment vehicles are similar, if not the same. Alternatively, stock market advocates will point to the longer-term performances of less speculative indexes like the Dow, as illustrated in Figure 3.1. They will also highlight the fact that some of the Nasdaq components declared dividends, albeit small ones, for that period.

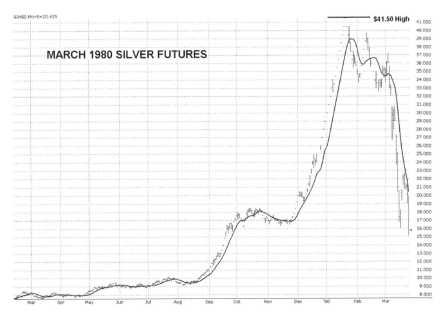

FIGURE 3.3   The Hunt brothers' manipulation of silver prices, coupled with the surge in gold and the platinum group, sent silver almost as far as $50 per ounce before the abrupt turn on January 21, 1980. (*Source:* eSignal.com)

Reasons for the Surge of the 1970s

What made precious metals such speculative successes toward the end of the 1970s? One reason was the legalization of gold in the United States. There was a new demand for gold and a bandwagon effect in silver, platinum, and palladium. Further, the Cold War encouraged rumors of strategic metals shortages that focused on platinum, palladium, and rhodium. The Soviet Union was the largest producer behind South Africa. Tensions remained high from the 1973 Yom Kippur Arab-Israeli War, which was the basis for the infamous OPEC oil embargo and subsequent energy crisis during the 1970s. The Soviet Union had sided with the Arabs, while the United States stood behind Israel.

The Western bloc had seen how the wrath of supplier nations could wreak havoc upon free-world economies. Memories of gasoline lines and odd/even purchase restrictions were fresh when U.S. automobile manufacturers posed the question, "What if we can't get platinum?" The United States was the first nation to strongly embrace catalytic air pollution reduction that relied on platinum. While a new development, it was in place by 1980.

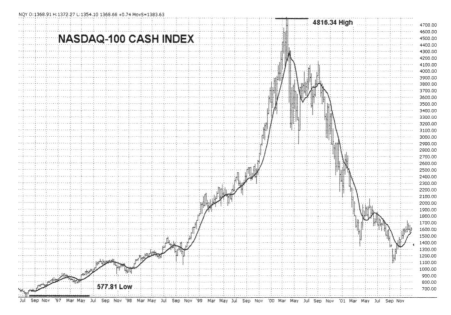

NQY O:1368.91 H:1372.27 L:1354.10 1368.66 +0.74 MovS=1383.63

FIGURE 3.4 From a July 26, 1996, base of 577.81, the Nasdaq-100 Index made its way to a 4,816.34 high on March 24, 2000. In a pattern almost identical to silver in 1980, the market turned bearish. (*Source:* eSignal.com)

At the same time, the world was making a difficult and uncertain transition away from metals-backed currency during a highly inflationary and politically tenuous period. This transition away from being monetary standards represented a monumental structural change for gold and silver. In fact, the break from currency can easily be considered the first true structural change of the post–World War II era. Within a single decade, we experienced the highest prices for grain, energy, coffee, sugar, pork, beef, metals, and other commodities. There were no assurances that the inflationary spiral would come under control. Money was floating for sure. Some economists warned that money was floating away. Consider that on an inflation-adjusted basis, these price records still stood as of 2004. Even three decades of inflation could not encourage silver prices to new highs. In fact, in the 1990s silver dipped below levels seen before the 1979–1980 climb.

There should be little wonder why the environment was ripe for a near panic into hard assets like precious metals. As established in earlier chapters, gold, silver, and platinum were already considered precious. It was a question of *how* precious. Simply put, there did not appear to be any alternatives to metals at the height of the buying spree. Even real estate had failed in the mid-1970s, as a deepening recession rolled back commercial rents and squeezed landlords who were forced to pay high utility bills during the energy crisis. A look back reveals that huge expenditures were made to retrofit buildings and homes to save energy. The true conservation movement was born out of the turmoil of the 1970s.

The United States also endured one of the most divisive and tense political periods. Young and old were polarized. The women's movement was in full swing. Black Power was reshaping ideology. Those who had protested the Vietnam War were now members of a highly fragile economy and workforce. Richard Nixon was disgraced and forced to step down from office. The U.S. withdrawal from Vietnam was chaotic and interpreted as a sign of weakness that plagued Gerald Ford and carried over into Jimmy Carter's administration. In the four years of the Carter presidency, inflation reached a new high and America's image seemed to make a new low. In particular, the Iranian hostage crisis appeared to render the U.S. military might and economic hammer impotent. Even President Carter's attempt at humanitarian intervention on behalf of Afghani rebels backfired, as the grain embargo against the Soviets permitted other producers to capture substantial portions of U.S. market share. U.S. leverage was all but lost.

Place yourself back in 1978. What might you have done? What investments were more attractive than venerable gold and reliable silver? Even Alan Greenspan, the economist turned Federal Reserve chairman, warned that abandoning gold might eventually endanger the ability to stabilize domestic and global monetary systems. Floating exchange was still a huge experiment.

This apprehension provided the incentive for commodity traders to take refuge in hard assets. Two high-profile oilmen, the Hunt brothers, embarked on a personal mission to shore up values by returning to a metal monetary standard. They chose silver. As later mentioned in Chapter 5, the Hunts began accumulating large quantities of silver and promoted the concept of silver certificates for global exchange—in particular, purchasing oil. This was the spark that ignited the extreme stampede into metals.

The effect was long lasting. Even in the aftermath of this period, a novice trader named Hillary Clinton allegedly turned $1,000 into $100,000 speculating in cattle and soybeans. Commodity speculation did not lose its momentum until interest rates offered a deal investors couldn't refuse: passive, assured, high returns on bonds.

The unprecedented surge in precious metals during 1979 and the beginning of 1980 marked the start of a second major structural change for precious metals that followed the departure as monetary standards. The first structural change was the move from fixed values to floating prices for gold and silver. No one knew what the eventual consequences of the monetary divorce would bring. Absent an immediate and sustained gold and silver price surge, economic incentives to explore for and mine these metals remained weak. According to some sources, mining costs for gold were between $80 and $150 per ounce in 1975. From the time gold opened that year at just under $200 through the first half of 1976, prices sharply declined to find support at a meager $125 an ounce as illustrated in Figure 3.5. This was attributed to poor investor interest and the slow economy. In addition, U.S. Treasury sales depressed prices in 1975 and 1976. Silver traded in a narrow range between $3.75 and $5. At the same time, mining costs had risen from 1969 through 1975 because of the energy crisis and global inflation. It was not particularly profitable to operate mines.

As demand heated up, new supplies were flat. By 1978, the picture was looking much brighter. At more than $250 an ounce for gold and $5.50 for silver, there were better incentives to expand marginal production up to costs of approximately $200 for gold and $3.75 for silver. It doesn't take a genius to understand that when prices rocket to more than $900 for gold and close to $50 for silver, producers will seek every possible way to boost

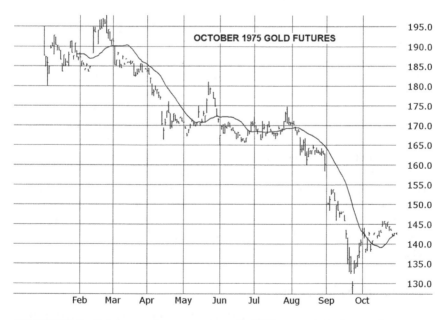

FIGURE 3.5 Gold opened at approximately $200 to much fanfare and projections of substantially higher prices. Recessionary pressures proved too great. Gold contracted to an unexpected dip to $127 in the October 1975 futures contract. (*Source:* eSignal.com)

production. New technology used solvents to remove trace amounts of metal from low-grade ores that had been considered unworthy prior to the price explosion. In time, these extraction techniques became increasingly efficient and the entire production environment changed. Deep-shaft mining gave way to surface strip mines. By-product production of silver and gold became a major focus for growing production. Along with rising precious metals prices were the base metals like copper, tin, zinc, lead, aluminum, and nickel. Each of these metals yielded ever-increasing by-product production of gold, silver, platinum, and palladium.

On the flip side of the equation, industrial users were forced to rapidly seek alternatives to silver, gold, platinum, and palladium as prices reached new highs. The huge price surge toward the end of the 1970s became the incentive for finding substitutes for gold coatings on glass, gold dental materials, electrical contacts, jewelry, and other applications. Use of silver in brazing materials, mirroring, electronics, tableware, and jewelry also came under attack. A huge recycling/scrap business was born and there were conflicts over who would collect X-ray negatives from hospitals and old film from lithographic printers. People lined up to sell silverware. Old bags of silver dollar coins became hot items.

The combination of better production, better exploration, new discoveries, better recovery, and alternative materials altered the way the world produced and used precious metals. Suddenly, there were increasing supplies at increasing rates. From 1980 to 1990, the United States increased its gold output by 1,000 percent. Ten times more gold was being produced in less than a decade. Within 12 years, South Carolina went from being a nonproducing state to being the ninth-largest gold producer, based on new mining and extraction technologies. Of course, this pace was duplicated in other parts of the world. For those following precious metals, this is a significant point. Throughout the 1980s there were countless schemes that lifted tens of millions of dollars out of unsuspecting pockets using the pitch that the world faced a pending shortage of silver and gold. There was the threat of a Soviet strategic metals embargo. There was the China Silver Syndrome, in which the People's Republic was going to corner the entire world production. The list of fables is almost endless. Throughout this period, very few news stories carried the truth about surging supplies.

Hitting the Skids in the 1980s

Unfortunately, investors wanted to hear that gold and silver would resume their upward spiral. Those who missed the moves of the 1970s were anxious for a repeat performance. In other words, people were easy victims. Also, inflation continued into the 1980s. It took half that decade along with unprecedented interest rates to bring prices under control. This represented a final structural change that substantially reduced the roles of gold and silver as inflation hedges. Although introduced in 1972, currency futures did not gain in popularity until the development of other financial futures and options contracts. The Chicago Board of Trade announced the first interest rate futures contract with the Government National Mortgage Association (GNMA—Ginnie Mae). Thereafter came Treasury-bills, Treasury-notes, Treasury-bonds, Eurodollars, and municipal bonds. Suddenly there was a paper alternative to gold and silver. If inflation were present, the sale of interest rate futures would ride the wave of rising interest rates, offsetting exposure. The deterioration of any currency could be countered by selling the appropriate futures contracts short or buying put options. These derivative vehicles obviated the need to use gold and silver as traditional inflation or uncertainty hedges.

Equally important, paper markets were more liquid and easier to use. Understand that physical precious metals markets are slow and cumbersome. It takes time to transfer and move metals. They must be insured and assayed. If bullion is transported, time and expense are involved. Essentially, trading large amounts of physical gold, silver, platinum, or palladium is not an investment activity for the modern age of paper markets.

Once gold and silver roles as inflation hedges diminished, interest in precious metals became dulled. Certainly, high interest yields in the 1980s made government debt more attractive than holding silver or gold bars that had no yield and, in fact, cost money to store and insure. The stock market's bull trend also offered far better returns than precious metals. Thus, even attitudes toward gold and silver structurally changed. Particular crisis events that would have pushed investors toward gold and silver failed to influence prices. Many believe the Falklands War between the United Kingdom and Argentina was pivotal. At the onset, gold surged more than $50 an ounce. However, enthusiasm for gold and silver immediately reversed, as demonstrated by Figure 3.6.

When the Soviet Union shot down a Korean airliner, metals did not respond. The August 1990 invasion of Kuwait by Iraq had only a modest influence on gold and silver. The subsequent Gulf War was a precious metals yawn compared with the reaction one would have expected in the late 1970s. Investors became less interested in moving into metals because the crisis hedge was no longer valid. In fact, stocks and bonds had more pronounced and long-lasting reactions to crisis, as illustrated by the impressive U.S. equity market recovery on the initiation of Operation Desert Storm in January 1991.

Well, if precious metals are not good investments, shouldn't the book end here? After all, history shows gold and silver do not perform well over time. Derivatives markets permit strategies to offset inflation and deflation.

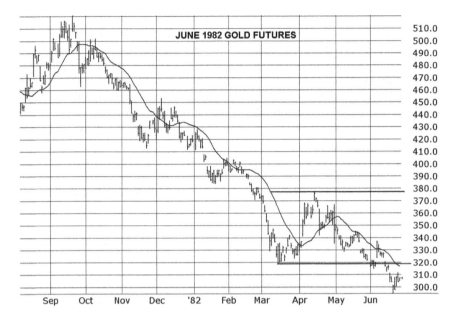

FIGURE 3.6 In April 1982, Argentina invaded the Falkland Islands, which were a British territory. Initially, gold reversed from a powerful downtrend to rally more than $50. But the underlying decline quickly resumed even before the situation was fully resolved. (*Source:* eSignal.com)

Central banks have eliminated charters and language linking gold to the monetary base as a reserve asset. The European Union's Maastricht Treaty specifically disavows gold as an official reserve asset. The *New York Times* and the *Wall Street Journal* abandoned gold as an economic indicator. Technology is finding ways to substitute lower-cost materials for gold, silver, platinum, and palladium. What purpose can precious metals serve other than their intrinsic psychological appeal?

THE NEW MILLENIUM

The word "revolution" is loosely used to describe innovation. We speak of the industrial revolution or the technology revolution. But the more literal definition of revolution is a return or revolving back to a previous condition. The association with rebellion and new government order is probably responsible for the interpretation of revolution as progressive. After all, the French and American Revolutions established new governments and governing structures. A more appropriate word for innovative or progressive periods might be "evolution." This is because new technologies evolve and impacts are evolutionary.

Derivative financial vehicles are founded upon new technology. The ability to convert an index into a futures or options contract is based on the nearly instant calculations of high-speed computers. The impact of derivatives upon investment theory and practices has been evolutionary. The Black-Scholes option pricing model evolved from the relationship between underlying securities and the relative value of puts and calls based on time, volatility, and price proximity. The model earned the Nobel Prize.

The evolutionary process cannot be underestimated. By some accounts, the development of derivative financial markets has been the single most significant leap forward since the concept of equity investing was developed centuries ago. Just when a move away from monetary standards like metals was experiencing serious challenges, investors were provided with the ability to hedge interest rates and fluctuations in currencies using brand-new futures and related options.

Moving forward, options now provide the ability to earn a return on commodities in the same way as a landlord earns rent on a property. The assumption that a commodity is in demand leads to the presumption that someone is willing to pay for the option to purchase that commodity. By the same logic, an owner of the commodity might be willing to part with that commodity if a satisfactory price is available. The owner has an incentive to sell an option. In return, the owner collects a premium that becomes a form of "rent" on the commodity with an option to buy at the right price. As covered in the next chapter, on strategies, options on precious metals convert them into income-generating assets that also have appreciation potential. The means metals have evolved from simply stores of value into potential investments using the traditional definition and concept.

Recall the concept of buying coins of the realm that have declared face values. The logic in buying a U.S. silver dollar is that it has the silver content *plus* a face value. If silver's price were to decline below $1, the value of the coin would remain $1 as guaranteed by the face value. Using that analogy, investors are able to buy precious metals relying on intrinsic values while using options for income. The strategy holds that if all else fails, nothing else is "as good as gold." Sound familiar?

The new millennium was supposed to be ushered in with the most spectacularly hyped modern-age disaster of all time. The infamous Y2K bug was going to shut down everything from banking to elevators and the world's electrical grids. In anticipation of this pending doom, the Federal Reserve eased liquidity and announced that it stood ready to feed the system if the need arose.

Before Y2K, gold was snatched up just in case. But as the event approached, widespread preparations and testing proved capable of transcending the Y2K bug. Computers could, in fact, deal with the double zero. As we know, the system did not fail and, in reality, the new millennium came with hardly a glitch. Still, we see in Figure 3.7 that a flight to gold took place, confirming the underlying belief in this metal as a disaster hedge.

Unfortunately for gold bugs, the degree to which gold responded or failed to respond to Y2K represented a significant setback. Once confidence in the paper system was reestablished, gold plunged back to interim lows. By the first quarter of 2001, gold made a new bottom at approximately $255. Few would deny that the potential of Y2K represented an extraordinary threat to financial systems. On that basis, the gold reaction was actually subdued. Place yourself back in 1979 with the same prospects. I am sure gold would have easily challenged $1,000 per ounce! Of course, we'll never know.

We know that immediately following the Y2K yawn, tech stocks represented by the Nasdaq-100 Index exhibited a burst of enthusiastic

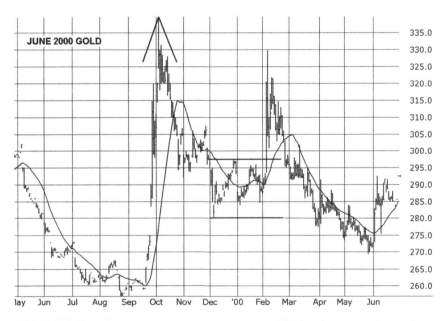

FIGURE 3.7 Gold experienced a surge in demand just prior to Y2K. As confidence began to build, gold prices retreated. On the actual New Year, gold was confined to an anticipatory trading range between approximately $285 and $295 per ounce. (*Source:* eSignal.com)

relief. We survived. But the euphoria was short-lived. By March, the Nasdaq ran out of steam along with other equity markets. While the reason for the rapid reversal remains arguable, conservative economists question whether the tax code was a catalyst. We see that there was a move away from traditional stocks like the Dow Jones industrials into the highfliers like the Nasdaq stocks during the last quarter of 1999. Everyone wanted to join the party. Apparently, tax consequences of this swap may not have been fully appreciated.

As the April 15 U.S. tax day loomed, investors were suddenly faced with an unexpected reality that capital gains taxes were owed on the former Dow positions that had been held for so many years. Alas, there was a liquidity crunch because investors did not have the money to pay the unexpected tax. They were forced to liquidate some stocks before April 15 and it appears the exodus took place in March 2000. The beginning of the recession had arrived. As we see by Figure 3.8, the Nasdaq-100 plunged and took gold along for the ride. Nasdaq stocks practically melted down, losing more than 72 percent within the following 12 months. At the same time, gold dropped from $320 to $255, a 20 percent decline.

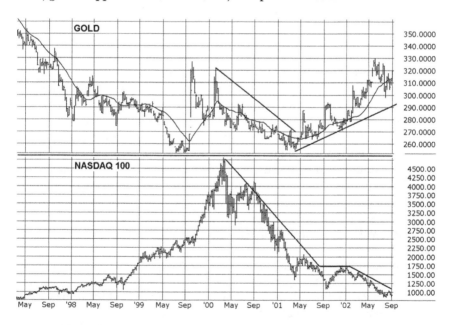

FIGURE 3.8 When compared with the Nasdaq-100, gold declined in tandem as liquidity dried up for investors. However, gold's decline was fractional when compared with Nasdaq stocks. Gold's reversal took place well ahead of the Nasdaq, which continued to fall after gold double bottomed in the first half of 2001. (*Source:* eSignal.com)

This positive correlation between stocks and gold demonstrates that liquidity affects *all investments*. When investors run out of money, they cannot invest in anything. (well, almost anything). There was a flight to quality that lifted principle values for U.S. bonds and notes. However, the Federal Reserve was simultaneously easing short-term rates to stem the red ink from stocks as well as the accelerating economic contraction.

What should be apparent and encouraging for precious metals advocates is the fact that gold began appreciating after making a double bottom in March/May of 2001. In comparison, the Nasdaq-100 deteriorated from approximately 1,800 all the way to 980. Thus, high-tech stocks lost 45 percent as gold increased by more than 17 percent.

THE BALANCED PORTFOLIO ARGUMENT

Whether we accept that precious metals are commodities rather than investments or we cling to the concept of metals as valuable assets within a balanced portfolio depends on our historical perspective. As mentioned earlier, gold and silver did not perform well since decoupling with money, with the exception of some spectacular reactionary run-ups. Yet, the decline in equity value experienced in the first three years of the new millennium reengaged the argument that gold and perhaps silver belong in a balanced portfolio.

Portfolio balancing seeks to reduce overall risk through diversification among noncorrelated investments. The assumption is that as stocks decline, bonds might rise. This is certainly the logic when the decline in equities is a consequence of rising interest rates because bonds would, by nature, increase in principle value. Low interest rates might also encourage rising real estate values as mortgage overheads fall. Portfolio balancing might seek to add a proportional share of bonds to equities, with a sprinkling of real estate investment trusts (REITs) for good measure.

Thus, adding gold to a portfolio can serve to balance against a plunging stock market *as long as the negative correlation between gold and stocks exists*. The problem is that we do not have a sufficient history of positive correlation to make an assumption that gold serves as a balancing mechanism. If we rely on only the first decade of the new millennium, we discount the years from 1972 through 2000. We cannot forget that gold was only released from its duty of representing monetary value in the last three decades of the prior millennium.

If a reverse correlation holds, we see that gold moved from $255 per ounce to $410 from the 2001 bottom through the first quarter of 2003. That 60 percent appreciation compares with the Nasdaq-100's 45 percent deterioration. In equal parts, a portfolio of Nasdaq-100 stocks and gold would have experienced a net gain of 15 percent. It is unlikely that a prudent investor would divide assets equally between gold and stocks; however, the example makes a point that precious metals can provide a counterbalance against stock market adversity.

More likely, a portfolio would be a mix of stocks, bonds, real estate, and precious metals. Like gold, bonds moved higher when stocks were moving lower. In fact, bonds experienced better than 30 percent gains as stocks dropped more than 50 percent. Some real estate soared more than 100 percent for the same period. While this text is not designed as a primer on portfolio design and management, the point should be taken that precious metals may have a valid and strong place in a balanced investment strategy.

MINING AS A KEY TO VALUE

Those familiar with precious metals should know gold mining stocks were among the best performers during the latter half of the 1980s, through the 1990s, and into the new millennium. Gold stock funds outpaced the S&P 500 and Dow Jones Industrial Average by hefty margins. Rather than abandon gold, the world embraced this metal and, in reality, demand appears to have kept pace with production. The hottest new issues are not just technology stocks related to the Internet and medical advances. Each time there is a new gold discovery, investors flock to the issue with fists full of dollars. Names like Royal Gold and penny stocks like Trend Mining prove the potential. At the same time, established names of the big companies exhibit consistent expansion. Why the investment interest? The fact is that today's gold mining is highly profitable.

Very few heavy industries boast spreads between production costs and selling prices that are as wide as in gold mining. More importantly, profitability is getting wider. Few products have such continuous demand and stable relative prices. Basically, gold is *good business.*

Silver, platinum, and palladium are also good business. As mentioned, most silver is produced as a by-product of other metals. Silver represents additional marginal profit on other metal production. If silver prices rise, marginal profits follow. Platinum is a unique metal. Far more rare than gold and silver, platinum is the cornerstone of value in terms of industrial demand. Although there may be technological threats to major platinum applications like automotive catalytic converters, new technologies like fuel cells and electronic storage can fill demand gaps. Finally, palladium has excellent prospects as either a platinum substitute in catalytic devices or certainly a complementary component. Taken as a group, precious metals are extremely versatile commodities.

We know there are many ways to invest and speculate in commodities. Depending on characteristics, you can invest in the means of production. When you buy a share of Proctor & Gamble, you are participating in the production and distribution of household products and health care accessories. When you invest in North American Palladium on the Nasdaq Small Cap Market, you are participating in the production and distribution of palladium. When you buy stock in Placer Dome, Agnico-Eagle, or Freeport-McMoRan Copper and Gold, Inc. you are investing in gold production and distribution. The same holds true for Apex Silver and Clifton Mining for silver as well as base metal mining companies. Therefore, it is important to understand the commodities produced by the companies in which you are investing. That is why you must understand the new precious metals markets and their evolutionary trends. After all, how can you properly evaluate a food company relative to a precious metals producer? Should you buy utilities or mining stocks?

Precious metals have the unique characteristic of being "semiconsumables." Unlike crude oil or agricultural products, a portion of each year's precious metals production is hoarded. In addition, gold, silver, platinum, and palladium are recovered from former applications ranging from film to catalytic converters to electroplated materials. In the case of gold, the majority is hoarded as bars, coins, and jewelry. Hoard accumulations play critical roles in the long-term prospects for precious metals. The process is a throwback to the monetary link and is likely to maintain a stability not found in other commodities. All signs point to a strong future for gold, silver, platinum, and palladium. This means you will have investment opportunities in stocks of producer companies and speculative opportunities in futures and options markets. In addition, the same derivative vehicles and strategies that dulled the luster of physical metals markets can brighten their comeback. It is possible to use gold and silver as the foundation for yield-bearing programs. Just as banks may trade options against cash balances, so can investors trade against gold and silver inventories. In fact, we could see precious metals producers using production as backing for market strategies rather than just selling into the physical market.

As semiconsumables, precious metals will always maintain roles as stores of value. They are still assets of last resort. In the coming years, humanity will see enormous technological and political change, and probably the most rapid age of human development in history. Some say humans are on a road to disaster. Frankly, if the entire world develops living standards set by the United States and Western Europe, Mother Earth could become nothing more than a revolving cinder by the end of the twenty-first century. If the pace of global industrial development continues, doomsayers will finally be vindicated. Obviously, something must change.

Technology must address population and progress. As later chapters reveal, platinum and palladium may play significant roles in changing the way people power the world. Although still highly controversial, new technologies based on special characteristics of platinum-group elements may provide solutions to an inevitable energy-related crisis. The world will need massive quantities of potable water. This may translate into widespread use of silver-based water purification systems.

How are precious metals affected? Most obvious will be rising values for the platinum group and silver. Even after being rebuked as "junk science," cold fusion based on palladium has not been completely abandoned as a pursuit of so-called fringe science. If, by some defiance of mainstream science, cold fusion becomes a reality, this metal could develop into the most valuable on earth. Given platinum's complementary role in the process announced by University of Utah researchers Stanley B. Pons and Dr. Martin Fleischmann in March 1989, investors could see equal opportunities for speculative gain. Stocks of platinum-producing companies would have extraordinary performance. Companies developing the new technology will offer equally impressive investment opportunities. All the while, precious metals, as a group, will be viewed as ultimate hard assets that maintain value.

Before moving on to new precious metals strategies, it is important to keep precious metals *investing* in context. As reviewed, the assertion that gold stabilizes a portfolio by acting as an insurance policy against monetary catastrophe has created recommendations for gold holdings ranging from 5 percent to 10 percent of total financial assets. This means that an individual with net financial assets of $100,000 would have between $5,000 and $10,000 in gold. This philosophy assumes that gold will perform during high inflation or a paper confidence crisis.

For those living in Western Europe, the United States, and the developed nations of the Pacific Rim, the need for a monetary hedge is questionable. Any 10 percent investment in gold bars or coins that can significantly underperform the stock market, bonds, and gold stocks must be carefully evaluated. The most conservative view holds a logical argument favoring sacrificing performance in return for security. If the time to own gold is during a monetary crisis, the market may not be sufficiently liquid to enter when instability is upon us. However, holding a solid portfolio that includes mining stocks can address the liquidity issue in advance.

No, stocks will not have the ultimate value of precious metals in a crisis, but holding 10 percent of one's total portfolio in bars with no complementary strategies may be imprudent. Raging inflation is not likely to appear overnight. If a progressive rise in the consumer price index develops, a move into precious metals may be justified while inflation is present. However, be aware that gold may not be as sensitive to inflation today as it was in the 1970s and 1980s.

PRECIOUS METALS AS PERFORMING ASSETS

Strategically, it is possible to turn metals into performing assets. This is where the line between speculation and investing blurs. The key is to recognize that the dynamics of precious metals markets have changed. We are dealing in new environments with new rules. Today, traditionalists can have their cake and eat it, too. If you hold physical gold, you can earn money on your inventory. If you know prices will remain stable, you can develop strategies that take advantage of flat price action. If silver persists in trading within a wide but limited price range, you have a way to make exciting gains with limited risk and exposure.

With the creation of new markets, financial vehicles, and strategies, precious metals could actually become better investments than they have ever been in the past. I find this somewhat humorous because gold and silver advocates spend millions of dollars each year to promote investing in gold and silver. The World Gold Council, representing producers around the globe, publishes detailed academic studies and reports dealing with the monetary aspects of this single metal. The Gold Institute and Silver Institute, located in Washington, D.C., actively promote gold and silver investing. The Platinum Guild and Johnson Matthey call attention to the benefits of owning platinum. These organizations do an excellent job of collecting, digesting, and distributing information. Most literature directed toward investors focuses on owning gold with sidebars on using futures, options, mining stocks, and leveraged transactions. There is little information about using gold and silver inventories to implement specific investment strategies.

Change is often difficult. We are all influenced by the past and we have limited access to the future. Thus, it is difficult to divorce our minds from traditional gold and silver thinking. You can view precious metals as money, investments, insurance policies, stores of value, or collectibles. The new metals markets combine past traditions with modern strategies. Of course, the global economic environment can change, and probably will. When you consider using new approaches, always keep in mind how and why conditions can change. A good fundamental background should help. So will an open mind!

CHAPTER 4

New Strategies
for
New Markets

Throughout this book, I refer to structural changes in precious metals markets. These changes create important strategy considerations. When Americans carried gold coins in their pockets, the market's structure foreclosed investing or speculating in gold. As covered, gold was money, not an investment. The postmonetary era brought about speculative potential for silver and gold. Silver, platinum, and palladium were traded as futures contracts in the 1960s. U.S. gold futures began trading in 1975. Access to U.S. gold options was introduced in 1982, after the precious metals frenzy of 1979–1980. Although options created entirely new strategies for precious metals investors, most of the emphasis was on buying as a bet that futures would go up or down. For the average investor, strategies were almost exclusively "buy call options and hope for the best."

Considerable literature on precious metals investing was developed between 1975 and 1981. This material does not necessarily cover the full range of strategies that include the most popular vehicles for investing or speculating in metals. We are all familiar with physical metal that includes coins of the realm, medallions, bullion, and collectibles. To a lesser extent, there is jewelry. Then there is near metal in the form of depositary receipts. Depositary receipts represent metal that is stored in a depository on behalf of investors. In some cases, the investor can buy metal on margin or on loan. Depositary receipts can offer safety and flexibility. The metal is in a secured facility. The investor does not require insurance and usually does not pay storage or assay fees. However, the investor must rely on the integrity of the depository. In a time of true panic, there is no assurance the deposits will remain the assets of the investor.

FUTURES CONTRACTS

Futures contracts are actual commitments to make or take delivery of a specific quantity of metal at a specific time in the future—hence the name "futures contracts." Futures are actual legal contracts that bind buyers and sellers in the same way as any other contract to buy or sell a car, boat, or house. Using a car as an example, you might go into a dealership and test-drive a new Toyota hybrid Prius that runs on gasoline and electricity. You like the test car, but you are interested in some extra features that are not installed on the cars the dealer has in stock. To facilitate the purchase of your new Prius, you enter into a contract to purchase the Prius for delivery in 180 days. You specify the color and features and make a good-faith deposit binding the contract. The legal term for your deposit is *consideration*. However, in futures contacts the deposit is labeled "initial margin."

Once you have signed the contract and made your deposit, the contract is in full force and effect as long as the parties adhere to the contract provisions. By analogy, you are *long* one car contract while the dealer is *short* one car contract. A common question that frequently perplexes new students of futures markets is, "How can you sell something you don't have?" As in the example, the car dealer has sold a car he does not have. He has further obligated himself to deliver the right color vehicle at the agreed-upon price at a "date certain" in the future. In essence, the dealer is *short* one car.

You, on the other hand, are *long* one Prius automobile. You don't have it yet. When it arrives on the San Francisco dock, you need to claim it and have it pass inspection. If the price of the car goes up between the time you sign the contract and the time you take possession, you have saved money because you locked in a lower price. If the price declines, you could have picked up the car less expensively. On the seller's end, a rising price before making delivery cuts into profit potentials. A falling price means the dealer can acquire the car more cheaply and sell it to you at the contracted price for additional profit.

Suppose you come to a builder with plans for a house. He uses his best estimate to formulate a quote for your completed house based on materials, labor, transportation, land (if not included), and interest on the construction loan pay-down. If the price of lumber soars between the time the contract is consummated and the time of construction, the builder loses money because he has quoted a fixed price for completing the home. If building material costs decline as the house is completed, you could perhaps have gotten a cheaper quote on the house; alas, the general contractor becomes the beneficiary of the price change. Before construction, the contractor is liable for delivery of one house built within a certain period and subject to the architectural specifications for configuration and finishes. Much like a futures contract, you are *long* one house while the contractor is *short*.

So, we define a futures contract as a legally binding agreement to make or take delivery of a specific quality and quantity of a commodity at an executed price and at a specified time called expiration. The buyer is *long* and the seller is *short*. One difference between a futures contract for delivery of silver and a contract to build a house is that the futures contract is easily transferred from party to party through a clearinghouse or clearing broker; in simple terms, any long can sell to any short, thereby transferring the obligation to either make or take delivery. An additional difference is that the futures contract immediately confers the gain or loss on the prospective transaction to the parties, whereas the homebuyer is not likely to see any day-to-day benefit from changes in the cost of building materials or labor.

The fundamental purpose of futures markets is to offset risk. This probably sounds contradictory to some who have heard that futures are "the most dangerous markets in the world." Actually, the risk is offset by transferring it from producers and users to speculators. As an example, suppose you are in the business of mining silver. Your cost of production is approximately $4.25 per ounce. Major elements of production include capital equipment, labor, energy, interest rates, and remediation. To satisfy shareholders, you need to pay at least a 3 percent annual dividend. Silver is quoted at $5.05. At this point, you have to make a decision. You can take your chances that silver will maintain more than a required $4.37 to meet a 3 percent return over cost, or you can lock in the $5.05 price by selling a futures contract with an expiration that coincides with your production schedule. If you take your chances, you are speculating on the price of silver remaining stable or moving higher. If you sell your silver forward with a futures contract, you are *hedging* against any price deterioration.

If the decision is to hedge, you are most likely to sell to a *speculator* who assumes your price deterioration risk, hoping that prices will rise and his speculation will pay off. The speculator is essentially insuring the price for you, the producer. Since you have the product and wish to sell it at some future date, you are placing a *sell hedge* and are *short* silver.

Now let's assume you are a jewelry manufacturer making gold and silver bracelets. You have just completed your Christmas catalog with prices based on the current gold and silver market levels. Since profit margins in your business are thin, your concern is that gold and silver prices could rise before you have acquired raw materials for manufacturing your inventory. Under these circumstances, you see that you need a gold price of $396 or less to maintain your profit margin. A glance at the August gold futures contract posts a price of $392. With an extra $4 under your required price, you decide to buy August gold as a hedge against a rising price that could wipe out your manufacturing profit margin.

As you might assume, the purchase of a gold futures contract is a *buy hedge* and you would be *long* gold. Logic dictates that the long gold hedger and short gold hedger should get together as they would in the cash or spot market. After all, the seller is the producer and the buyer is the user. Why have an intermediary known as the speculator? The answer is that the time each may need to secure a buyer or seller can differ, and prices can change before the actual time the commodity needs to be delivered. During the time between producing and manufacturing, someone needs to assume the risk of an adverse price change *in either direction*. That is why long and short speculators are helpful.

Markets can work without speculators. If the commodity is highly stable with little price fluctuation, speculators are not required. Interestingly, such would be the case if gold and silver prices were, once again, fixed. Producers would always know what they would receive, and buyers would pay the prices fixed by decree. Yet, prices of today's raw materials tend to be highly unstable. From commodities like soybeans and corn to crude oil and gasoline, we see enormous swings of double-digit proportions. A price move of silver from $6 to $7 represents a 16.6 percent change that can happen in less than two days. When gold pops from $393 to $412, you have a 4.8 percent change. These numbers may seem insignificant unless you have a small 5 percent profit margin!

The concept of hedging is important for understanding how precious metals markets work. When evaluating the potential of a gold, silver, platinum, or palladium mine, it is essential to review the company's hedging policies and positions. Too frequently, investors jump to the conclusion that they should buy a gold stock because the price of gold is rising. However, if the company has sold its production forward using futures or long-term delivery contracts, there will be no advantage. In fact, mining stocks have been observed declining when metals are rising because they have been overhedged. This means they have sold in excess of actual production and the loss on the hedge takes a toll on the balance sheet!

With the brief description of the dynamics among hedgers, speculators, and futures markets, we can review the role of options on futures. For some, the distinction between an option and a futures contract is confusing. Both can be bought *long* and sold *short*. However, a futures contract is an *obligation* to make delivery (seller) or take delivery (buyer) of the commodity under the terms and conditions of the futures contract. The buyer of an option has the *right* but not the obligation to make or take delivery of a futures position at a specific price and time. The price is called the *strike* and the time is the *expiration*. The right to buy a futures position is a *call* while the right to sell is a *put*. In order to acquire the right to buy or sell, the purchaser pays a *premium* to the seller. Here's where it becomes a bit tricky. A buyer of an option can be long either a put or a call, while a seller can be short a put or a call. The option buyer has the right to assume a long futures position if the call strike is reached or to take a short futures position if the put strike is reached.

The option seller is often called the writer because he is writing the put or call. If the strike price is reached for a call, the option seller automatically assumes a futures position because he must deliver a long futures position to the option buyer. This places the seller short. If it is the put that reaches the strike, the buyer becomes short and the seller must take the opposite long position.

What happens if the strike price is not reached before the option expires? Under that circumstance, the buyer loses his rights and sacrifices the premium paid. The seller pockets the premium with a smile!

As a prelude to our discussion, consider that central banks know gold inventories should have income-generating potential. During the past several decades, a system of lending gold at nominal interest rates has been developed to help producers and consumers hedge. The gold loan rate is the interest charged on these transactions that permits the borrowing of inventory for replacement at some future date. Because gold is held as a quasi reserve asset, the opportunity risk on the part of the lender is theoretical. There is no intention to part with the inventory or speculate on price movements; the gold is simply lent out with an interest charge.

For example, the State Bank of India offers to lend gold to jewelry manufacturers at rates lower than a normal rupee loan. The process provides metal for fabrication at the current gold price. The bank views the loan as less risky because the metal is the collateral. Once sold, the receipts are deposited with the bank and the cash acts as security for the loan. Many financial institutions offer this type of transaction. Even mining companies can hold a portion of production off the market for gold loans.

This loan process is the cash equivalent of selling a call at a premium equal to the interest rate—with one *big* exception: The gold price remains variable. The reason I draw the similarity is because small investors do not have the capacity to buy gold and lend it out. If they did, gold would become a performing asset that more appropriately conforms to our definition of an investment. When we examine option strategies we see that there is a way to convert metals into performing assets and, better still, ways to synthesize various postures through combinations of options and futures. Here's how it works.

CALL OPTIONS

If you own physical gold in excess of 100 ounces, you can create a return in a way similar to that of the State Bank of India by selling call options against your inventory. For example, during August 1996, an October 400 gold call was quoted at $490 while gold was trading at approximately 39200. (For those unfamiliar with futures quotes, 39200 represents $392.) Gold options trading on the Commodity Exchange Incorporated (COMEX) division of the New York Mercantile Exchange (NYMEX) represent 100 ounces. Recall the strike price of 400 is the price at which the option buyer can purchase gold. Consider that the value of 100 ounces trading at $392 per ounce is $39,200. Therefore, the $490 premium represents a 1.25 percent return. This is derived by dividing $490 by the total contract value of $39,200.

By selling the 400 call, you collect $490. Of course, timing might yield a better or less attractive premium. October gold options expire in mid-September. Therefore, you earn your 1.25 percent premium during August and September—approximately six weeks. Annualized, these earnings amount to 10.83 percent (divide 1.25 percent by six weeks and multiply by 52). When compared with 1996 interest rates, 10.83 percent was competitive. Moreover, there would be the added safety of owning gold.

As an update, this example of a 1996 transaction was presented in the first version of this book (*The New Precious Metals Market*). The 2004 example is virtually the same. Gold was trading between 38600 and 41000, as seen in Figure 4.1. The September 410 call traded at $4.40 while gold was trading at approximately 40100. Notice that gold had a slight upward bias on the chart; however, the swings within the range appeared reasonably consistent. Selling the 410 call yielded $440 on a contract worth $41,000 for a 1.07 percent return.

A major difference between 1996 and 2004 is the number of months traded. Formerly, gold expired in February, April, June, August, October, and December. The contract was revised for monthly expirations and monthly options. This means that the transaction is not as limited in frequency because all 12 months are now available.

Although the replication of the 1996 transaction in 2004 is probably coincidental, it demonstrates a potential consistency in gold's behavior and pricing. There was no way to predict that this would happen other than to review gold's historical stability and volatility profile.

It should be noted that the 410 call *went into the money*. This means that the option was exercisable for a short period and the position (i.e., short 410 call) showed a loss. Yet, the highest the price moved while the position was held was 41550 on August 20, 2004. This means that the option holder (i.e., the person you sold the option to) had the right to buy

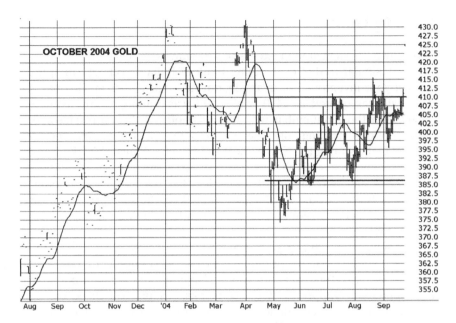

FIGURE 4.1 October gold traded in a range between 38600 and 41000. The wide range and short-term volatility provided high option premiums that allowed the sale of 410 gold calls at an attractive premium. (*Source:* eSignal.com)

gold from you at $410 when the price was $415.50. You would have been exposed to a $550 loss on the futures contract ($5.50 × 100 ounces = $550) because you were obligated to deliver at the $410 strike price. However, that $550 exposure would have been offset by the $440 you collected in premium for a net $110 loss.

As the transaction turned out, gold retreated back below the $410 strike and the option expired out of the money. You would have profited with the entire $440 premium.

Option premiums are a function of time, volatility, and proximity. The closer the strike, the more likely it is to be in the money. This increases premium values. The longer the time period, the higher the premium, under the assumption that time carries risk and/or the possibility of achieving the strike. Thus, time has an associated value. The greater the volatility, the more likely a strike price can be achieved. Over the course of a year, gold can exhibit reasonable volatility and provide healthy option premiums. Options are available for each calendar month and are based on the corresponding or next consecutive futures expiration. Gold futures generally trade bimonthly beginning with the February contract. With options, in contrast, there can be 12 separate opportunities to sell gold options during the year. Even if the best premiums averaged only 0.5 percent for each expiration, a 6 percent annualized yield would result.

What are the risks and exposures? The inherent risk in owning gold is that its value will decline. You may have purchased your metal at $400 an ounce in March or April of 1996 or August of 2004. By September of either year, you could have lost approximately $15 per ounce or 3.75 percent. Over the same time, you might have sold call options in October, November, December, January, and out to the following August for various premiums ranging from $3 to $25. Even with the 3.75 percent decline, there were enough option opportunities to provide impressive net positive returns. Of course, gold prices can always plunge. Although it's not historically evident in data during the past 10 years, there is always a chance the metal could seriously decline. Under such circumstances, the question would be whether call options could still provide enough premiums to offset falling values. In contrast, gold prices could rise above your strike price. You would be exposed to losing your gold . . . having it called away. In this case, you would still achieve the positive appreciation from the price at the time you sold the option to the strike. Thus, if you sold a $400 call when gold was selling for $385, you would make $15 an ounce plus your premium. If you are sufficiently nimble, you can simply repurchase the gold around $400 and start the procedure all over again.

There are defensive strategies that can keep you in the game. As long as people are willing to buy gold options, you can trade against your inventory. This is a form of "covered write." It is called this because your option exposure is offset by your actual gold inventory. Some successful practitioners of this methodology have been accumulating gold over the past few decades. Despite the lack of price appreciation, properly timed option selling has yielded comfortable returns ranging between 6 percent and 15 percent per year. At the same time, there is the underlying comfort of knowing you hold the quintessential asset of last resort. In some cases, traders buy futures to cover the call with a stop at or near the call strike for protection against price failure. It is a balancing act between option premiums and inventory exposure. Professional traders make money this way.

You may have guessed that you do not need a physical gold inventory to practice selling calls. If you have the cash equivalent of a gold inventory, you can sell calls and cover with *futures* if the strike is exceeded. Under this scenario, you are making your return on cash with the presumption that cash will be used to buy gold or gold futures. Here, your transaction can be leveraged. A gold futures contract might have a margin as low as $2,000 per 100 ounces. A $20 premium on a covered write based on futures represents $2,000 on $2,000, or 100 percent. The amount of leverage you use is a subjective decision that should be based on objective criteria. The fact that you may have $2,000 for the futures contract and there is a $20 premium offered does not mean you can afford the exposure. What if you sell a $400 call at $20 and the price moves to $420? Your premium will be wiped out. Any move beyond $420 will cost you $100 for every $1. This is because the futures contract and related option both represent 100 ounces of gold.

SELLING A CALL AND BUYING A PUT

On occasion gold moves higher, providing an opportunity to sell a call while buying a put for a credit. This strategy reduces the amount you make on the call by the amount you must spend on the put. However, you are protected if prices collapse because the call becomes less valuable or even worthless as the put appreciates. Gold may remain confined to a trading range, but if the range is wide with swift and frequent swings from tops to bottoms, you might be able to sell both calls and puts above and below the range.

Consider the market from 1993 through 1996 (See Figure 4.2). Gold traded in a range between $370 and $400 per ounce. This provided put and call strikes at 360, 370, 380, 390, 400, and 410. Gold options are traded in $10 increments. Few commodities were supported as well as gold during this period. The stability coupled with the possibility of a breakout or bust was just the fuel needed to heat up premiums on a regular basis. Strategically placed sales of calls and puts could have yielded returns in excess of stocks, bonds, real estate, and other investments for the period.

The danger came in 1997 when prices fell below the 37000 support. This had become a critical technical level. Once breached, gold assumed a downward momentum that lasted halfway through 1999 when a bottom was finally established. Under these conditions, the put provided a hedge against the depreciating price. What was lost in the value of physical gold was made up by the profit from the long put, which became a short futures position.

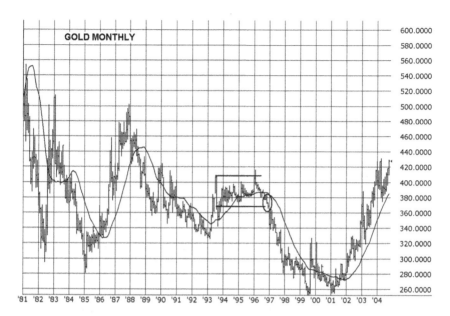

FIGURE 4.2 Gold monthly price action from 1981 through the first half of 2004 shows a wide range of prices with periods of extended stability as seen from 1993 through most of 1997. The bust below this range saw prices double bottom in 1999 and 2001 at approximately $255 per ounce. The decline represented less than 50 percent, which compares very favorably against the Nasdaq-100 Index from 2000 through 2003. (*Source:* eSignal.com)

BUTTERFLIES AND CONDORS

To supplement covered call writing, there are strategies that can protect inventories against dramatic breakouts or failures. Such strategies apply to holders of physical metal or those anticipating owning metal using a cash reserve. If you own 100 ounces while gold is trading at approximately $390 per ounce, you can sell (write) 390 calls and 390 puts while buying 400 calls and 380 puts. This transaction is commonly referred to as a *butterfly* where the two 390 options are the body or inside options and the 400 calls and 380 puts are the outside options or wings (see Figure 4.3). When advantageously placed, premiums earned on the body should exceed the amount paid for the wings. This is called a credit transaction or credit spread because you receive more premium than you spend.

The reason is as explained earlier. An option's value is based on three criteria: proximity, volatility, and time. The closer an option is to the current selling price, the more premium it will command. Since the body of

FIGURE 4.3 The center of the butterfly is an option straddle that involves selling the same strike for both the put and the call. In this illustration the "body" consists of the 390 call and 390 put option. The "wings" are placed for protection against a breakout or bust. Buying the 380 put protects against a decline below 380 while buying the 400 call protects against a rise above 400.

the spread is at the money, it will have a higher value than the wings. The short call and put alone would be called a *short straddle*. An option straddle refers to the sale of the same strike for both the call and put.

Only one inside option can be in the money. Exposure is limited to $10 on either side less the net credit premium. The closer the price is to the body upon expiration, the more premium you will earn. If gold's price is exactly $390 at the options' expirations, the entire credit premium is your profit.

The wings protect against any move outside of the trading range between $380 and $400. Your inventory will not be called away because you are protected by the $400 call. If gold prices soar, you still own it. For the holder of metal, an alternative strategy is to finance buying a put with the sale of a call at a credit as mentioned earlier. This protects your gold from a price decline while yielding a premium if the price remains stable. If you bought a 380 put and gold declined below $380, your inventory would be protected by a short futures position. If gold recovered above $380, you would be back at square one. Your exposure would come when opportunity profits were lost on rising prices.

Assume you sold a 400 call. A move above this level would mean your gold could be called away at $400 and you would sacrifice any profit above this price. Keep in mind that you can replace your inventory by paying the difference between your strike and cash gold. If you are efficient, your lost opportunity will be small.

On July 19, 2004, October gold was selling between a low of 40660 and a 40920 high. The 400 call sold for $1,300 while the 400 put was at $500. The combined premiums for selling this straddle were $1,800. The 425 call was available for $250 while the 375 put was at $150. The combined cost of buying outside protection was $400. The net premium collected was $1,800 less $400: $1,400. Subsequent to placing the trades, October gold traded as high as 41550 and as low as 38600. Since we were short both the 400 call and the 400 put, the potential loss at 41550 would have been $1,550 less our net premium of $1,400 or $150. At 38600, our exposure was $1,400 less $1,400 or $0.

The maximum exposure as per our example would be from 40000 to 42500, or $2,500 less the $1,400 collected: $1,100. The same exposure existed on the short 400 put and long 375 put. When the options expired, gold was trading at approximately 40600. Since the 400 call was in the money, we were short at 40000 with a $6 loss. However, we collected $1,400. Covering the short would have yielded $800.

Prudence dictates that the short should be immediately covered to avoid jeopardizing the remaining profit. As it was, gold appeared to be declining and we decided to place a 41100 stop while seeking a decline below 40000. Indeed, the price dipped below 40000 and we were able to cover at 39990. This real-life example serves to support the strategy. Figure 4.4 provides the October 2004 gold chart for reference.

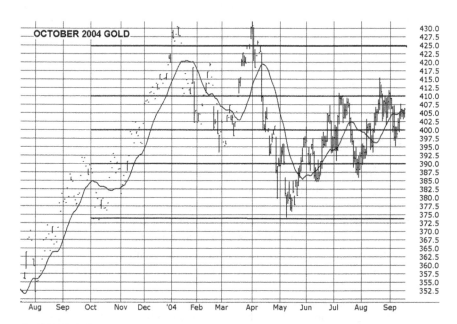

FIGURE 4.4 October 2004 gold was in a wide channel uptrend with a midpoint averaging 40000. The thick line at 40000 is centered between the 310 put and the 410 call as well as the 375 put and 425 call. Based on the interim behavior from May through June, it appeared gold would stay within the 39000 to 41000 range through the October option expirations. (*Source:* eSignal.com)

SELL

400 CALLS
370 PUTS

BUY
360
PUTS

BUY
410
CALLS

FIGURE 4.5   The condor has a body consisting of different call and put strikes with wings that protect against a breakout or bust. The objective is to give some room from the current futures price to lessen the likelihood that either the short call or put will be appreciably in the money.

Further variations on the theme involve selling different inside strikes while buying different outside strikes. This is almost the same as a butterfly, but the body consists of different put and call strikes. Assume gold is trading at $390. You might sell the 400 call and 370 put while buying the 410 call and 360 put (see Figure 4.5). The trade will yield a credit because the closer options have higher premiums. If prices remain between the two inside options by expiration, your premium is your profit. If prices rise above the 400 inside call, you make the amount of the price rise up to the 410 outside call while your puts become worthless. A breakout above $410 caps your profit at $10 plus your premium. This strategy is frequently called a *condor*.

RATIO SPREADS

With our growing understanding of options, we can experiment with combinations and permutations of call and put strikes to achieve very refined objectives. When we look at the personality reflected by a chart, we may see a propensity for extended trading ranges as exemplified by the 1993 through 1996 period. Using $400 as an assumed median, we could have an opportunity to buy the 410 call and 390 put while selling *two* 420 calls and *two* 380 puts. The goal is to achieve a credit for the call and put sides of the total transaction.

This strategy assumes that gold has the potential to break out above the 410 strike or bust below the 390 strike, but will be constrained below 42000 and above 38000. Strategically, a move above 41000 activates the 410 call's earning potential. As prices rise, the 380 put premiums should rapidly deteriorate. This provides an opportunity to cover the short puts at a deteriorated price, thus favorably removing any downside exposure.

If gold rises above 41000 but stays below 42000, the 410 call earns a profit while the 420 calls expire worthless. The position can be covered and the premiums added to the position's success. Alternatively, if the market crashes but fails to penetrate 38000, a profit is realized on the 390 put while the two 380 puts expire worthless. All the while, the surplus premium (i.e., the credit) is collected, too.

What happens if the price breaks out above the short 420 strikes or falls below the short 380 calls? Since you are short two outside options, you will progressively lose money the further the price moves beyond the strikes. However, one of the two options is covered by the long inside option. You have made the combined premiums *plus* the $10 from your long 410 call up to the 420 calls. Since one of the short 420 calls is covered by the long 410 call, you lose on only one of the 420 calls. You have collected the premiums on all short sales and you have made $10 from 41000 to 42000. This means the price must exceed 42000 by $10 plus any collected premiums to cause a loss. You are still a winner up to approximately $430/43500, depending on the collected premiums.

This approach is philosophically saying that you don't know where gold will be upon expiration, but you are reasonably confident that it will end up between 38000 and 42000. With no breakout or bust, you collect your premium.

In the real world, October gold traded from a 40350 low to a 40780 high on July 14, 2004. The 400 call was at $1,500 while the 400 put was $1,050. The 410 call was at $1,100 and the 390 put was $620. The ratio spread involved buying one 400 call and one 400 put for $2,550 while selling *two* 410 calls and *two* 390 puts (a total of four) for $3,440. The net credit was $890. If the market moved within the range, either the 400 call or the 400 put would move dollar-for-dollar up to $410 or down to $390. Beyond these wings the positions would lose dollar-for-dollar, but there would already be $1,890 collected from the $10 appreciation in the long option plus the credit premium. Gold would need to move above 42890 or below 37110 before losses would accrue. When gold dipped to 38600, there was an opportunity to reduce long-side exposure by covering one of the short 410 calls. This ensured a profit on the long leg if gold recovered above 40000, no matter what. When gold rallied above 41000, there was the same chance to reduce short-side exposure by buying back one 390 put. The cost came to $410, which still left a $480 credit. Again, reference Figure 4.4.

There was still the prospect for either the call or the put to exceed the strike. As mentioned in the previous real-life example, the options expired with gold at 40600. Since gold was declining at the time, we liquidated our futures position that resulted from our exercised 400 gold call for a $600 profit. The total result was $480 in premium plus the $600 futures profit: a total of $1,080.

A trading range market usually offers a chance to cover the short positions of each leg. As prices move higher, the put premiums deteriorate and you can cover to remove exposure. If prices retreat, you can do the same with short calls. Eventually, you may be left with only the long put and call. A breakout can be liquidated for a profit followed by the same for a bust. Over time, positions are legged in or out. This simply means that the position is added to or reduced over time.

In some cases, you will find a net positive transaction involving futures and options combinations. In the case of silver, anticipation and false breakouts created the perfect environment for selling options without underlying inventory. In August 1996, I recommended selling December silver 525 calls and 500 puts for combined premiums of 25 cents. Although silver traded above the calls and below the puts, the transaction was lifted after premiums had deteriorated to below 10 cents. Exposure was confined to a move above $5.50 or below $4.75. In other words, either strike would need to be exceeded by the 25-cent premium collected on the transaction. By the middle of September, the 525 calls and 500 puts were yielding a combined 30 cents. (See Figure 4.6.) Although the call or put would be highly likely to be in the money by December expiration, the price would need to exceed $5.30 or fall below $4.70 before the transaction would begin losing on an expiration basis. Thus, if the price dipped to $4.75 on expiration, there would still be a 5-cent profit, assuming all positions were properly liquidated. The silver contract represented 5,000 ounces. Therefore, every penny was worth $50. A 5-cent profit was $250. Margin on the transaction was as low as $1,000. Your gain was 25 percent. These are not hypothetical trades; all of these opportunities actually existed within the time frames mentioned.

A unique characteristic of precious metals markets is their remarkable price stability. Trading ranges generally extend over moderate to long interim periods. This behavior has been extremely reliable. Equally important, when prices for silver and gold do break technical support or resistance, premiums usually become sufficiently rich so that adverse price movements can be offset. During the 1970s, metals were so reactionary that exposures were too great to consistently assume trading range strategies. In addition, liquid options did not exist. Some economists believe options strategies have actually confined prices within ranges. Professional traders who implement selling strategies in calls and puts may try to trade futures into their ranges. Because speculators and hedgers work off the same historical patterns, ranges can become self-fulfilling prophecies.

FIGURE 4.6 September silver traded in a range from approximately 52500 to 50000. Selling the December 525 calls and 500 puts yielded as much as 30 cents. (*Source:* eSignal.com)

Certainly, everyone who is short options wants to preserve the range. The question is whether they have the power to accomplish this objective.

INTRACOMMODITY STRATEGIES

Even before options, there were ways to earn money on inventories using futures. You may be familiar with the term *basis* used in commodity markets. The difference between the cash price and a futures contract price is the basis. There are also differences between consecutive expiration months, called intracommodity spreads. For example, April gold will have a lower price than June, June will be lower than August, August lower than October, and so on. The basis and spread difference represent a cost of holding gold that includes an assumed storage charge, assay fee, insurance premium, and interest rate. In a normal market, the further the month is from the present time, the wider the spread or basis. This price difference will converge on the cash price as expiration approaches. Producers and consumers use futures to protect against adverse price movements. If you own gold and are afraid prices will fall, you could sell futures short. Any negative price movement yields a profit on a short sale. Suppose the current gold price is $450 per ounce in January. You notice February gold has a price of $455. There is a $5 difference. By selling short February gold, you automatically earn $5 more than the current selling price and you have locked in the $455 price.

What if prices continue to go up? You have the gold to deliver and you have sacrificed the opportunity profit above $455. If gold remains static, the $5 spread will eventually shrink to zero and you have earned $5 in about one month on 100 ounces ($500 on $45,000 worth, or 1.1 percent). Calculated over 12 months, this process could earn 13.2 percent if each spread were uniform at 1.1 percent. In reality, the spread will closely reflect a short-term interest rate like that of a 90-day Treasury bill. The hedge income generated from consecutive short sales is likely to be low, but it is still income. The purpose of this strategy is to earn a modest return while protecting against disaster. Further, if call option premiums are low, you can finance call purchases from the hedge income. If a breakout materializes, you are long at the call strike and you profit from any bull market.

In the immediate aftermath of peak 1980 precious metals prices, investors were torn between holding silver and gold for security and buying Treasury notes and bonds for high yields. Spreads were below bond yields, and traders found it comforting to buy futures on margin while investing the remaining cash in government securities. This allowed interest to accumulate on cash reserved for precious metals purchases. Unfortunately, gold prices declined and the futures positions lost money. However, the losses were the same as if the cash had been used to buy the actual gold or silver.

INTERCOMMODITY SPREADS

Aside from intracommodity strategies, you can take advantage of intercommodity spreads. Historically, platinum prices exceed those of gold. However, there have been instances where the price difference between platinum and gold became narrow. The merging of the COMEX and NYMEX has allowed traders to economically "spread" the platinum group metals against gold and silver. Spreads involve the purchase and sale of commodities in anticipation of a change in the difference between prices. In the case of platinum versus gold, one would buy platinum and sell gold when the price difference became small or negative. Spreads are quoted with the long leg or buy side first. Therefore, a platinum/gold spread involves buying platinum and selling gold. If the spread were referred to as gold/platinum, you would be buying gold and selling platinum.

In theory, precious metals move in tandem. In practice, this has not been the case during the past several years. Fundamental forces affecting platinum are substantially different today because platinum is a highly industrial precious metal. The majority of platinum is used in catalytic converters and petroleum cracking. As the volume of automobiles increases, so does demand for platinum. As more refineries come on line, platinum demand will grow. However, platinum is a resilient metal that is not actually consumed in its catalytic role. The metal used as a catalyst can be recycled. This simplistic view is covered more fully in Chapter 8. For the purpose of justifying a platinum/gold strategy, it is important to understand that industrial demand for platinum coupled with limited supply tends to hold the platinum premium over gold.

A strategy of buying platinum and selling gold when the spread narrows to a $5 platinum premium and lifting the spread at $25 has worked well over time (see Figure 4.7). There were two instances when the spread went seriously negative. However, in all instances through 2004, platinum has recovered its premium over gold. Here, a careful review of the structural differences between platinum and gold must be continuous. As later

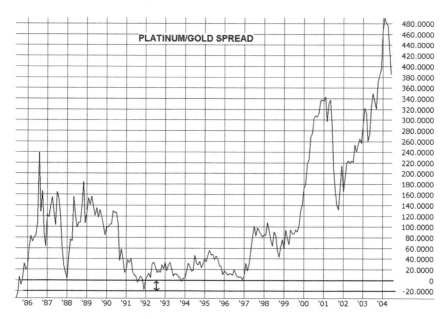

FIGURE 4.7 The platinum/gold spread shows platinum consistently above gold. Reversals in this relationship are rare and brief. (*Source:* eSignal.com)

chapters reveal, certain demographic patterns imply that gold requirements could accelerate during the next several decades. In particular,
China and India could become major consumers for religious and cultural
reasons. The key is to observe consumption patterns in both metals relative to supply. Although gold demand may have good prospects as wealth
increases in China and India, there are huge central bank reserves that
can act as a buffer.

Platinum has no such reserves. Based on this one structural difference, platinum prices can be more sensitive to shifting supply and demand fundamentals. Gold, in contrast, is influenced by potential central
bank or International Monetary Fund (IMF) sales.

Platinum's sister metal, palladium, also offers spread opportunities.
From 1989 forward, palladium has experienced the most interesting relative strength, rising more than 1,000 percent in a few decades. Technological advances in the use of palladium as a substitute for platinum in
catalytic converters boosted the price ratio between these metals. The
purchase of palladium against the sale of platinum was an incredibly
profitable strategy when palladium suddenly rocketed to more than
$1,000 per ounce.

The extreme reaction after 1998 suggests fundamental change in the
platinum/palladium relationship. The change was attributed to a concentrated effort to use palladium as a substitute for platinum in catalytic converters. The reason should be obvious. Platinum held a $240 to $282
premium over palladium and a 1998 price range from 35000 to 43000. Palladium was much cheaper and appeared to be capable of meeting emission standards.

However, as soon as palladium demand began to grow, the spread
started to reverse, as seen in Figure 4.8. In particular, companies like Ford
and Toyota began palladium accumulation programs that eventually resulted in massive losses on their palladium inventories.

As the palladium transition was gathering momentum, Russia began
limiting exports. The results were unprecedented and totally unexpected.
For the very first time, palladium surpassed platinum and just kept going.
In fact, palladium achieved the highest price of any member of the Big
Four precious metals in the beginning of 2001 as it blasted beyond $1,050
per ounce. This was an absolute shocker. However, the bust below the
$240 platinum premium represented a technical signal to buy palladium
while selling platinum.

Interestingly, this potential situation was covered in the first iteration
of this book published in 1998. As we cover in later chapters, the balances
between platinum and palladium supplies and demand are delicate and
tight. Until there is some form of surplus and swing inventory, these vital

FIGURE 4.8 From 1986 through 1989, platinum maintained a premium over palladium between $350 and $480 per ounce. This relationship was consistent until narrowing from 1989 through 1991 after the announcement of revolutionary cold fusion. The spread settled between $240 and $282 from 1991 all the way to 1998. Thereafter, the relationship completely destabilized. (*Source:* eSignal.com)

industrial metals are likely to have many extreme price movements capable of generating outrageous profit potentials.

It is interesting to note that only 20 percent more palladium was produced than platinum in 1994. Moving forward, palladium's production growth appeared stronger, with approximately 6.21 million ounces mined in 1995, compared with 4.89 million ounces of platinum. During 1996, the spread between platinum and palladium widened in favor of platinum because of a surplus differential. How quickly things can change!

The platinum contract represents 50 ounces of metal, while the palladium contract is 100 ounces. Hence, the proportional spread is two contracts of platinum for every one of palladium. Platinum is worth $50 per dollar fluctuation whereas palladium is worth $100. With a 2-to-1 ratio, the values are equalized.

Strategically, one could consistently profit by selling platinum and buying palladium each time the spread widened to a $450 platinum premium. Then, the spread would be reversed when it narrowed to approximately $350. The actual instruction would be:

> *Buy 1 [March contract month] Palladium—Sell 2 [April contract month] Platinum at $450 Platinum over or greater. Add to position on widening to $460 using a $485 stop.*

The contract month needs to be inserted as indicated. One of the idiosyncrasies in the spread is the different futures contract expirations. Platinum trades January, April, July, and October, while palladium trades March, June, September, and December. The difference is not overwhelmingly significant, but it forces the timing and requires some consideration for the difference in carrying charges—if we want to be precise. (What we generally find is that precision is not necessarily worth the effort).

The months would be paired as March/April, June/July, September/October, and December/January. In our example, the exposure from initial entry to stop was $25 or $2,500 per spread. The swing objective represented $100 or $10,000 per spread. Margins were low—around $1,000 per spread. The profit possibilities are obvious and impressive when referencing Figure 4.8 from 1989 through 1991. The strategy generated five swings with two stop-outs. That represents $50,000 in profit against $5,000 in losses. In the later part of the trading range, there may have been another two stop-outs; depending on the specific months selected and whether the spread was rolled if expirations forced liquidation.

When the $350 support was violated, the strategy was to hold palladium while selling platinum. It worked sporadically until the new trading range was established from 1991 through 1997. This was the long stretch of relative stability and balance. Unfortunately, the spread was not as dramatic and it did not offer the same sensational ratios. From my own experience, the transactions were a wash, although I am sure some traders fared better.

As reviewed in the Introduction, the real action came when palladium broke out relative to platinum in 1998. Using $240 as resistance (having been former support), it looked like a very reliable trading range was setting up between $220 and $240. However, that was too narrow for me, and other spread traders probably agreed. Admittedly, I recommended trading the bust below $200 platinum over palladium. Since the chart was in new territory, the strategy was simply to ride the spread as it narrowed and reversed to place palladium over platinum.

The swing was $680 in the almost three years from March 1998 to January 2001. That represents $68,000 per spread or 6,800 percent on $1,000 initial margin. In reality, I was stopped out twice in 2000 when the market double bottomed. The first was a profit. The second was a loss. By the time the spread resumed favoring palladium, most traders were in disbelief. How could the relatively unknown palladium surpass platinum to such a huge extent?

The next opportunity came when platinum climbed $200 relative to palladium in the beginning of 2001. This was the signal to buy platinum and sell palladium. Once again, the results exceeded the wildest expectations. Platinum moved to a $700 premium over palladium over the next four years. The fundamentals supported a case for this relationship because automobile manufacturers moved back toward platinum when palladium had taken such an enormous price lead. This was the granddaddy of all the intercommodity spreads. The spread yielded approximately $20,000 per year if ideally rolled from months to months.

Why trade the spread when the gross move in futures seems substantially similar and easier? Platinum had a gross move from approximately $340 per ounce in 1999 to about $940 at the 2004 peak. That's $600 compared with the spread that moved from just under a negative $440 (meaning that platinum was selling for $440 per ounce *less* than palladium) to a positive $760 (meaning platinum was selling for $760 *more* than palladium). That's a $1,200 swing for the same approximate period using less margin and having (presumably) less volatility and risk.

These are sensational imbalances, and it is likely industry will not tolerate such price behavior on any consistent basis. The danger in these swings is the possibility that science will be financially motivated to find a total substitute for both metals in their primary roles in auto and truck catalytic converters. Computerized ignition and fuel mixture systems are just such a longer-term threat.

Understand that platinum's popularity as an investment metal and in jewelry can still cause positive swings against the palladium ratio. The palladium/platinum spread carries more risk than platinum/gold because the history is less stable and developments favoring palladium took hold after the turn of the millennium. Investment accumulation of palladium is almost nonexistent relative to platinum, gold, and silver. Therefore, investors must rely on its industrial demand for significant price enhancements.

As with gold, a cash platinum inventory lends itself to option writing. Platinum futures and options represent 50-ounce contracts in contrast with 100 ounces for gold and 5,000 ounces for silver. If platinum is trading at $420 per ounce, the total contract value is $21,000, whereas gold at $400 per ounce represents a contract value of $40,000 on 100 ounces. Platinum's smaller contract size makes it more manageable. In many cases, option premiums can be attractive. However, platinum has offered a less liquid market than gold and silver. Again, circumstances can quickly change. Commercialization of any new platinum-based technology can quickly shift investor interest toward platinum. Platinum can easily gain liquidity.

TECHNICAL ANALYSIS BOOST

Strategies designed to give precious metals a yield can be enhanced through certain timing mechanisms. You are probably familiar with technical analysis and chart interpretation. Since the development of high-speed, low-cost computers, technical analysis has gained enormous favor and respectability. Once viewed as hocus-pocus by the academic and investment establishment, technical analysis has virtually taken over from fundamental analysis as the tool of choice. The random walk theory that contends past performance cannot predict future events has been significantly discounted in our new computer age. There is sound evidence that certain technical market approaches work.

With this in mind, option and spread strategies can be optimized by more accurate timing and pattern recognition. For example, there are new computer systems that apply human problem-solving logic to pattern recognition. These systems, called neural networks, have displayed uncanny accuracy in predicting market behavior. Although the jury is still out on neural network performance, scientists know that these powerful programs can tell investors the probability that markets are in trending or trading range patterns. This can be extremely useful information for writing (selling) call options against metal inventories.

If you can have a certain confidence that gold will remain within certain price boundaries, your timing of option strategies can be more accurate. Obviously, call premiums will be higher if the strike price is closer. Neural networks can measure the probability of a breakout based on certain market patterns, which may include an analysis of price momentum, open interest changes, and volume. In the past, the artful technical analysis practitioner would eyeball a chart and use intuition to determine support and resistance price levels. It is true that certain individuals seem to have a sixth sense for picking tops and bottoms, but for the average investor, mechanical systems and statistical tools are the next best thing to clairvoyance.

As the publisher of the daily COMMODEX® system, I am familiar with using technical analysis for accurate timing. COMMODEX was developed during the 1950s by my father, the late Edward B. Gotthelf. The system is designed to automatically trade commodities based on certain price forecasting formulas and trading rules. Although the system is sufficiently robust to have withstood the test of time, applications for this mechanical approach have changed with market dynamics. There were no options when the system was developed. COMMODEX provides buy and sell signals for futures contracts. Because options are derivatives of futures, the system can apply to new strategies. A buy signal for futures can translate into the purchase of a call option, the sale of a put, or both. A sell signal can lead to the purchase of a put, sale of a call, or both. Then, you can apply the combinations of options and futures to buy and sell signals. COMMODEX is a trend-following system, looking for markets that are moving consecutively higher or lower on balance. If no price trend is recognized, COMMODEX remains neutral with no position. This is different from a reversal system, which is always long or short, but never neutral.

When COMMODEX was introduced in 1959, neutral signals could not be traded. Today, neutral signals can be the basis for selling both calls and puts above and below the futures price or applying the butterfly and condor strategies previously covered. If the market remains trendless, the options will lose value and the investor can collect the premiums as the options expire worthless. This is particularly good for trading precious metals. Given the long dry spells when gold, silver, and the platinum group remain in ranges, it is comforting to know there is no technical basis for a breakout or bust. Whether you apply the COMMODEX system, moving average crossovers, relative strength, stochastic indicators, Market Profile®, or a host of other technical tools is not important. The key is to use these tools in an integrated strategy for collecting revenue from the new precious metals markets.

INVESTMENT METHODS

The World Gold Council has published "A Guide to Investing in Gold," an informative pamphlet that touches on traditional approaches without discussing strategies. The council highlights 10 ways to invest:

1. Bullion
2. Bullion coins
3. Numismatic coins
4. Statement accounts
5. Accumulation plans
6. Mining shares

7. Mutual funds
8. Futures
9. Options
10. Forwards

Except for forwards, which require large financial commitments, these areas apply to individual investors and are available for silver, platinum, and palladium, too. Platinum and palladium have few, if any, numismatic coins because these metals were hardly ever used for coin of the realm. In addition, palladium does not have sufficient popularity for the development of statement accounts or accumulation plans. These facts aside, the 10 investment methods can be broken into four categories:

1. Physical holdings
2. Custodial holdings
3. Derivatives
4. Equities

I consolidate these further into the traditional, progressive, and participatory. If you own coins or bullion, you're a *traditionalist*. If you trade futures and options, you are *progressive*. If you own equities, you are *participatory*, involved in the rewards of production and distribution.

Strategically, there are times to own metal, times to trade progressively, and times to participate in equities. Further, all three have a measure of overlap in today's precious metals environment. This is to say that a precious metals advocate can justify owning metal or having a custodial account simply as disaster insurance. If the purpose is to protect against a financial panic, physical metal is favored over a custodial account because the integrity of the custodian like a bank or brokerage house might be challenged. When all else fails, the investor would need coins or bars. There is a serious question as to whether anyone would be safe in a crisis of such proportions that it requires a flight to gold and silver.

Leaving philosophical questions and intellectual exercises aside, nothing would be more secure than physical metal. If some technological breakthrough like cold fusion becomes a commercial reality, demand for palladium and platinum could be so explosive as to justify owning metal for fear of a complete market lockout. Based on current palladium production, its price could climb to $5,000 an ounce while remaining economically viable for supporting the cold fusion process. The original literature touted that as little as a half ounce of palladium could power an entire home for a thousand years. If true, $5,000 an ounce might be a bargain. At the first hint of commercial feasibility, you and I would probably be foreclosed from participating. Yet, if we own 10, 20, or 100 ounces of palladium at prices ranging from $100 to $200, this modest investment can grow into a small fortune. There is no doubt you would be making a bet on unproven technology. But the gamble is worth the price for those who can afford it.

A more likely scenario is the prospect of platinum fuel cells for home and automotive use. Fuel cell technology will be reviewed in greater detail when we cover platinum fundamentals in Chapter 8. Hypothetically, we could see a serious move toward stationary fuel cells for home and office use as a result of the war on terror and the vulnerability of our power distribution grid. Fuel cells can run on natural gas and propane, which are widely distributed through public service companies. As an alternative to the grid, individual cells can be placed in homes for local power generation. This model is more efficient because most of the power generated by utilities is dissipated and lost through the grid. Local generating presents huge efficiencies.

Details aside, the demand for platinum could become extreme while new discoveries remain sparse. The result would be a huge price surge. Again, a small amount of platinum can go a long way when prices rocket from $600 to $6,000.

As later chapters demonstrate, equities may easily represent the best precious metals investments. When you own mining stocks, you participate in production and distribution. You make your gains the old-fashioned way—through earnings. In a reasonably stable stock market environment, stocks and mutual funds are sound and effective. In particular, gold stocks and mutual funds have the advantage of widening profit margins based on stable prices and falling production costs. Yes, the ratio between price and cost can fluctuate. Some companies will have better numbers than others. But the process of mining and selling gold, silver, platinum, and palladium in a free and open market should maintain better than average performance as demand for these commodities grows.

When trading equities, an investor must be aware of the general market environment. Even gold stocks suffer during an overall market collapse, as seen in 1987 and during the 2000 recession. When picking individual stocks, the investor must consider properties, location, management, technology, financial strength, political environment, and a string of other fundamental factors. Should one invest in a dedicated mine that specifically produces gold, silver, platinum, or palladium? For example, North American Palladium concentrates on palladium, as the name implies. However, gold, silver, and platinum are a usual consequence of palladium production. Alternatively, should the investor look at a base metal producer that spins off large by-product precious metals production? Freeport-McMoRan produces gold as a consequence of copper, although the company also pursues gold mines.

What technology is in place? Are investors looking at deep shaft or strip mines? What are the ore grades and how much does the metal cost to refine? When later chapters review specific metals in greater detail, you will see how many considerations exist. Selection is a complex process.

If you choose a mutual fund, you should determine the management philosophy. Is it a small-cap fund? Are choices highly speculative, or are investors investing in an established mix of companies? The most popular funds deal exclusively in gold stocks. There are international funds, country-specific funds, and sector-specific funds. Speculative or venture funds may invest in start-up companies, partnerships, or even property rights. You can even seek out funds specializing in mining technology stocks. The variety is almost endless.

I should point out that equities have associated options, too. Speculating in stocks can be linked to the general market environment or the specific metal price trend. Understand that production costs are relatively fixed compared to product price fluctuations. Although that statement may appear obvious, rising metals prices will eventually lead to rising profit margins. However, if a company has hedged, it may not participate in the rewards of price appreciation. This has been particularly perplexing to investors who have jumped into mining companies with both feet, only to find that the stock declines because of a poorly placed hedge or badly conceived forward selling.

Sometimes you might miss the move in physical metal but catch the reaction in subsequent stock movement. That is why relationships call for integrated strategies. In the old days, precious metals did not involve so many strategic considerations. Obviously, market structure has changed. It is now far more complex.

It is unfortunate that so much of the promotion of gold, silver, and (to a lesser extent) platinum and palladium is based on an assumption of doom and gloom. There is an inherent tendency to link the need to invest in gold and silver with a pending hyperinflation or global monetary meltdown. The truth is no such disasters are required to inspire precious metals higher. Facts indicate that population patterns and general global wealth are the more likely motivators for these markets during the next several decades. Yes, inflation can be the catalyst for a new major bull market. Yes, a monetary crisis can drive people back to hard assets. Yes, a change in political atmosphere can ignite a panic. No, these are not the absolute requirements for rising precious metals prices.

Consider that gold made a contraindicated recovery beginning in 2001 when inflation was low. The definitive price rise began before oil made its war-related move and before 9/11. Retrospectively, many believe weak stocks and falling interest rates were the motivators. However, accumulation patterns point to another possibility. The combination of gold and associated options created strategies for making gold a performing asset. Like bonds, gold could have a yield in the form of premium, as we have illustrated in this chapter. Using gold as an ultimate hedge while earning a return represents a structural change and a new opportunity. The same holds true for silver, platinum, and (to a lesser extent) palladium.

Thus, we see that the ever-changing economic environment can be the ultimate foundation for new strategies using precious metals.

CHAPTER 5

Price
Action

Research associated with this book guided me to hundreds of sources. Throughout my investigations, I found the majority of readily available information came from individuals and organizations that were subjectively interested in promoting bullish prospects for precious metals. Facts and figures associated with precious metals are often obscured by an ever-continuing optimism about higher prices. During the mid-1990s, there was an increasing awareness among producers that their markets are elastic and price sensitive. As commodities, the higher the price, the more restricted the demand. The lower the price, the more affordable the metal. This contrasts with the theory that demand for precious metals can and does increase with price. This corresponds with the theory of luxury pricing. The most common example of luxury pricing is seen in the automotive market. The Lexus and Toyota line have virtually identical vehicles from power plant to options to body type. For example, the Toyota Highlander SUV and Lexus RX 300 are virtually the same with the exception of small body details. Yet, Lexus commands a higher price because it has been positioned as a premium vehicle with an associated higher status. In some cases, the demand for certain Lexus models is greater than for the comparable Toyota despite the higher price because of the luxury appeal.

Certainly, the precious metals buying frenzy of 1979–1980 established a precedent for the positive correlation between rising prices and rising demand. Refer again to Figure 1.1 in Chapter 1 to examine the effect of a herd mentality in silver when prices make their extreme advance. Of course, the circumstances of a panic are not the same as those of a normal market. In reality, silver and gold had no commodity identities in 1979–1980. People simply did not understand how pricing should be correlated.

Price sensitivity became clear when industrial consumers screamed for alternatives to silver, gold, and platinum following the 1980 price peaks. From 1977 through 1984, gold and silver were event driven. Prices would react to specific events with very little supply consideration. This extraneous and reactionary performance was the incentive for users to seek alternatives. You may recall that Europe did not require catalytic converters on cars and trucks through the 1970s and 1980s. The surge in platinum prices played a strong role in their delay toward cleaner air. At the time pollution control was being examined, technology was at a fork in the road between "lean-burn" engines and the conventional catalytic converter. As platinum prices began retracing to reasonable levels, catalytic devices appeared more economical than implementing entirely new combustion technologies.

What would have happened if Europe had adopted lean burn over catalytic converters? Considering the amount of platinum and palladium dedicated to automobiles and trucks, it is fair to say price margins for the platinum-group metals would have been seriously challenged. With today's increasingly powerful computers, lean-burn technology is more feasible. Ignition, fuel/air mixture, fuel monitoring, suspension adjustment, and gear shifting can be more precisely controlled by tiny automobile "brains." Assuming manufacturers do not move to an entirely new power system, don't be surprised to find yourself driving a vehicle that operates more efficiently without the use of a catalytic device. Such cars are already in production.

As strange as it may seem, dynamic price histories for gold, silver, platinum, and palladium are extremely short. From a marketing perspective, none of these metals is mature. It is as though gold and silver were introduced as commodities in the 1970s. Platinum and palladium actually have more product maturity. Yet even these metals have a brief price history. There is evidence platinum was used in ancient Egypt and by Native Americans. Whether they knew the distinction between platinum and silver is unknown. Certainly, platinum is a harder metal than silver and is more difficult to work. As an element, platinum was analyzed in the 1700s. However, commercial production was not feasible until the nineteenth century.

This is an important consideration when one examines price patterns. With so little historical behavior to analyze, we cannot be sure of consistency. What may appear as a pattern or trend today can easily change tomorrow. This is why precious metals remain so interesting and exciting. The lack of dynamic pricing has hardly been raised as an issue. I believe it is one of the *main* issues! Incredible as it may sound, governments still maintain a market-independent official price for gold and silver. This suggests these markets are still not fully weaned from fixed pricing to dynamic pricing. Indeed, the subtle links may never be completely broken.

The vice chairman of the U.S. Congress Joint Economic Committee, Representative Jim Saxton of New Jersey, wrote an August 1999 report entitled "IMF Gold Sales in Perspective." The report reviews requests for the International Monetary Fund (IMF) to sell its 103 million ounce gold hoard. One of the interesting problems with the postulated sale was the fact that the metal was booked at the official $48 per ounce price. Carried as an asset, this metal was, and remains, improperly valued and, of course, undervalued. The obvious question is how the profits from the sale at the market price would be allocated. Should gold profits accrue to the originating country?

This is not unique to the IMF. Virtually all government-held gold is accounted for at the accumulation price. There can be two price bases: one at an official *fixed* price and the other at the *market* price. This is why we see central bank holdings referenced by quantity more frequently than by price. Reports tend to be static like the inventory. Price action is not.

Adding confusion to price fundamentals is the fact that so much precious metal is a by-product of base metal production. This means that costs are somewhat amorphous because they are derived from various allocation methods. For example, considerable silver is produced as a by-product of extracting copper, nickel, zinc, and other base metals. The primary focus is mining the base metal. The consequential extraction of silver and other precious metals may have limited direct cost, which is fractional compared with allocated costs. From an accounting standpoint, by-product metals should share in general overhead and capital allocation. But silver and gold would be there regardless of any allocation.

Given these facts, it is difficult to determine how low prices can sink before it is no longer economically feasible to produce precious metals. This is exactly why so many analysts and metals advisers were wrong when they predicted silver production would shut down if prices dipped below $6.50 per ounce. There was too much emphasis on dedicated silver mining and too little attention to by-product production. Some silver mines *did* shut down. But their production was picked up by increases in other mining operations.

PRICE AND DEMAND

What is a realistic market price for gold and silver? The markets tell us. Suppose the average cost of an ounce of gold sinks to $50. Would the market price fall in tandem? Price behavior suggests gold and silver pricing is *demand skewed*. This means that demand plays a more important role than supply in determining value. It is a fact that the average cost of gold extraction has declined. It is a fact that demand has held gold's market price relatively steady from the mid-1980s forward. I use "relatively steady" because gold has had less overall volatility than currencies and stock markets like the Nasdaq. Even with large central bank sales, gold has managed to hold its value. In addition, there has been a steady increase in production that demand has easily mirrored.

In contrast, the platinum group is *supply skewed*. This is to say that demand remains within predictable ranges based on growth within specific industries. Thus, when palladium prices reached beyond $1,000 in 2000–2001, it was then linked to Russia's export restrictions as opposed to any immediate demand increase. There was a movement away from platinum and toward palladium because platinum was more expensive. This steady demand increase for palladium helped Russia manipulate prices to the 2001 high.

With this in mind, we can take a fresh look at precious metals pricing to derive a better perspective. How realistic are expectations for prices of $500, $750, and $1,000 per ounce of gold? What is the probability silver will soar to $25, $50, or more than $100? Will platinum rocket toward $1,500? Can palladium follow or lead? Examining price patterns cannot tell us what circumstances will eventually determine prices. However, we can judge volatility, sensitivity, stability, seasonality, cycles, and trends.

Our study of fundamentals for each metal will elaborate upon pricing potential. You should have a sense of where supply and demand might go in the years ahead. Any attempt at long-range forecasting is guesswork, at best. However, my prediction that gold and silver would experience steady declines through the 1980s and 1990s proved correct in the face of dozens of contradicting forecasts. Everything from the fall of the Soviet Union to the new South African government to strikes in Chile and Peru was the basis for phantom bull markets. My 1998 prediction that palladium could achieve a price above $1,000 per ounce if supplies were disrupted proved true in 2000–2001. The same call for platinum came to fruition in 2003–2004.

For investors following the advice of so-called experts, the road has been rough and frustrating. I have worked with people in the precious and base metals industry to formulate long-term marketing plans and hedge strategies. I cannot tell you how difficult it is to convince a major gold or silver producer that the price is going down, down, down! In contrast, I suggested lifting gold hedges in 2001, after perceiving a double bottom and a longer-term reaction to 9/11. In some cases, I was fired, hired, and fired again! In all cases, my consulting services proved highly profitable for those willing to accept reality.

In my precious metals work, I discovered the true meaning of "expert opinion" and "research study." At the day-to-day investment level, they translate as "useless." I read the most detailed reports on supply and demand and the most scientific forecasts from the most respected consulting groups. In almost all instances from 1985 forward to 1996, the bias was for higher prices. The very people who sponsored so much of this analysis and research were substantially responsible for price declines. The whole industry stood in amazement when silver prices broke down below $5 an ounce in 1990 and proceeded to test 15-year lows by 1991! It was the industry that continued selling into this market. So, why was the downward spiral such a surprise? The structural change in silver production that shifted from primary to secondary production encouraged using this metal as a sacrificial lamb in support of other operations. Yet report after report indicated that supply was in serious trouble. In particular, the post-1987 stock market crash was supposed to tip the scales in favor of higher silver prices. There had already been a spike up in prices beginning in the second quarter of 1987 from approximately $5.50 to almost $10. The market was expected to follow this pattern as investors sought to shore up paper portfolios with hard assets.

In reality, the liquidity crunch associated with the crash caused hard asset liquidation to shore up paper. In some cases, metal was the only thing left to sell in order to raise cash to meet margin commitments. Although some may argue this logic comes with the benefit of 20/20 hindsight, the writing was on the wall immediately after equities hit bottom. None of the metals were responsive. The heaviest campaigns to promote silver and gold failed to raise investor interest.

This is important because investors hold the "swing demand." Investors are the unknown factor that can instantly change. Investors can absorb or expunge metal without regard for industrial circumstances. Investors drove prices to extremes in 1979–1980. Investors abandoned metals in favor of paper assets through the 1980s. Investors returned to metals in the aftermath of 9/11 and when sufficient liquidity was established by record low interest rates beginning in 2001.

This is not to say that industrial hoards cannot play a swing role. Companies like Eastman Kodak that hold silver or car manufacturers that inventory platinum and palladium can certainly influence supply and demand. However, these inventories can be considered part of the investment stash when not immediately committed to production.

Factors Affecting Price

In (*The New Precious Metals Market*) I stated,

> *It is reasonable to assume that investors will regain confidence in precious metals only if there is a significant change in market environment. Even if demand from Third World nations accelerates, the price rise must be coupled with some fundamental alteration in investor psychology. This comes with two types of events. First, a general currency devaluation; inflation. Second, a confidence crisis. Absent these two developments, investor interest is likely to be related to interim ups and downs. Participation in the market will continue to be sporadic.*

This first suggestion that investor confidence might be shaken came after stocks faltered in March 2000. The subsequent recession was compounded by the War on Terror. The consensus shifted and precious metals were viewed as more attractive because they represented physical value rather than value by decree. If the "full faith and credit" of currency should falter, precious metals are assumed to hold value. It remains that simple.

Having been confined to fixed prices during the time of monetary linkage, gold and silver values can be measured only in terms of a purchasing standard. Figure 5.1 plots the actual silver price against a price in 1987-indexed U.S. dollars from the period 1850 through 2004.

It is immediately apparent that silver's cash price was virtually flat through 1960. For more than a century of consecutive years, the price hardly budged. With the exception of the 1979–1980 price hike, silver prices were contained at less than $10 per ounce. From 1910 through 1965, the relative value of silver in 1987 dollars was declining. After the shock of 1979–1980, silver returned to its range that averaged around $5.89; the apparent secular trend continued down from 1980 through 1996. The fact that silver prices display such a poor performance on an inflation-adjusted basis is intriguing because most individuals believe silver prices should track the price index. Silver was as cheap in 1996 as it was in 1976 without an inflation adjustment. Thus, through 20 years of constantly rising prices, *silver failed to keep up with inflation.*

What does this say about silver? It should be clear that this metal was neither an inflation hedge nor a good investment for more than 150 years. Any long-term silver hoarding provided a negative return on an adjusted

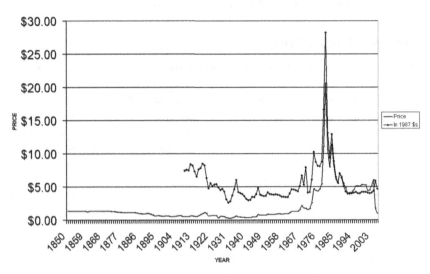

FIGURE 5.1   Silver values in real dollars and in 1987-adjusted dollars from 1850 through 2004. The plot of 1987 dollars comes into play after 1905. (*Sources:* U.S. Treasury and COMEX division of New York Mercantile Exchange)

and nonadjusted basis. Silver, in effect, is "just a commodity" and it is typically responsive to supply and demand relationships. Therefore, the most important emphasis for this market must be consumption and production. Unless there is an unexpected and dramatic structural change in silver, this is not a metal to buy and hold. Unfortunately, too few investors take the time to actually examine silver's long-term price history. When you do, you must ask yourself, "Why would this metal make a good long-term investment?"

Short- versus Long-Term Prospects

Refer again to Figure 5.1, and you can be the judge. Does the price pattern look encouraging to you? This is an important perspective because the sales pitch for silver frequently relies on a narrow slice of history—from 1974 through 1984. You are supposed to believe what all investors hope for—that silver will return to and exceed its most lofty levels. If you examine silver's economics as presently structured, such a price rise is not industrially feasible because it would severely stress commercial applications. At $50 per ounce, the price for silver-based technology would rise beyond elasticity. At $100 per ounce, industries and consumers would definitely seek other technologies.

Would you pay $25 for a roll of 35mm color film? Silver solders, electronic contacts, pastes, alloys, mirrors, purifiers, and other products would be priced out of their markets. At the very least, there would be strong financial incentives to find alternatives.

Based on price behavior through 2004, there appears to be more of a chance prices will deteriorate rather than advance over the longer term. To be sure, silver could pop up to $6, $8, and $10 during market dislocations. But price analysis points toward real values as low as $2 or $1.50. If silver can break below the $2 barrier, there is a possibility it can return as a monetary metal.

Does this sound strange? The lower the price, the greater the incentive is to use silver as coinage. Silver coins accomplish two goals. First, silver gives the appearance of value. Second, at low prices, silver is as good as any other metal! Governments would be slow to adopt silver coinage because there is always a fear that some shortage will drive prices up. At any time, industrial consumption may rise. Unless there is some way to control prices, there is too much exposure to arbitrage.

American mints experienced such problems with copper pennies when market value exceeded face value. There was an incentive for the public to hoard pennies, which reduced supplies in circulation. This is a problem treasuries will continue to face as industrial demand for any form of metal raises market value beyond a practical face value. At some stage, plastic may be the only alternative. Consider that plastic coins can be encoded to prevent counterfeiting. Plastic is lightweight and durable. It is unlikely there would ever be an incentive to hoard or melt down plastic coins. Other practical alternatives might be steel and aluminum.

Futurists tell us the entire coinage scenario is completely wrong. Eventually, we will have no need for money because our transactions will be conducted using handprints, fingerprints, voice recognition, or some other high-tech approach. In response to this, I would advise anyone to hide some gold. You never know when you may need it!

SILVER

Figure 5.2 illustrates silver price behavior from 1972 through 2004. The graph reveals that silver has a tendency to consolidate into narrow trading ranges over extended periods of between three and five years. With the exception of the 1968–1972 consolidation, prices settled within similar ranges around $5 per ounce. Given a span of approximately three

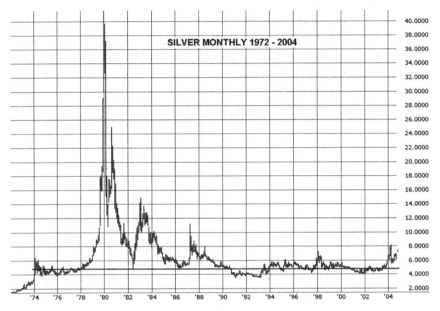

FIGURE 5.2 Silver's price action from 1972 through 2004 reveals equilibrium around $5 per ounce. (*Source:* eSignal.com)

decades, the observations suggest silver has a natural equilibrium around the $5 level. Any movement significantly above $5 eventually returns, whereas any dip below that price results in a recovery. This assumption is based on consistent fundamentals. If there were a discovery that silver could cure cancer or purify the world's water supply, the equilibrium level could be raised. By the same token, if digital photography completely displaces conventional film, the equilibrium price could find a lower level. Either way, we can expect the same price behavior whether silver finds a higher or lower consolidation range.

This steady price behavior probably carries over from the time when silver prices were fixed. Perhaps it is habitual. There was a great deal of conjecture throughout the amazing price spiral of the late 1970s. This event was correlated with two developments. There was the famous attempt by the Hunt brothers of Texas to corner the silver market. They tried to control sufficient supplies to manipulate prices. The Hunts were not alone in this wild speculation. As oil producers, the Hunts formed an alliance with Middle East interests and planned to reestablish silver as a monetary instrument. Some may recall that crude oil was being rapidly devalued by dollar inflation during this time. Because oil was priced in

U.S. dollars, producers were concerned that they were not receiving payment in a stable form. Hence, the focus was on silver.

Adding to this was the inflation itself. Investors joined in the silver bonanza because currency was considered in crisis. What would have happened if the Hunts had succeeded in their plan? History implies that prices would have settled back into a trading range. There is no indication prices would have moved appreciably above the 1980 top of just under $45 per ounce. Thereafter, the Hunts as well as the investing world would have been surprised to find silver seeking its normal levels. This is because Western Europe, the United States, and Japan would have implemented the same plans to stabilize currencies and economies. Eventually, confidence in currency, silver-backed or not, would have returned. While the high price might have been extended, silver's inherent price behavior should have forced a return to the approximately $5 level.

For those inclined to speculate in silver, the ratios are obvious. At $5 per ounce, the most you can lose is $5. Clearly, this is theoretical because it is impossible to think that silver would be thrown into the streets for free. There is a practical downside lurking around $1 to $1.50. Below these prices, the process of extraction, assay, transportation, and storage would be adversely affected. If you must own this metal, levels of $5 or less represent a comfort zone. Buying metal above the comfort zone increases risk and exposure. Certainly, you might trade a price reaction. Caution is in order when purchasers consider an accumulation program.

Bull Markets

When prices do break out into a major bull trend, history shows a relatively short duration: approximately one year. The bull market of the late 1970s began in 1978 with a move above $5 (see Figure 5.3). Prices reached only $6.25 by 1979. From 1979 to January 1980, prices reached almost $42. Within two months, silver retraced below $11. Technically, silver displayed a classic pattern. Following the 1980 plunge, prices recovered approximately half the distance from top to bottom. This follows a 50 percent retracement rule.

By 1982, prices reached back down to the good old $5 level. From July 1982 to February 1983, silver staged another rally to a high of almost $15. Within a year, it was back down to near $5 (see Figure 5.4 and Figure 5.5). This propensity to return continued when silver hit a low of $4.15½ on July 18, 1997, and pushed to $7.50 by February 6, 1998. This was another infamous intervention by a powerful investor named Warren Buffett who began accumulating physical silver and speculating in futures during the 1997 summer. Buffett proceeded to announce that he was buying silver in

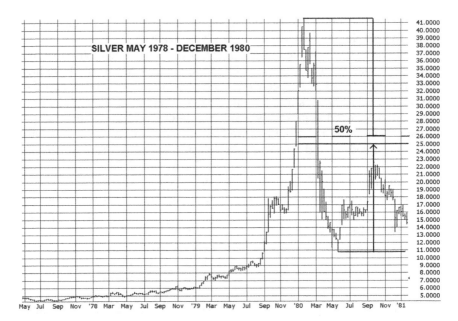

FIGURE 5.3 From a low below $5 in 1978, silver was propelled to more than $41 per ounce by January 25, 1980. By May 23, prices had plunged below $11. The approximate $30 decline was followed by a $14 recovery representing an approximately 50 percent retracement that follows a technical assumption. When using the intraday values, the 50 percent was exactly reached. (*Source:* eSignal.com)

anticipation of a major move higher. This "going public" sparked a brief, but potent buying frenzy that contributed to the thrust to the $7.50 high. While not specifically confirmed, volume and open interest patterns suggest that considerable *selling* was taking place in the July futures contract. The selling was attributed to Buffett himself in the postmortem analysis. It appeared as though he was pushing prices higher by buying the near months while selling for protection in the far months.

In the carnage that followed, many investors wanted an inquiry into Buffett's trading. However, there was nothing illegal about what he did or allegedly did because he owned large quantities of silver and was legitimately entitled to hedge his inventory. An inquiry might have been in order, though, since Buffett had publicly announced that he was accumulating silver. If he had been selling silver while misinforming the public, there might have been a breach of the Commodity Exchange Act. Alas, we will never know!

FIGURE 5.4 Silver reached a $14.93 high on February 18, 1983, and proceeded to decline to 7.83 on January 13, 1984. Within a year, silver dropped back near its $5 equilibrium. (*Source:* eSignal.com)

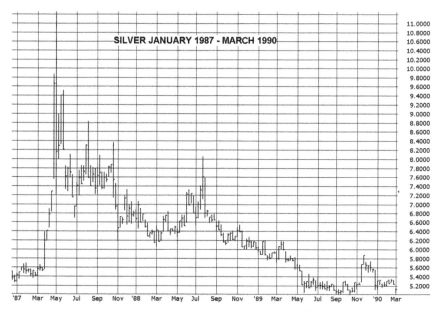

FIGURE 5.5 Silver made another run to $9.79 on May 1, 1989, and dropped to $5.06 by May 26. (*Source:* eSignal.com)

Silver collapsed to $4.01½ on November 23, 2001, and rocketed to $8.21 by April 9, 2004. Thereafter, silver made a typical sharp reversal to test $5.50 on May 14, 2004.

While I cannot profess clairvoyance, I suspect this pattern will repeat with reasonable certainty until there is a fundamental change in this market or a major dollar realignment.

Interim Action

Regardless of silver's long-term price prospects, interim movements have been exciting and significant. A jump from $5 per ounce to $6 is a 20 percent increase. When translated into profit potential in the futures or options markets, leverage multiplies profitability by as much as 100 percent. Assuming a silver margin of $2,000 per futures contract, a $1 gain represents a $5,000 profit for a 250 percent return. Examine yearly ranges for silver from 1981 through 2003 as shown in Table 5.1.

TABLE 5.1 Silver's Yearly Ranges from High to Low for 1981 through 2003

Year	High	Low	Range
1981	1,653	797	856
1982	1,130	481	649
1983	1,474	838	636
1984	1,753	624	1,129
1985	1,230	570	660
1986	799	503	296
1987	1,015	544	471
1988	1,089	598	491
1989	886	508	378
1990	643	393	250
1991	455	351	104
1992	433	363	70
1993	544	352	192
1994	579	453	126
1995	616	434	182
1996	585	464	121
1997	539	415	124
1998	750	456	294
1999	580	482	98
2000	560	455	105
2001	588	401	187
2002	515	421	94
2003	579	434	145

The smallest range of 70 cents occurred in 1992. Even this lack of movement represents a $3,500 fluctuation in contract value. Obviously, your profit opportunity would depend on the consistency with which silver moved from high to low, coupled with your transaction timing. An examination of silver price movements from 1981 through 2004 as shown in Figure 5.6 reveals good trending tendencies and reasonable seasonal consistency.

Thirteen of the 24 years exhibit seasonal downtrends within the first quarter. The second quarter provides strength, whereas the last quarter begins the weakness that is carried into the first quarter. Three first quarters were essentially flat. Nine years exhibited uptrends from January through March. Of course, these generalizations are not the rule. Certainly, 1982 provided a strong exception, with prices rallying into 1983. We see strong uptrends in 2002 and 2004; however, be careful to pay attention to the different vertical scales for each year in the condensed illustration offered by Figure 5.6. The 2002 move was from 42600 to 52000 in the December silver futures contract, whereas the 2004 range was from 60000 to 85000.

As the saying goes, "What goes up must come down." This is not necessarily an axiom that applies to commodity prices or paper investments. In the case of silver, the 44 years spanning 1960 through 2004 held to this axiom. Silver advocates are frequently upset when confronted with this historical reality. The charts speak for themselves. Equally important, silver experienced significant price deterioration when measured in constant dollars. The 44 years of inflation from 1960 forward did not see an indexed increase in silver prices. Thus, silver had an equivalent *value* of $2 in 1998 when compared with the price in 1978.

What does this mean? Once again, we are forced to objectively conclude that silver was a fluctuating commodity and not a good long-term investment. With the facts in mind, I fail to see why so many die-hard silver fanatics insist that the "big one" is just around the corner. Even if the big one comes, it is likely to have a return trip to historical normalcy. It is the two-way ticket up and down that holds the most profit potential for anyone willing to take the ride trading futures and options.

Strategically, our objective is to formulate trading programs that can take advantage of annual volatility. Interestingly, a 30-day moving average was applied to prices as a method for "deseasonalizing" price data. The relatively long interim price trends suggest you can approach this market with a seasonal filter. This simple method seems to generate handsome profits over most of the 24-year period covered by Figure 5.6.

When confronted with silver's price behavior, the application of a penetration factor or a longer moving average may yield better results because intermittent crossings of price and moving average can be

FIGURE 5.6 Silver displays consistent seasonal and cyclical patterns from 1981 through September 2004. The 30-day moving average appears remarkably accurate in tracking changes in price trend.
(*Source:* eSignal.com)

FIGURE 5.6 *(Continued)*

FIGURE 5.6 (Continued)

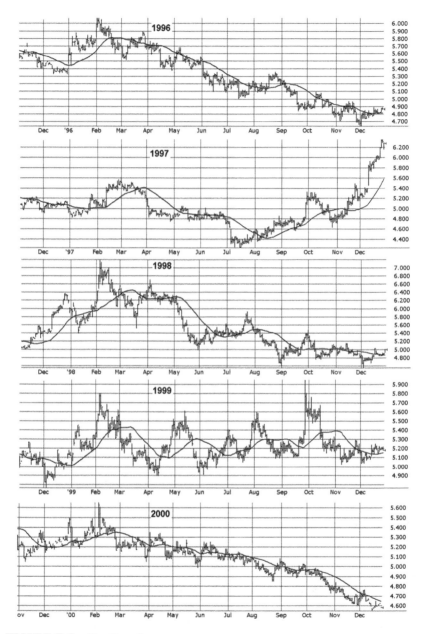

FIGURE 5.6 *(Continued)*

FIGURE 5.6 *(Continued)*

eliminated or minimized. A penetration factor is simply an adjustment made to the moving average to confirm the validity of any crossing by the price. In some cases, the factor is statistically derived by back-testing to determine the level of penetration required to have confidence that the trend will follow through. Experience shows that a penetration factor can be more efficient because longer moving averages have a tendency to give back too much profit in a fast-moving market. Equally important, silver's tendency to remain in wide trading ranges supports strategies using options, as previously covered. It is fair to say that silver is not like a good company stock. You cannot necessarily "buy and hold."

Examine the last two quarters of 1981, 1983, 1984, 1985, 1986, 1987, 1989, 1990, 1991, 1992, 1995, and 1998. Consider how the trading ranges in those years lend themselves to option writing. The essential ingredient of short-term volatility coupled with longer-term trading ranges present the ideal environment. Admittedly, the resolutions in Figure 5.6 are not the best for discerning retrospective trading strategies. Yet, the illustration should be apparent.

As a trading vehicle, silver has occasional displays of upside volatility that provide opportunities for trend following. For example, the 2004 market provided excitement when prices broke out of an extended trading range as seen in Figure 5.7. From July through August 2003, prices were confined between 48200 and 58000 ($4.82 to $5.80). In early November, the price broke out above the 30-day moving average and challenged the 58000 channel line. Once silver broke out, it steadily progressed ahead of the 30-day moving average until reaching resistance at 61000. The side-

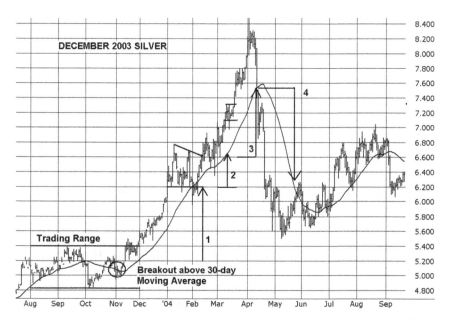

FIGURE 5.7 The December 2004 silver futures contract displays a wide range of behaviors from a trading range to an upside breakout and a downside bust. (*Source:* eSignal.com)

ways action at 61000 from January into the first week of February 2004 allowed the moving average to converge upon the vacillating price until the average was violated to the downside. From breakout to the January consolidation is shown by arrow #1 on the chart and extends from 51000 to 62000. At $50 for every penny, the move was worth $5,500.

Prices went on another brief upswing labeled by arrow #2, and extending from 62000 to 64500. This added another $1,250. A breakout from 65000 to 75500 is labeled #3, and represents another $5,250 change in the silver contract's value. The top of the move actually extended to 85000; however, the bust was so dramatic that the price declined almost 50 cents to reach the 30-day moving average.

Thereafter, there is an assumption that you would have sold short for the decline labeled by arrow #4 that extended from 75000 down to 61000. This move yielded $7,000. We see that the downside was as impressive as the upside. All we were following was a simple 30-day moving average coupled with widely known charting rules.

Undoubtedly, there were a few interim stop-outs as prices briefly touched the moving average line. However, the breakouts and busts made up far more than the staccato trades that resulted from quick bouts above and below the 30-day moving average. This is why some traders use the penetration factor referenced earlier. A slight adjustment can make a significant difference, as Figure 5.7 demonstrates.

Alternative Technologies

Economic and political uncertainty is likely to present cyclical patterns and extended profit opportunities for silver traders. However, fundamental prospects for decreasing photographic usage can translate into lower lows and lower highs over time unless new applications can close the gap left by film. In all cases, there must be a sound reason for investing in physical silver like coins or bullion that extends beyond any temporary inflation or monetary adjustment.

The discussion of silver's fundamentals and prospects provides more details about underlying trends in production and consumption. Any comprehensive review must evaluate the potential impact of new silver technologies associated with mining and usage. I have briefly mentioned digital photography as an alternative to silver halide film. How realistic is the prospect for total digital substitution? If digital technology does displace film, how much silver consumption will it impact? Can other technologies pick up where photography leaves off? What about silver batteries, silver water purification systems, silver memory devices, and silver photovoltaic cells? These are some impressive technologies that can employ increasing amounts of silver in years ahead. Later chapters explore the possibilities.

GOLD

If you haven't guessed by now, I'll tell you. I really do love gold. I said it at the beginning of this book. My personal affinity for this metal pains me when I am forced to take an objective view and conclude that gold, like silver, has not been a good investment since it was legalized in the United States in 1975. I confess the coins and bars I keep tucked safely away defy my better judgment. I admit that I have told others to divest or not to invest when I refuse to part with my personal (albeit small) stash.

Emotions aside, Figure 5.8 plots gold prices in fixed dollars, 1987 dollars, and the floating price from 1971 forward. From 1900 through the post–World War I recovery, gold's purchasing parity declined as measured against 1987 dollars. The pronounced parity spike following the 1929

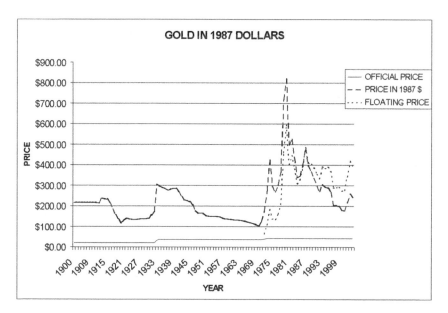

FIGURE 5.8 Gold's price plotted in contemporaneous and 1987-indexed U.S. dollars from 1900 through 2004 reveals very little net appreciation since values were fixed through 1971. A floating U.S. price was permitted in 1975. (*Sources:* U.S. Treasury, and World Gold Council)

stock market crash reflects the extraordinary deflation of the Great Depression. In reality, this was one of gold's finest hours. Its "real value" as a function of buying power reached the second highest levels of the twentieth century. Of course, we must keep in mind that gold's price was fixed through the first three-quarters of the 1900s.

It is interesting to note that gold's value during the Great Depression surprises many investors. Consider that the gold price was still fixed, meaning the dollar was still linked. Here is the example where gold circulated as money. With price constraints in place, the massive deflation drove gold values to pre-1900 highs. The purchasing power increase correlating to President Roosevelt's official gold price hike to $35 is proportionately greater. This should tell you something about owning gold. Although the consensus is that gold is an inflation hedge, it is really a deflationary asset, too. Consider the average gold price from legalization in 1975 through 2004 as illustrated in Figure 5.9.

We certainly know inflation continued from 1972 forward. If, indeed,

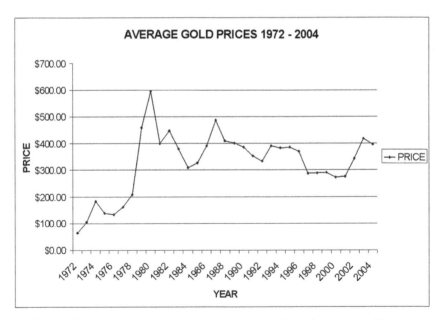

FIGURE 5.9 The average annual cash gold price from the time world prices began to float in 1972 through 2004 reflect a relatively stable price ranging between $300 and $400 per ounce despite continuing inflation from 1972 forward. (*Sources:* Gold Institute and COMEX division of New York Mercantile Exchange)

gold provided an inflation hedge, why did the 30-year average remain at approximately 55 percent of the 1980 high average? Gold's inflation-adjusted purchasing parity actually declined. The 1980 high was, in fact, an overreaction relative to inflation from 1975 through 1979. Even as an overreaction, gold was able to attain its highest purchasing parity of the twentieth century. Many analysts attribute this to a more powerful correlation to oil prices during that period. Therefore, it stands to reason that gold would seek a more realistic level on a true inflation-adjusted basis. The crossover was approximately 1983 as seen in Figure 5.8. Thereafter, gold prices still declined.

Look how the 1987-indexed gold price declined in response to the post–World War I economic boom. Even after the official gold price was boosted, parity deteriorated. This is why so many conservative economists condemn President Roosevelt's New Deal. When the government began to play with monetary alignment, the so-called natural alignment of purchasing parity was infringed.

In 1990, I wrote an article for a precious metals company on the virtues of owning gold. In keeping with objectivity, I pointed out poor price performance and the lack of investment return. The audience for the article was a group of hard-asset buyers who wanted to believe gold represented a safe financial haven. I presented two scenarios that seemed to appease readers. If an investor bought gold futures in 1990 on an unleveraged basis, the difference between the required margin and unused balance could have been used to buy U.S. Treasury debt or highly rated corporate paper. Thus, the unused portion of the funds would earn a return that would be added to the overall gold appreciation . . . if it appreciated. If gold remained stagnant, it would be no worse than a bond with a steady interest rate.

Assuming a $100,000 commitment to gold at $300 per ounce, the investor could buy approximately 333 ounces. Since futures contracts represent 100 ounces, there would be a purchase of three contracts—the equivalent of 300 ounces. There is a 33-ounce leftover. Assuming a $2,000 initial margin per contract, the amount posted for the futures positions would be $6,000, which leaves $94,000 in cash that can be used to buy the interest-bearing instruments. It is wise to leave an amount in cash to cover variation margins because we know gold can easily vary by 5 percent to 10 percent within modest periods. A 10 percent swing on $300 is $30, or $3,000 per contract. With three contracts, the amount left in cash would be $9,000.

This transaction provides the security of gold with the yield of bonds, notes, bills, or commercial paper. Since the intent is to own gold, there is no difference between buying 333 physical ounces and holding 3 futures contracts, save the 33-ounce differential. Some may recognize this as "notional trading." In effect, the cash for the transaction is notionally available.

An additional twist would be the use of options as described in the previous chapter. If another 1 percent per month can be generated by selling three call options against the open futures positions, we add 12 percent to whatever the interest-bearing investments are yielding—say 5 percent. This could yield a total of 17 percent plus or minus any appreciation or depreciation in gold's price and some minor adjustments for the cash held in reserve.

I admit that the suggestions of notional gold trading did not appeal to those who like to *own* gold. Futures contracts do not look or feel like the real thing. There is always the possibility commodity exchanges will collapse in a *real* disaster. There is no argument against an extreme scenario.

Based on the data, I also reported that gold would be the asset of choice during a monetary realignment. We are all familiar with the concept of a formulated currency exchange. For example, the U.S. government might issue a new $1 bill requiring the exchange of five old $1 bills. The exchange formula is five for one. Unlike a genuine deflation that is driven by market forces, an exchange of old money for new is realignment. Because it is unlikely all prices will adjust to an exact formula, gold can act as a standard until prices seek new levels after the exchange.

In 1990, a currency swap remained conceptual. Yet this is exactly what occurred in 1999–2000 when the European Union introduced the euro. To smooth the transition, the euro was established as a book entry in 1999 and became live physical currency in 2000. This was, perhaps, one of the riskiest government ventures since Roosevelt nixed the gold standard and Nixon closed the gold window. I sincerely doubt whether anyone can say the euro became a reality without trepidation!

As we know, the euro was exchanged for massive amounts of member currencies. There were price discrepancies. However, the movement into a unified European currency actually went smoothly—with hardly a glitch. Some traders are quick to point out that the euro plunged from its introductory high of more than $1.23 against the dollar to a November 2000/July 2001 double bottom around 83 cents. Certainly, a 32 percent parity swing illustrated by Figure 5.10 is nothing to sneeze at! Yet, once the apprehension was alleviated, the euro gained against the U.S. dollar in a show of strength and confidence.

Prices and Hoarding

As previously mentioned, gold is unlike any of its sister precious metals because it is almost entirely hoarded rather than consumed. Some may say this makes price analysis easier. I would disagree. With silver, plat-

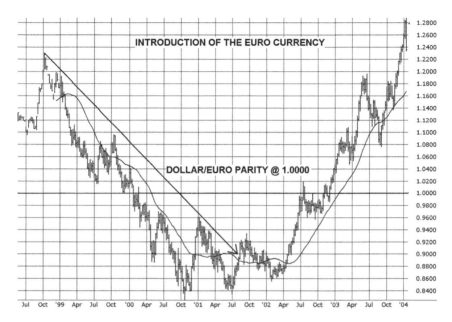

FIGURE 5.10 The euro currency was established as a book entry in 1999 and went live as physical bills and coinage in 2000. The initial reaction was nervous as reflected by the 32 percent decline in euro/dollar parity. The drop lasted just over a year. (*Source:* eSignal.com)

inum, and palladium, investors can attempt to measure supply and demand. With gold, investors face duality in supply and demand. Pricing is based on a combination of new gold and divested gold. Assuming no potential for divestiture, gold prices could be judged in the same manner as wheat or copper. Simple price forecasting would examine mining and divestiture for each period and compare against consumption (usage).

Alas, dynamics are not so simple. At any moment, the "instant" gold supply can double, triple, or increase tenfold. Obviously, central banks can sell reserves. Private hoards can be liquidated. Extreme crisis can drive gold into and out of the market. Extreme tranquility can produce a similar effect. Therefore, gold represents the ultimate financial game of chess. It is an environmental, political, and economic instrument that is unlikely to fade from the investment forum.

As of this writing, there remains a debate among International Monetary Fund (IMF) members regarding the disposition of approximately 103 million ounces of gold that had been accumulated prior to the dissolution of the Bretton Woods fixed exchange rates. This represents approximately

33 percent of the original hoard that was substantially liquidated during the 1970s after gold was abandoned as a reserve asset. At an assumed price of $400 per ounce, the IMF has approximately $41.2 billion as of 2004. This is not an inconsequential amount. However, the official price set by formula has been $48. Consequently, the IMF carries an undervalued asset on its balance sheet of approximately $4.5 billion.

The stock market boom experienced toward the end of the twentieth century raised the pressing question, "Why hold gold when paper is doing so much better?" The answer came after equities began their infamous meltdown in the spring of 2000. The argument that there were storage and opportunity costs associated with the IMF gold inventory met resistance when gold began to rise while global equities and interest rates were precipitously falling. Still, a $41.2 billion asset in the face of an increasing need for IMF financing represents a potential threat to the supply side of gold's pricing equation.

The IMF inventory is only one of many that hang over gold's ultimate price. As we will see, official gold sales make a noticeable impression upon price. Is this a good thing? For those who wish to accumulate gold at favorable prices the answer is "yes." For producer nations, the answer is "no." If gold's recovery from official sales is any indication, effects are temporary.

Figure 5.11 plots the Dow Jones Commodity Index from October 31, 1933, through the end of 1981 as an illustration of how raw commodity prices responded from the Great Depression through the Great Inflation. The index is calculated on an average between 1924 and 1926 equaling 100. Although a futures price index does not directly consider labor, capital, and other important inputs affecting inflation, commodity prices generally respond during inflationary, deflationary, and stable periods. Note that the post-Depression recovery clashed with commodity shortages, which resulted in a general commodity inflation. This increase was accelerated by World War II, which imposed rationing to curb extraordinary price spirals. Once the war economy settled down, commodity prices remained virtually flat from 1955 through 1970. Of course, gold bugs will say that this stability was the result of Bretton Woods and the global adherence to gold. This does not explain why commodity prices shot up in 1971—before the gold standard was fully abandoned.

Commodity price action was linked to a series of natural, political, and economic events. Yes, there was a food crisis in 1971 that extended through 1973. For example,there was a 1971 U.S. corn leaf blight and subsequent Russian crop failures. Underpinning these natural price events was the rapid rebuilding of Europe and industrialization of Japan following World War II. There was a time in the late 1960s and early 1970s when

DOW JONES COMMODITY INDEX OCTOBER 1933 - DECEMBER 1981

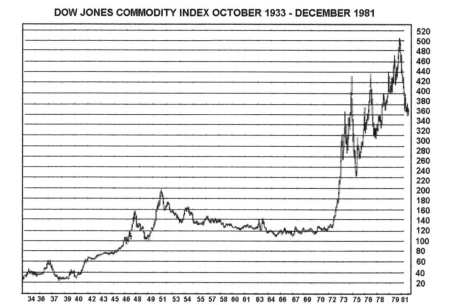

FIGURE 5.11 The Dow Jones Commodity Index illustrates raw commodity price movements during and after the gold standard. (*Source:* Commodity Research Bureau)

"Made in Japan" was synonymous with cheap and poor quality. Americans bought a Japanese-made car when they could not afford anything else. Postwar Japan was not on a par with other industrial countries. It did not take long for Japan to change this situation.

In the process of building industrial capacity and a unique process-driven economy, Japan exerted structural pressures on raw material prices, energy, and labor. The world had to keep up with Japan's accelerating ability to convert raw materials into finished products. At the same time, Germany was building its capacity and image whereby Americans moved from their focus on the Volkswagen Beetle to the Mercedes-Benz coupe. In short, half the world was building wealth at an increasing rate.

One of the most popular campaign slogans echoed from the Nixon years forward by U.S. presidential incumbents and challengers has been, "Are you better off now than you were four years ago?" This question can be posed to industrialized nations in general. Has wealth increased as a function of living standards from 1933 to the present? The most recent U.S. Census clearly reveals a positive answer. Further, global wealth is undeniably rising. Any suggestion that the size of the world's poor population is indicative of negative wealth expansion is spurious. Even though population growth and nonuniform wealth distribution mean there are more poor people in the United States, Canada, Mexico, Western Europe, or other regions, the overall global standard of living is rising at an increasing rate as the direct result of increasing wealth.

Increasing wealth creates its own economic and monetary structural change. Wealth leads to demand. Demand leads to production. The inherent lack of synchronization between demand and production correlates with inflation and deflation. Technology and capacity caught up with wealth during the 20 years preceding the end of the twentieth century. Yet the very structural change that caused inflationary pressures during the 1970s could repeat as the Third World gains first-class status over time.

Although an imperfect correlation, the link is clear here between the substantial breakout in gold and the steady rise in the commodity price index. It is interesting to note that gold was sleeping from 1975 through 1976 despite the pronounced jump in commodity prices. In fairness to gold, consider that prices jumped from the official price of $42.22 an ounce to more than $200 when trading began on December 31, 1974. One could argue that this 473 percent climb reflected the Russian wheat deal and Arab oil embargo. But how can this trend explain the lack of performance during the next two years? The fact is that inflation alone was not sufficient to excite precious metals. The ultimate requirement was a monetary confidence crisis.

Price Patterns

Absent unusual disturbances, gold price action is the same as silver price action with a slight twist. Gold's unofficial role as a reserve asset buffers reactions to changing supply and demand fundamentals. Regardless of this fact, gold as a commodity exhibits distinct price patterns to use for speculation. Figure 5.12 presents a year-by-year price history from 1975 through 2004. A monthly moving average was applied for seasonal price smoothing. The years 1976 through 1978, 1982, 1987 through 1990, 1993, and 2002 through 2004 show gold's tendency to rally into the fourth quarter. With reasonable consistency, gold sells off in the first quarter as seen in 18 out of the 30 years. This seasonal pattern has been correlated with the fourth-quarter holidays. Surveys show jewelry fabricators begin accumulating inventory toward the end of August. Demand increases through October. By November, goods are manufactured and shipped. Any excess inventory is liquidated during the first quarter of the following year.

FIGURE 5.12 The December gold futures contracts from 1975 through the first nine months of 2004 depict consistent behavior over three decades. Gold has a powerful tendency to form seasonal trends as well as trading ranges. (*Source:* eSignal.com)

FIGURE 5.12 *(Continued)*

FIGURE 5.12 *(Continued)*

FIGURE 5.12 *(Continued)*

FIGURE 5.12 *(Continued)*

FIGURE 5.12   *(Continued)*

Without the benefit of fundamental interpretation, Moore Research Center, Inc., of Eugene, Oregon, conducted technical research that determined the best time to sell gold futures was toward the end of January. This coincides with peak inventory liquidation and a slowdown in forward purchasing activity. The greatest profit potentials from short sales occur between mid-February and mid-March. Interestingly, the most significant interruptions in gold's seasonal tendencies came when central banks sold off reserves. This is extremely important to keep in mind as investors develop their trading strategies. The real danger in trading gold comes from political uncertainty or intervention.

From a longer-term perspective, traders have been particularly impressed with gold's cyclical tendency that is illustrated by Figure 5.13. From inception into 2004, a five-year cycle from peak to trough repeated until the 1996 high. At that point, we were in the accelerating phase of the Clinton boom and global conditions were improving. Stocks, bonds, and real estate were far more enticing than gold. Clinton had the advantage of

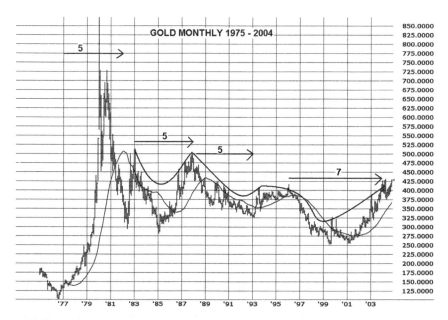

FIGURE 5.13 The monthly gold continuation chart shows a smoothing moving average and cyclical trace with horizontal arrows that annotate the length in years of each identified cycle. The last period extends between seven and eight years depending on how the chart progresses beyond 2004. (*Source:* eSignal.com)

the first peacetime economy since the turn of the nineteenth century. Thus, extraordinary conditions might be the cause of the extended cycle from 1996 to 2004.

As emphasized in the beginning of this book, we have very little price history for precious metals because platinum and palladium are relatively new, while gold and silver were restrained by fixed pricing until the latter half of the 1900s. With 20/20 hindsight, we have the ability to identify only three five-year trends since gold was legalized in the U.S. in 1975. If we were to have relied upon these three observations to formulate a strategy for 1996 through 2001, we would have bought the 1999 low that represents two and a half years into the cycle. We would have sold at approximately $300 in 2002 and suffered losses as prices continued rallying into 2004!

Enhanced technical precision might have been gained using a moving average as is superimposed upon Figure 5.13. We might have delayed our decision to sell in 1999 because the average remained below the 2003–2004 monthly price line. Depending on when you are reading this chapter, conduct your own experiment by going to any charting service and plotting a monthly continuation gold chart. Use a 50-period moving average and see if a violation of the average line achieves a follow-up decline in prices after 2004 as seen in Figure 5.13.

The United Kingdom and Portugal announced gold sales in the last quarters of respective years and changed the seasonal patterns. It is important to understand that seasonal patterns do not offer sufficient consistency to develop specific rules. Examine any of the contraseasonal years and you will see that the divergence from the majority behavior is frequently extreme. In 1994, gold reached above $400 in late September and proceeded to drop to approximately $375 by early December.

Seasonal commodities lend themselves to a moving average filter corresponding to the most common seasonal subunit: the month. This is why we use a 31-day moving average to smooth gold price data for identifying intrayear trends. Review each year and you should be impressed with the number of trends identified by this technical technique. Even during a year like 1987, which displayed 10 months of trading range conditions, we see a late February upside breakout that takes prices from $410 to $500 in about two months.

As central banks change their political outlooks for gold, seasonal patterns can be altered. Any trading plan that seeks to use seasonal patterns must keep a careful watch for untimely central bank sales.

When we statistically normalize gold prices from 1989 through 2004 around constant U.S. dollars, we see an interesting pattern suggesting that toward the latter half of the 1990s, gold actually increased in purchasing value despite its obvious decline in dollar parity. As a parallel, recall that gold purchasing value increased during the Great Depression. This was a deflationary period. If the technical indicators are correct, steady gold values from 1989 forward tell us Americans had balanced economic growth against the money supply. We can also conclude that the fall in gold prices during 1995–1996 was offset by a deflationary increase in purchasing parity. Because the price is recorded in U.S. dollars, we know that disinflation was accurately reflected by the gold market.

By indulging in broad hypotheticals, a case can be made for an economic shift that establishes new rules for today's economic environment. Assuming governments continue maintaining control over our perceptions, technological progress may play catch-up with economic inadequacies. It is becoming less expensive to manufacture goods, deliver services, communicate, track, control, manage, and even entertain. This eco-environmental progress integrates with monetary instruments like gold. This is an anti-inflation environment. If, in fact, we eventually change the cost-push spiral, gold's value will probably sustain any realignment. Thus, gold's apparent consistency stands like the Rock of Gibraltar. There is no better constant than gold.

PLATINUM AND PALLADIUM

If gold provides consistency while silver offers speculative intrigue, platinum and palladium are perfect complements to the precious metals complex. Since neither platinum nor palladium has played any monetary role, price analysis does not need to consider central bank intervention or monetization. The analysis can be simplified. Although there is a modest amount of hoarding, the bulk of these metals is used for industrial purposes. This distills analysis down to basic supply and demand. We have little concern over the impact of free stocks—inventory similar to gold and silver held by central banks and monetary agencies. As covered in subsequent chapters, the platinum group metals have unique properties that are vital in particular industries. Aside from well-known requirements for automotive catalytic converters, there are extremely important applications in chemical processing and manufacturing for which no substitutes appear on the immediate horizon.

Price Action

As a direct consequence of the industrial demand for and consumption of platinum group metals, we see a well-defined secular trend for platinum prices as reflected by Figure 5.14. I am confident price action is primarily linked to the development and widespread adoption of

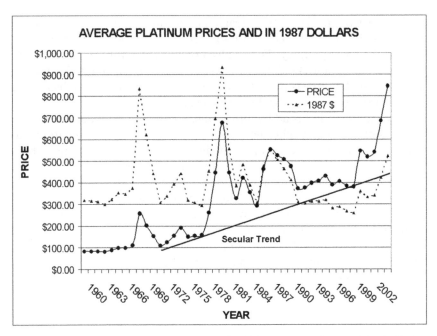

FIGURE 5.14 The monthly average platinum price plotted from 1960 through 2004 shows an upward secular trend in contemporary dollars. When indexed to 1987 dollars, the secular trend flattens and we see a median price around $300. (*Source:* Johnson Matthey, Ltd)

antipollution devices in most of the developed countries. From 1975 through 1978, prices traded in a narrow range between $135 and $180 per ounce. The inflation-driven breakout in 1979–1980 clouded the picture to some extent because the price spike is not related to industrial supply/demand fundamentals. Europe did not adopt catalytic devices until the late 1980s.

From late 1977 through 1996, platinum prices increased from approximately $135 to $400. This represents a 196 percent increase in 19 years, for an average increase of 10.32 percent per year. Absent an inflation adjustment, demand has pushed platinum steadily higher. Although platinum's price performance as an investment may have compared poorly with the Dow Jones Industrial Average, S&P 500, and other market indexes during the late 1980s and 1990s, stock market performance did not exceed a straight-line average annual return of 15 percent during the 1970s and early 1980s.

We see that platinum has not displayed the same consistency as gold nor has it reverted back to an equilibrium price like silver.

Price Cycles

Underlying demand fundamentals favor rising platinum prices providing there is no structural change that adversely impacts platinum consumption. Increasing global wealth is driving platinum demand as nations adopt increasingly stringent pollution constraints that necessitate catalytic converters. Even in the face of rapidly rising gasoline prices, the United States adopted ever-larger sport-utility vehicles (SUVs) as the mainstay of the American fleet. Such vehicles require more heavily loaded catalytic devices than conventional passenger vehicles. Europe's move toward high-efficiency diesel vehicles also places additional demand on platinum moving forward.

Of course, the situation can change on both a temporary and a structural basis. A severe economic downturn might affect auto sales and, in turn, platinum demand. Rest assured that stocks would encounter more adversity if such a severe recession occurred. Such downturns are episodic. Thus, we would expect the secular trend to resume as illustrated in Figure 5.14, just as we have seen equity values recover from recessions and even depressions.

Habits, fashions, and demographics change in ways that can influence platinum. Recall that the muscle car was popular during the late 1950s all the way into the early 1970s. Within a matter of three years, necessity became the mother of invention as smaller, more efficient cars speedily replaced the big-engine-block gas-guzzlers. The energy crisis forced conservation upon the American consumer. Suddenly, the "K" car was in and the semi-hemi was out. The Volkswagen Bug captured a generation of frugal drivers. Automotive historians point out that the SUV is a reiteration of the station wagon. It is the accommodation of the growing American family. This raises an important observation.

Baby boomers born between 1945 and 1955 were in their 20s in the 1960s and 1970s. They were a disproportionately large population resulting from the population boom that followed World War II. The station wagon succeeded when this generation was growing up within the parental household. Once out of the house, these young adults faced the post–energy crisis recession of the 1970s combined with inflation and stagflation. The economic environment was ripe for a transition away from extravagant cars. Since they did not yet have families, there was no need for the station wagon (unless it was a hand-me-down). The move was toward economical transportation. As boomers began to raise families, the need for a family vehicle returned and, hence, the SUV became popular. The Jeep was the first popular "utility vehicle." When the Grand Cherokee was introduced, it became mainstream.

I bring this up because the cycle of big to modest cars is inherent in our demographic swings. Youth enters urban areas in search of career and exits in search of a sound family environment. From no car to small car to SUV seems like the logical progression. Indeed, car companies have spent millions on research that attests to this pattern. In fact, the Toyota Scion line was specifically introduced to target the youth driver. The impact upon platinum demand has been a cyclical increase and decrease relative to loading requirements. (*Loading* is an industry term for the amount of reactive metal required to effect a satisfactory catalytic process.)

The Clinton presidency was highlighted by excess. Despite the belief that the 1980s was the decade of indulgence, the 1990s proved far more so as attested to by the size of everything from SUVs to homes to electronic niceties like television screens. I seem to recall hearing a news commentator say that three out of five poor urban families owned a personal computer, high-end video equipment, and electronic games like Nintendo and X-Box. The poor enjoyed a higher standard of living in the 1990s than in the 1950s, 1960s, or 1970s! This economic indulgence contributed to surging platinum and palladium demand. From catalytic converters to chemical processing, our hunger for a higher standard of living automatically included platinum and palladium in the equation.

Changing attitudes and tastes came with the post-9/11 era of uncertainty, austerity, and extreme gasoline prices. In response to cries of global warming, car companies developed ultralow emission vehicles (ULEVs). Concurrently, these cars came with ultrahigh fuel economy. The Toyota Prius hybrid (gas/electric) car that was sparsely introduced in 2000 became wait-listed by mid-2004. The list exceeded 12 months in many areas. The introduction of the Lexus hybrid SUV, Highlander hybrid SUV, Ford hybrid Escape, and some hybrid Honda models suggested a paradigm shift away from gas guzzling toward efficiency. The hybrid power scheme uses lighter platinum and palladium loadings that, in turn, can impact demand for these metals.

This trend was just beginning to come into play as platinum's supply/demand balance was pushing prices toward new extremes. The move toward efficiency had yet to make an impact upon prices. As covered in the first rendition of this book, both platinum and palladium have extremely tight relationships between supply and demand. Any modest shift in either supply or demand could cause doubling, tripling, or even quadrupling of the price. Indeed, platinum and palladium reached toward four-digit pricing after the book was released in 1998.

Figure 5.15 shows that platinum is susceptible to multiyear cyclical behavior. Although the data does not appear on the chart, the first price cycle of the 1980s began in 1978 and ended in 1982: four years. The next cycle was from 1982 to 1985: three years. The years 1985 to 1991 marked the next cycle (six years), and from 1991 through 1995 there was a less

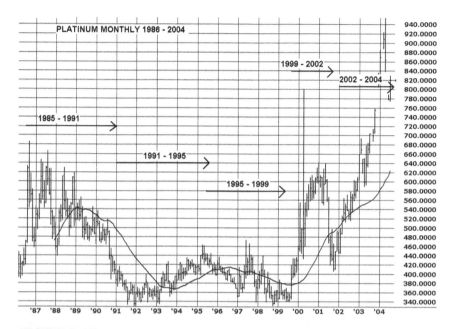

FIGURE 5.15 Monthly platinum prices based on near futures from 1986 through the first three quarters of 2004 illustrate the potential for multiyear cyclical behavior. (*Source:* eSignal.com)

dramatic four-year rise and fall. The year 1998 represented a turning point for platinum supplies, which peaked at approximately 5.4 million ounces and proceeded to drop like a stone in 1999 to 4.87 million ounces. At the same time, 1998 demand hit a record high of 5.37 million ounces to leave a very narrow 30,000-ounce surplus. Understandably, by 1999, prices were being squeezed. From a low of $340, platinum rocketed to $800 by April 1, 2000. A 720,000-ounce shortfall in 1999 drove the price into a buying frenzy. Companies with small hoards made big fortunes!

The trend toward deficit production continued pressuring platinum prices through 2004. Prices made a $954 high by April 1, 2004, before settling back by more than $160 an ounce by June of that year. The sharp correction in 2001 was too brief to be considered cyclical. The deficit from 1999 forward actually defined a continuing upward cycle that remained into 2004.

The historical perspective revealed by news articles dating from 1980 to 1995 suggests interim platinum price movements were more supply-sensitive than demand-correlated. This is because platinum consumption patterns have been relatively steady and reasonably correlated with automotive, chemical, and energy industries. Simply put, a burst in platinum demand is not as likely as a decline in supply when considering the complexion of industrial users. This does not rule out a speculative frenzy. When traders see deficit production, they pounce on the opportunity as Figure 5.15 illustrates. There are major reasons for arguing the case for speculative instability:

- Platinum is far less liquid than are gold and silver. Participation lacks diversity. The number of producers is relatively small, and their ability to swing prices has been demonstrated from 2000 forward.
- Several industry analysts have called attention to the fact that the total quantity of platinum mined in 2002 and 2003 approximated 12.08 million ounces. Even at a high price of $800 an ounce, the total value of annual output comes to less than $9.664 billion. In effect, a speculator would be capable of accumulating a substantial quantity of this highly strategic metal with very little capital. Assuming the use of futures or options, as little as $10 million could tie up 20 percent of deliverable supplies on a leveraged basis.

Thus, platinum has been sensitive to real and rumored supply disruption. Because there is no easily mobilized platinum reserve, production must closely track consumption. A key platinum characteristic that may mimic a reserve is derived from the metal's resilience. As a catalyst, platinum facilitates chemical reactions rather than being consumed by their processes. Although the metal's efficiency can deteriorate within a catalytic device, generally, most is recoverable. Assuming the domestic car fleet in the United States has an average age of seven years, recovered platinum should follow a somewhat muted seven-year and 3.5-year cycle. In addition to auto and truck catalytic converters, platinum is also recoverable from chemical plants and oil refineries. As an increasing amount of platinum is reprocessed, the industry has a propensity for an industrial hoard. The more efficient the recovery process, the less new platinum is required to supplement scrap.

Assuming there is a decline in catalytic usage as automotive and truck engines become more efficient and/or hybrid technology becomes more popular, recovered platinum can establish a surplus in the supply equation. Even with this potential, we know platinum technology is highly dynamic. The decline in catalytic use can easily be offset by demand for fuel cells, electronic storage devices, and chemical processing.

Seasonally, 7 out of 18 years display a pronounced July-August rally followed by a retracement. In 1986, 1987, 1989, 1992, 1994, 1997, and 2000, there was a tendency to rally into the first quarter. In 1981, 1982, 1984, 1989, 1990, 1991, 1996, 1998, and 2001, prices took a downward track in the first half as seen in Figure 5.16, suggesting platinum does not display a

FIGURE 5.16 Annual platinum performance as represented by the January futures contract from 1986 through 2003. (*Source:* eSignal.com)

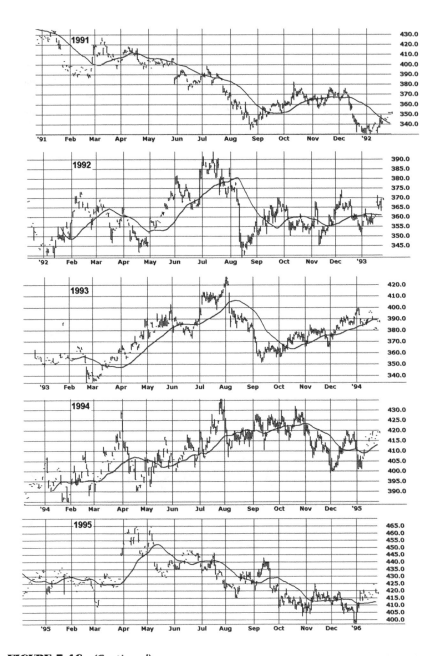

FIGURE 5.16 *(Continued)*

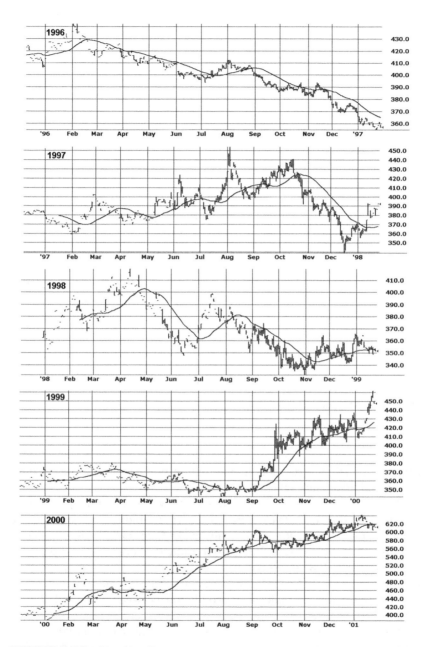

FIGURE 5.16 *(Continued)*

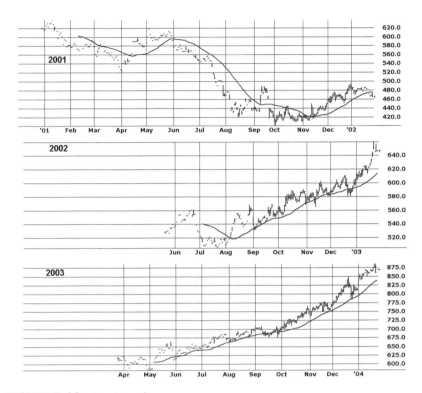

FIGURE 5.16 *(Continued)*

strong seasonal pattern. Indeed, platinum prices appeared to follow automobile and light truck sales.

In 1987 I conducted a study to determine where platinum prices were heading over the next 10 years. Based on cyclical indications and patterns in the automotive/truck industry, my projections called for two events that proved quite accurate. First, I determined platinum would probably retrace its 1985–1987 price rise from $240 to $660 by at least 50 percent. This would return prices to approximately $450. Indeed, prices declined to $450 and below to make a consolidation between 1991 and 1993 at around $360. My second conclusion was that prices would become less volatile as retired cars and trucks began to feed the scrap market. I based this on the fact that catalytic converters were introduced in the mid-1970s. Using turnover estimates, it seemed the first significant recycled platinum would begin to feed the market by 1985 and build thereafter. Platinum recycling would create a revolving door whereby scrap would increase overall supplies on a continuous basis. By 1988, recovered platinum accounted for 12 percent of the amount used for automotive catalytic devices. Within five years, it had risen to 16.4 percent with a pronounced acceleration in 1994 and 1995. By the following year, it reached 17 percent.

Most industry information comes from two sources. The Platinum Guild is the primary industry group, operating in the same way as the Gold Institute and the Silver Institute. Then, Johnson Matthey, PCL, produces the annual *Platinum Report* with quarterly updates. These reports are similar to GFMS Limited's *Gold Report*. GFMS Limited began producing extensive research reports similar to those of Johnson Matthey in 2003 and serves as another excellent information source for platinum and palladium. Because industry-related literature is produced on a current basis looking forward, there is little retrospective coverage addressing the price cycle over several decades. Platinum bulls claim figures as reported by Johnson Matthey, PLC, may be understated because they concentrate on automotive catalysts. Considerable recycling of platinum also takes place in the petroleum industry, where peak demand for platinum reached 150,000 ounces in 1991 and declined to 90,000 ounces by 1994. Recognizing these patterns, I concluded platinum price action would calm in the absence of any extraordinary events.

Indeed, platinum prices did calm from 1997 through the first three quarters of 1999. The pattern that I extrapolated forward materialized and prices reacted accordingly. As we see in Figure 5.16, prices narrowed to a $40 range from $340 to $380 between 1998 and 1999. The proud moment came when the supply deficit more than doubled prices in less than a year. Translated into profit potential, the contract value soared from $19,000 for 50 ounces to $40,000—a 210 percent gain. On a leveraged basis, a $2,100 initial margin could have carried that same profit for an extraordinary 1,000 percent return. There are not many investments that can perform so well on a regular basis.

There is a strong industrial link between platinum and crude oil because platinum is used in the refining process. This leads some analysts to believe their price actions are interdependent. With the exception of the 1990 Gulf War oil price spike, we see a correlation beginning after 1995 as illustrated by Figure 5.17. However, a quick look at crude oil from 1983 through 1995 indicates mixed price action.

Looking behind the scenes, platinum's price action is frequently related to politics. The two largest producers have been South Africa and members of the Commonwealth of Independent States (Russia); both were prone to political turmoil and experienced major political transitions during the 1980s and 1990s. Both were involved in reformulating labor forces. Thus, price cycles can be statistically linked to developments within these producing countries. Even with the post-9/11 War on Terror

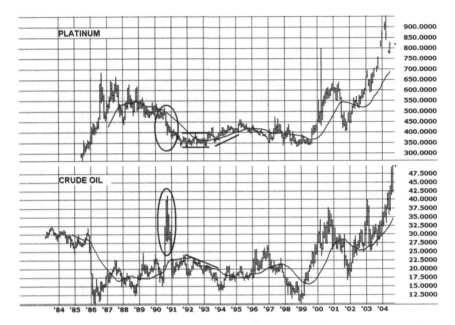

FIGURE 5.17 Monthly comparison of crude oil and platinum prices from 1985 to 2004. (*Source:* eSignal.com)

and uncertainty over Iraqi oil supplies, the politics of Russia and South Africa carry the most significant weight. Longer-term forecasting tracked demand, whereas price events like spikes were highly correlated with labor unrest or political developments in South Africa and Russia.

The 30-day moving average smooths price action sufficiently to indicate that "buy-and-hold" or "sell-and-hold" tactics work for long-term technical trading as seen in Figure 5.15. Overall price trends have sufficient duration and distance to profitably accommodate this trading strategy. Unfortunately, we live in fast times with anxious expectations. Few individuals are willing to adhere to long-term trading using moving averages of 30 days or more. Today, it is almost unconscionable to hold a position in excess of a few weeks, let alone several months. Yet the charts clearly indicate that most years would have yielded handsome returns using long-term technical filters.

It is possible that platinum's less volatile personality from 1991 through 1996 was a coincidence. As Chapter 8 points out in reviewing fundamentals, other areas of consumption can grow to balance against recovered supplies. However, I suspect that the calm before the storm was related to the lack of speculative participation. Attention was focused on stocks and bonds. Supply was in balance with demand, and industry groups reported little incentives for investor participation. When considering the volatility sparked by deficit production, the key to assessing platinum's continuing profit potential is the fundamental consumption trend. The secular trend we see in Figure 5.14 remains on track and can accelerate. Depending on the slope of this underlying trend, platinum might be a buy-and-hold proposition.

Under such circumstances, the physical metal would make the most sense because rolling a futures position would have higher transaction costs. Platinum can be stored for a few pennies an ounce. According to mining sources, it is not likely that we will exponentially expand platinum production. This is why I believe the overall trend will drift higher.

It is important to note that the total history for platinum prices extends back only to the 1800s when the metal was specifically identified. Therefore, any attempt to hone a cyclical or seasonal study is prone to statistical error. Our data is not sufficient to draw any absolute conclusion. Further, applications for platinum are young and developing. This is why any study of platinum must be progressive rather than retrogressive.

PALLADIUM

Palladium is a relatively new and different animal among the precious metals. It began trading as a futures contract in 1968, but received very little attention until a dramatic announcement in 1989 that fusion at room temperature was possible using palladium cathodes in a solution of heavy water: the cold fusion process. Thus, palladium's price movement has been highly correlated with technological advances that significantly increased industrial or speculative demand within relatively short periods. This can have a dual impact on the platinum group because the increasing demand for palladium has exerted a negative effect on platinum when palladium is used as a platinum substitute. In the early 1990s, car manufacturers developed auto catalytic devices that relied on palladium as a platinum substitute. This tipped the scales in favor of palladium prices and caused spread relationships to dramatically narrow. In 1991, palladium made a low of $78 per ounce. By 1995 the price touched $160 for a climb just exceeding 100 percent. In comparison, by 1995 platinum moved only $40 above 1991 lows for less than an 11 percent change.

By the same token, the extreme price rise experienced by palladium in 2000–2001 drove industrial users away from palladium and back toward platinum. These wild gyrations (reviewed in Chapter 4) have the potential to structurally alter palladium and platinum markets because a majority of both metals is consumed in auto and truck catalytic devices. When palladium was cheaper than platinum, there was a strong incentive to research ways to use palladium as a substitute. Indeed, several breakthroughs elevated palladium as the dominant metal for auto catalysts. With a price tag for palladium above $1,000 per ounce, there was a mad scramble to reinstitute platinum, which was trading at three-fifths the price!

As with many extremes, the shift to platinum was met with a subsequent price spike, placing users on notice that both metals have extremely unstable supply/demand equations. By 2004, the platinum group remained a necessity for clean air compliance in the United States and Europe; however, technologists were busy investigating alternatives that included nickel catalysts, electrostatic filters, afterburners, and "homogenous-charge compression ignition," which increases efficiency through high-compression gasoline engines. Undoubtedly, there will be progress toward eliminating or substantially reducing the use of platinum, palladium, and rhodium for pollution control.

Palladium has exhibited approximate five-year cycles, as evident in Figure 5.18. An obvious interruption came with the enormous price infla-

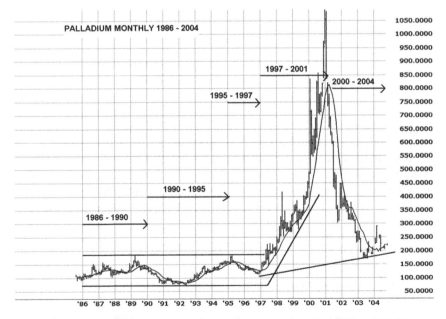

FIGURE 5.18 Palladium shows a flat trading range between $75 and $182 from 1986 through the breakout in 1997. There is a tendency for a five-year cycle from peak to peak. An upward secular trend appeared after the meteoric rise from 1997 into the beginning of 2001. (*Source:* eSignal.com)

tion from 1997 through 2001. The huge divergence between platinum and palladium signaled deterioration in the assumed positive price correlation, as proven in Figure 5.19. Both metals have been mined in similar quantities. From 1992 forward, the pace of palladium extraction picked up over platinum whereby there was approximately 20 percent more palladium mined by 1996. Figure 4.8 from the previous chapter demonstrates that these metals can diverge into opposite price trends. We see the huge spread differentials achieved after periods of relative stability. Notice how palladium moved from lows in 1997 to highs toward the end of 1999. At the same time, platinum reached highs in 1997 and declined to an interim low in 1999. Palladium was plummeting from 2001 forward while platinum was flying. This is an important observation because fundamentals are likely to create such situations in the future. Prior to palladium's enhanced role in catalytic converters, we had an assumed 5-to-1 price parity, decreasing to 4-to-1 within the 1990s. Projected usage for both metals suggests this ratio is now as low as 3-to-1. Thereafter, platinum's superior efficiency in automotive catalytic devices should hold the ratio steady.

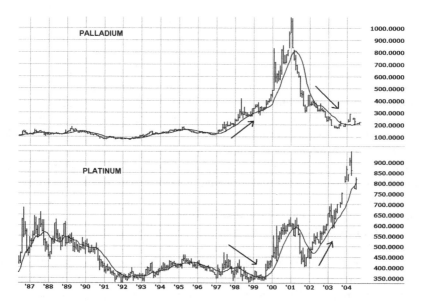

FIGURE 5.19 Comparisons of palladium and platinum reveal divergence. (*Source:* eSignal.com)

As previously mentioned, a speculative frenzy could be induced by silver, gold, and platinum. This would probably change ratios in favor of platinum because palladium has lacked speculative interest. However, it is interesting to note that palladium actually exceeded all metals in its spectacular appreciation during the run-up of 1979–1980. Analysts attributed this to the fact that palladium had farther to go. This logic is faulty because it assumes price level by itself can determine the velocity and distance of a move. This would challenge the most established principles of the random walk theory. As of this writing, no statistical evidence of price level dependence has been published.

Indeed, palladium's repeat performance in 2001 confirmed that this obscure sister metal packs the most punch during any supply dislocation. During both price spikes, palladium exceeded platinum on a relative basis and in 2001 on an absolute basis. The move from approximately $180 to more than $1,075 took place in about three years. The 497 percent increase represented about 165 percent per year. Trading futures on a leveraged basis, the 100-ounce contract went from $18,000 to $107,500 for an $89,500 change in value on initial margin of $2,200. The return might have been a staggering 4,068 percent! Of course, that trade would have required a crystal ball or enormous luck. However, just participating in a part of the trade would have yielded spectacular gains.

When considering that palladium retraced the entire move within another three years, an equally impressive profit potential existed on the short side of futures. All in all, the gross move represented a swing that exceeded 8,100 percent. Admittedly, some lottery tickets have done better, but not with the same odds!

Perhaps palladium's most intriguing price event took place in the spring of 1989 when two professors from the University of Utah announced they had produced a nuclear fusion reaction at room temperature using a palladium cathode wrapped with platinum wire in a heavy water solution. As mentioned, the process was appropriately labeled "cold fusion." The announcement quickly propelled palladium to highs of more than $180 per ounce in the cash market after wallowing below $80. As quickly as palladium rallied, it crashed in response to allegations that cold fusion was, at best, a mistake and, at worst, scientific fraud. Figure 5.20 demonstrates the speed of the market reaction.

The unusual breakout witnessed in February 1989 gave rise to suspicions that cold fusion was a sophisticated attempt at market manipulation. It appeared obvious that someone was accumulating palladium just prior to the highly controversial cold fusion press conference. However, investigations revealed that the suspicious price rise was linked to Japanese accumulations related to auto catalysts. If Profes-

FIGURE 5.20 The June 1989 palladium futures contract displays an unusual pre–cold fusion press conference rally leading up to a quiet period in March. Once the announcement was made, prices rushed above $180 per ounce. Enthusiasm quickly waned when the process was debunked as junk science. (*Source:* eSignal.com)

sors Pons and Fleischmann had been speculating in palladium prior to their announcement, it was never proven.

Cold fusion prospects did have a structural impact on pricing. From 1989 forward, there was a steady, albeit small amount of palladium allocated for fusion experimentation. In addition, cold fusion perked speculative interest in accumulating the metal—just in case. By 1990, estimates for cold fusion experimentation ranged from 5,000 ounces to as much as 50,000 ounces. In 1992, the range expanded to between 50,000 and 250,000 ounces. Those numbers were significant when one considers that they can represent as much as 1 percent to 5 percent of total annual production. Thus, even if cold fusion was a hopeless illusion, the pursuit still generated enough demand to influence prices. By 2000, cold fusion was hardly mentioned in any reports or studies involving palladium. Yet, each year since 1989 there have been cold fusion conferences where experimenters insist that a viable commercial process is just around the corner.

Palladium is a thin market, making speculation difficult. Further, it has not been easy to buy the physical metal. A modest amount is struck into investment bars by Johnson Matthey, Stillwater Mining Company and Pamp Suisse. Some Russian "Ballerina" coins are available through dealers, and some specific "cold fusion" medallions were minted shortly after the 1989 announcement. A trip to eBay on the Internet may list palladium ingots with selling prices from $17 to $50 over the spot price. Essentially, investors are left with the futures markets or deliveries in quantities with 100-ounce increments in order to get the best price.

Seasonally, palladium is erratic with first-quarter rallies seen in 1979, 1980, 1983, 1986, 1987, 1993, and 1994. The more consistent pattern is a lower drift through the last quarter, observed in 1980, 1981, 1984, 1985, 1986, 1987, 1990, 1995, and 1996. As with other metals, price trends tend to span three to five months; this supports a strategy using long-term filters like an advanced 30-day moving average. There is a basic misconception that once metals break out into a major trend, it is impossible to catch the action. This is merely a psychological aversion to buying in a rising market or selling in a falling market. In palladium's case, certainly, smooth transitions occur from rising to falling prices. Although there are spikes, the extent of these extremes has not been sufficient to retrace most preexisting trend movements. Unfortunately, the profile of precious metals traders reveals an impatient crowd. Mainstream investors do not seem to adhere to a longer-term buy-and-hold or sell-and-hold policy regardless of its proven historical efficacy. Figure 5.21 illustrates palladium's price patterns over more than 18 years from 1986 through September 2004.

Palladium's propensity for large price swings in each of the years from 1979 forward suggests this metal is a better candidate for speculative trading than the more stable gold. Understand that this observation is based on price volatility without any consideration of fundamental factors that can alter gold's inherent picture. History, alone, cannot warn us of pending change.

When Chapter 8 examines the platinum group in greater fundamental detail, you will see that its roles as a catalyst remained critical from the mid-1970s forward. In a 1998 debate on the CNBC television network, I engaged a representative of the Platinum Guild regarding the possible elimination of auto catalysts shortly after the transition into the twenty-first century. I held up a hard disk that was being used to record specific driving habits and adjust engine function accordingly. The response was that no such technology was being developed to any extent that would curtail platinum and palladium usage. Yet, my research indicated that progress in controlled engine ignition represented the single

FIGURE 5.21 Annual palladium performance as represented by the December Futures contract from 1986 through the first three quarters of 2004. (*Source:* eSignal.com)

FIGURE 5.21 *(Continued)*

FIGURE 5.21 (Continued)

FIGURE 5.21 *(Continued)*

most significant threat to platinum group price stability. Just as digital photography will decrease silver demand, so must digitally controlled fuel and ignition systems eventually impact prices and demand for platinum and palladium. Yet such developments will not detract from tradability. You should simply be aware of vulnerability when considering those wonderful platinum coins frequently advertised in national newspapers and magazines.

CONCLUSION: TREAT METALS AS
THE COMMODITIES THEY HAVE BECOME

I have spent countless hours consulting with individuals and corporations about pricing prospects for gold, silver, platinum, and palladium. Too often, reality is obscured by false perception. How often can we claim we have actually examined price history? I believe the basic chart illustrations in this chapter challenge several widely held illusions about stability, volatility, seasonality, and cyclical patterns. With the right perspectives in mind, we can see that precious metals do act like commodities. They are highly tradable and lend themselves to modern price analysis and speculative strategies. Much of the literature covering precious metals fails to divorce itself from monetary roles and linkages. This failure is so prevalent among mainstream thinking that it distorts reality.

In the 1996 U.S. presidential election, some debate centered around Republican vice presidential candidate Jack Kemp's affinity for a return to a gold standard. Whenever there is a conversation about precious metals, it is almost inevitable that former monetary applications become a topic. In the broadest sense, such references may be appropriate. Successful investors deal in the present rather than the past. The time to deal with metals as monetary instruments is when (and if) nations return to hard asset valuation. Without that development, investors should view metals as the commodities they have become.

When we explore precious metals' price history, we see obvious profit opportunities from speculative participation or covered option writing. The industrial precious metals like silver, platinum and palladium have distinctly different patterns based on supply and demand fundamentals for each. Gold has remained reflective of monetary conditions, yet it also responds more to commercial applications from jewelry to electronics.

It seems truly remarkable that the precious metals have maintained such steady prices through so many years of inflation. As a personal comparison, I recall when a slice of pizza in New York City was 15 cents. Now a New York slice is about $2. This means a slice of pizza has increased by more than 13 times since I regularly enjoyed it as an essential food group in my younger years. If I take the official gold price in 1975 of $42 per ounce and multiply by 13, the price of gold should have been $546 by 2005. Taking the average 1975 market price, the value would have been $1,820.

Silver traded at approximately $5 when pizza was 25 cents a New York slice. This suggests that if silver had kept pace with pizza, it would have risen by approximately eight times for a value of about $40 by 2005.

Platinum reached toward a reasonable price in 2003–2004 based on the pizza comparison. However, both platinum and palladium have maintained only brief parity in conjunction with pizza. Thus, even the inflation argument fails when we put historical price data to the test.

Whenever I make this point at precious metals meetings and conferences, there are cries of foul. I am bombarded with all the reasons why silver and gold have been manipulated to reflect artificially low prices. Whether real or manipulated, the price is what it is. You cannot profit from what a price *should be*. With this in mind, we now continue with an examination of market-driving fundamentals.

CHAPTER 6

Gold
Fundamentals

G old is a particularly unique precious metal. Aside from its beauty, weight, and rarity, gold embodies exclusive characteristics including being a noble metal with unparalleled ductility and malleability. According to descriptive literature from the World Gold Council, a single ounce of gold can be extruded into a viable wire exceeding five statutory miles in length. Alternatively, an ounce of gold can be flattened into a sheet covering more than 100 square feet. As the most malleable and ductile of all known metals, gold can be extruded in leaf as thin as .00013 millimeters. Gold leaf can measure 400 times thinner than a human hair. My earlier allusion to gold as a "constant" goes beyond its monetary association. Gold is virtually indestructible. It never tarnishes, is highly resistant to any form of corrosion, and is totally recyclable. These properties are the backbone of gold's industrial value. Although there are no absolute statistics covering gold production and consumption throughout the ages, industry groups estimate that as much as 90 percent of all gold mined over time still exists as tangible supplies today.

Gold is an awe-inspiring metal that has been attractive since recorded history. Even before the written word, there was evidence that gold represented the ultimate commodity. This is not to say that a gallon of water would not become far more valuable than gold during a drought. A pound of food would carry more immediate value to someone faced with starvation. But whenever we are asked to name commodities of value, gold invariably tops the list.

HOW GOLD IS USED

Gold's first and foremost use is ornamental. It simply looks good. There are few, if any, substitutes for this metal's unique color, appearance, weight, and texture. This is why gold appears throughout history as artwork and body ornamentation. From jewelry to the famous burial mask of Egyptian Pharaoh Tutankhamen, gold has made an impression throughout the entire world over all generations.

Gold has exceptional reflective properties and selective transparency as a thin coating, making it useful for optical coatings and spectrum-specific mirrors. There are rumors that the world's most powerful "sunbeam" was designed around a highly polished gold concave mirror. The mirror was shaped like a satellite dish to reflect sunlight in the golden spectrum toward a focusing lens. The device was supposed to have been developed in Israel, but the tests were conducted in the United States. Gold is used to coat window glass and space visors. The list of special properties continues with gold's remarkable heat and electrical conductivity. Gold is highly coveted as contact material in electrical and electronic switches. Even with the enormous move into fiber optics, telephone companies rely upon gold as the critical element in sensitive switching mechanisms.

With all of gold's exceptional characteristics, the greatest demand comes from fabricated jewelry and hoarding. Table 6.1 and Figure 6.1 provide a snapshot of gold usage as of 2003. Figures are based on estimates derived from GFMS Limited, the United States Bureau of Mines, the Gold Institute, and the World Gold Council.

Jewelry

As global wealth increases, we can expect a dramatic rise in gold jewelry fabrication. Of all potential growth areas, jewelry holds the most promise

TABLE 6.1 Categories of 2003 Gold Consumption

Category	Tons
Jewelry	1,805
Bar hoarding	183
Electronics	238
Dentistry	68.7
Coins	105
Medallions	27
Other	80

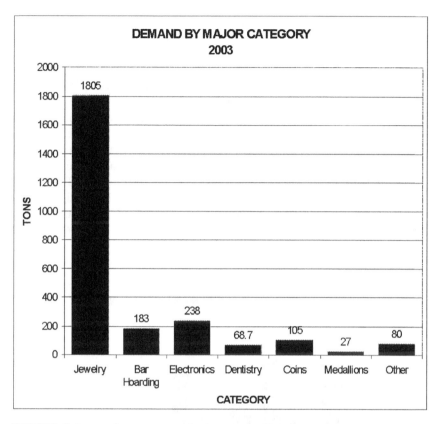

FIGURE 6.1 Jewelry represents the largest consumption category followed by investment accumulation. (*Source:* GFMS, Ltd. All rights reserved)

in the absence of any monetary crisis. As mentioned in the opening of this book, gold has particular symbolic and religious significance in many cultures. After World War II, the distribution of wealth was divided into four categories: Western industrial, Eastern bloc, Pacific Rim, and Third World. However, for the purpose of understanding gold demand, a more refined perspective is helpful. This is because cultural impacts on gold are likely to be extremely important as our world moves toward more uniform wealth distribution.

As an example, we know that Chinese customs place a heavy emphasis on gold as a symbol of marriage. To be sure, China's gold jewelry fabrication moved from approximately 89 tons in 1987 to more than 485 tons in 1997. This 445 percent increase can be compared with U.S. usage, which grew from 80 tons in 1987 to 316 tons by 1997—only a 295 percent increase. The rate of growth in China and nations with similar customs is indicative of an important pattern. Figure 6.2 shows the rate of increase in China's fabrication for the 12 years from 1991 through 2002.

Since the liberalization of investment restrictions in China from 1990 to 1998, gold experienced an increase in fabrication demand. However, by 2002 Chinese fabrication returned to the 1991 levels. It is important to note that fabrication statistics may not reflect an accurate consumption picture because fabrication can be targeted for export. In addition, some statistics report fabrication net of scrap recovery to portray a more accurate demand assessment. This is particularly true for Italy, which stood as the number-one fabricator in the mid-1990s, but lost rank as Turkey and other countries stepped up participation and production. Italy was the world's largest manufacturer of gold chain for export. Unfortunately, internal consumption statistics are estimates based on observed exports

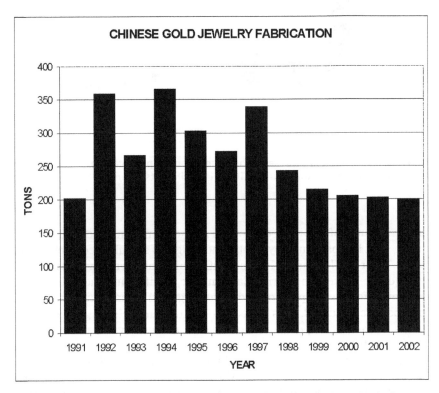

FIGURE 6.2 China's gold jewelry fabrication showed growth in the mid-1990s, but tapered off after the turn of the millennium. (*Source:* GFMS, Ltd. All rights reserved)

and reported gross consumption. Using this basis, China's internal usage moved from 202 tons in 1991 to 339 tons in 1997. This 68 percent increase supports the fact that gold jewelry fabrication demand was expanding in China at an increasing rate. By 2003, the amount declined to approximately 200 tons.

Shortly after the turn of the millennium, there was mounting concern about the rapid Westernization of China as its economy moved toward capitalism. A new China Syndrome raised fears that China's expansion was going to consume massive quantities of vital raw commodities. This would generate a huge global inflation as the Chinese economy revved up. In particular, news media called attention to China's energy requirements and painted a dire picture of dangerous world shortages and soaring prices.

In contrast to these predictions, China's wealth was not reflected in accelerating gold jewelry fabrication or consumption. In fact, China's gold jewelry demand appeared to peak in 1997 and steadily declined through 2003. This was true for China's gold investment demand, too. In truth, there were very few statistics that substantiated China's insatiable appetite for raw commodities. Even predictions for crude oil demand fell far from the mark moving forward from 2002.

What inspired this paranoia about Chinese demand and global shortages? As has become increasingly apparent, the Western news media (in particular, the United States media) thrives upon sensationalism. Ill-informed reporters gather generalities and draw unsubstantiated conclusions to formulate stories. Some examples are the adverse impact aerosol sprays have on the ozone layer. As the story goes, the 1970s show *All In The Family* aired an episode in which the ultraliberal son-in-law, "Meathead," shouted that fluorocarbons were destroying the ozone layer. The media immediately picked up on the possibilities.

While fluorocarbons do react with ozone, from research reports I have reviewed, a jet flying across the Atlantic does more damage to the upper atmosphere than 100,000 14-ounce spray cans using fluorocarbons. A single volcanic eruption like Mount Saint Helens belches more greenhouse gases into the upper atmosphere than all the cars and trucks can muster running continuously for a decade. This is not to pass judgment on either the ozone problem or global warming. It is simply to point out that there are two perspectives.

The China Syndrome is based on the assumption that China's enormous population will immediately adopt the abusive and wasteful U.S. lifestyle. If we accept this logic, we should see increasing Chinese demand for goods and services. In response, price level can rise if China's demand outstrips global availability.

Yes, China's oil demand will grow proportionately with its economy.

However, just as the total depletion of oil by 2000 never materialized after the bleak forewarnings of the 1960s and the world's population did not decimate the planet within the same time, I expect China's growth will be measured against technological advancement and continuing development of global resources that include energy.

What is implied by China's evolution into a Westernized economy? There will be a new export player with import needs. China might possibly dwarf Japan as an industrial powerhouse if China follows the Japanese and Hong Kong model. China may eventually pressure commodity prices, and we are likely to see rising demand for precious metals. At some point, China's increasing wealth will lead to a growing middle and upper middle class that will spend more on jewelry. For gold producers, this is good news!

China is joined by India as the second largest potential gold consumer. In India, gold also carries a strong religious significance. Like China, it is customary to give gold bangles to a bride. As of 1996, India was estimated as the largest consumer, with internal usage approximating 326 tons and total fabrication at 400 tons. Within its enormous population, gold adornment is the custom from the smallest nose pin to the most lavish necklaces and bangles. As with China, India's consumption will increase in proportion with expanding wealth. From 88 tons in 1986 to 304 tons in 1995, India experienced a 245 percent increase in fabrication demand during 10 years. India's jewelry consumption reached an interim peak in 1998, topping 658 tons. This fuels the argument that gold is on a collision course with surging prices. Although production experienced impressive expansion between 1986 and 2004, slopes of various consumption lines took a lead over gross global output.

Any forecast based on these facts requires caution. As gold prices slumped in 1985, several reports called attention to the same circumstances. Based on information available at that time, many investors concluded that prices would leap higher within that year because industry sources claimed production had reached a peak. In fact, production was accelerating. Any contention that gold production could not be expanded was clearly as wrong then as it would be now.

Total world jewelry fabrication derived from these regions moved from 1,277 tons in 1986 to 3,187 by 1998 for a 149 percent increase. Consider the overall growth as represented in Figure 6.3. We see peaks in fabrication that seemed to mirror investment performance from the 1980s forward. When equity markets reflected the recession that began in March of 2000, gold continued to mirror the reflection with a retracement back to the 1997 level. This raises an interesting dichotomy between gold's price performance and jewelry fabrication demand. While

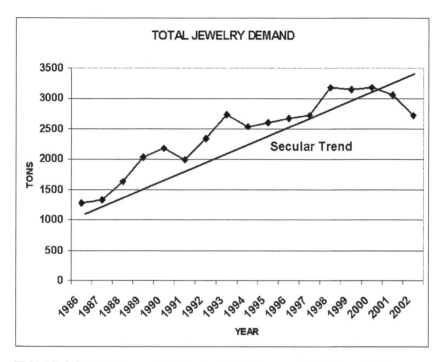

FIGURE 6.3 Total demand for jewelry fabrication worldwide from 1986 through 2002. (*Source:* GFMS, Ltd. All rights reserved)

gold's price may not reflect this component of demand, the rate of consumer buying appears linked to economic health, *independent of gold's price.*

This is interesting because analysts were perplexed by the lack of correlation between demand and price. They were looking for some correlation between jewelry accumulation and value. Examine the pattern of the Dow and you see the same upward slope in the secular trend moving from 1986 to 1995. When the Clinton economy began reaching its stride, the Dow developed a steeper interim trend that lasted until the first quarter of 2000. From the longer-term perspective, the Dow would need to sink below 6,500 to bust the secular trend—depending, of course, on when you are reading this.

Notice that jewelry fabrication breaks trend in 2000 also. But in gold's case, the secular trend is breached because no interim trend can easily be derived. We observe that regardless of China and India, the world economy seems to drive jewelry consumption independent of price.

FIGURE 6.4 The Dow Jones Industrial Average exhibits a similar pattern to worldwide gold jewelry fabrication from 1986 through 2004. (*Source:* eSignal.com)

If this is a factual correlation as opposed to a coincidental observation, we might derive a model for forecasting gold jewelry demand based on the Dow or a composite of paper asset performance. (See Figure 6.4.) This might provide a basis for forecasting price when supply is added into the equation. Mining output is generally known to the extent that economic forces do not change the production dynamic. Even a large gold discovery takes time to cultivate into production so that the impact can be measured over time. It is rare, if not impossible, for a new source of gold to immediately become available and weigh upon the supply/demand equation. This gives us the opportunity to analyze changing demand patterns as they relate to production.

Nine recognized regions comprise the global gold market:

1. Europe
2. North America
3. Latin/South America
4. Middle East

5. India

6. Far East

7. Africa

8. Turkey

9. Commonwealth of Independent States (Russia)

These nine regions can be divided into two markets: mature and developing. North America is a mature region with modest expansion compared with developing nations like China, India, and the Far East. In the background are sleeping giants like the Commonwealth of Independent States and Latin America. Based on emerging industrial markets, it is fair to assume monetary stability will come, allowing citizens to accumulate wealth at an increasing rate. The key to any long-term evaluation relies on the speed and consistency of the actual accumulation rate relative to any decrease in demand among mature markets. Although detailed data for each country within each region are available, such analysis mainly serves as an exercise rather than a conclusive study. If anything is known about jewelry demand, it is that patterns change quickly. For our perspective, it is sufficient to attempt an assessment of more general patterns. Figure 6.5 plots fabrication for the major regions from 1980 through 2002. It appears that demand is being led by developing regions.

Gold enthusiasts quickly point out that demand patterns suggest explosive upward price movements when considered alone. Obviously, supply must enter the price equation. Yet there are extremely strong arguments for a pending shortage if jewelry sector demand follows slopes in Figures 6.3 and 6.5. Demographic studies support prospects for continuing demand. However, wealth and purchasing power depend on price. As previous chapters explain, pricing from 1986 through 1995 was static to lower while purchasing power was just breaking out in developing markets. When demand offsets supply enough to increase prices, elasticity enters the equation.

Aside from the war on terror and economic uncertainty, one of the most significant developments impacting gold and many other markets is the Internet and related communications evolution. When information flows freely, governments struggle to control markets. At best, two-tiered systems controlled by governments fall victim to black markets. At worst, governments fall victim to revolution. As the global market for goods and services emerges and matures, most gold barriers are likely to dissolve. Gold can be quoted, bought, and sold electronically. Deposits can be held in any location and electronically transferred in an instant. How can governments regulate ownership in our information age?

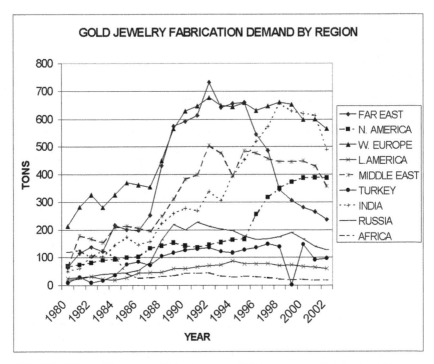

FIGURE 6.5 Gold jewelry fabrication from 1980 through 2003. It should be noted that figures for Russia are estimates based on multiple sources because official numbers are not available. (*Source:* GFMS, Ltd. All rights reserved)

Two-tiered markets like those maintained in India become virtual impossibilities. This means that exponential growth markets like India, China, and the Far East will be driving forces on the demand side of the price equation. The Commonwealth of Independent States and Latin America must also be considered to be powerful forces as societies mature and accumulate wealth. Although the slope of the Russian curve stalled into 1991, with time this huge producer will consume more of its production. An upper class and middle class are forming. The population diversity suggests that an elite "white Russian" class cannot grow sufficiently to absorb substantial amounts of gold jewelry. I believe this theory is misplaced because it is based on the former Soviet Union. The large Muslim population has gained status with the formation of the CIS. Their affinity for the yellow metal is strong and supports an argument for a reversal in buying patterns well into the twenty-first century.

While somewhat esoteric for this book, political scientists debate whether Russia can maintain the structure and continuity as the Commonwealth of Independent States. Pointing to the large difference between the Russian ruling class and the increasingly independent Muslim states, there are questions about how much control can be maintained. The Chechnya revolt, as well as the original Afghani revolution against Soviet influence, demonstrate the CIS structural vulnerability in a time when Islamic fundamentalism threatens Westernized and/or Westernizing societies. Time will tell if major differences in population and ideology can survive.

In conjunction with political science postulations, we should keep in mind that the majority of Russia's precious metals resources are substantially within the control of the non-Muslim population while oil resources are the opposite. This suggests that Russia's gold supplies will remain stable. The question is whether the white Russian or the Muslim population has the greater affinity for gold jewelry consumption. Given the religious significance of gold in the Muslim ceremonies of marriage and circumcision, I tend to believe demand will grow as the Muslim population's wealth increases. Without splitting hairs, however, it should be safe to assume that Russia, as a whole, will have increasing wealth if simply based on its enormous natural resources.

Any discussion of jewelry demand should take extraordinary events into account that influence local or regional economies. For example, the decline in Far Eastern and Chinese jewelry fabrication demand at the turn of the twenty-first century was attributed to the severe acute respiratory syndrome (SARS) virus outbreak. This potential epidemic significantly altered local perception, plunging luxury goods into a depression. While SARS had not materialized into a continuing economic threat by 2004, the disease remained a danger into the third quarter of that year. Conceptually, any epidemic that affects (or infects) a large regional gold consumer is going to have a significant impact on jewelry demand.

As Figure 6.5 illustrates, jewelry fabrication demand can have wide and abrupt swings. It is fair to observe that the general complexion has been upward since 1980. The recession that began in March 2000 is clearly reflected on the plot and impacted the major gold-consuming regions. This is a striking development because the large decline in jewelry demand *did not cause prices to plunge*. To the contrary, prices firmed up as speculation filled the deficiency in jewelry accumulation.

Bar Hoarding, Coins, Medallions

Physical gold investing encompasses bars, coins, and medallions. Together, they make up the second largest demand category. However, physical investing represents a double-edged sword because hoarding can lead to "dishoarding." Indeed, this is a confusing area because it must always be analyzed on a net basis. The gold industry recognizes that investment bars can fuel supply as well as demand. In contrast, coins and medallions have not been viewed as a source of supply even though they can be freely exchanged. As was seen during the early 1980s, the rate of exchange can impact prices. Evaluating investment accumulation is made more complex because figures are difficult to derive.

Two statistics provided a basis for reasonable estimates. First, there is new annual gold bar fabrication. This indicates the amount of new supply. Of course, these bars can become jewelry, dental material, coins, medallions, or electronic contacts. There is also an attempt to identify bars placed into investment holdings through storage and transfer statistics. Some accuse the industry of double counting; others claim significant transactions remain clandestine. What is certain is that investment demand is the most critical for generating dynamic price movements. This is the emotional arena that is inevitably responsible for shifting the supply/demand equation.

Unlike jewelry fabrication, which can be viewed as true consumption, hoarding lacks definitive long-term patterns. Today's accumulation can easily become tomorrow's distribution. Therefore, long-term analysis of this critical area is, in many respects, target practice. However, it is important to consider some basic fundamentals. The majority of private gold is held in Western Europe, the Far East, the Middle East, India, and China. The United States entered the private investment scene late because U.S. citizens were not able to legally own investment bars until 1975. Surveys reveal that U.S. gold investors opted for coins over bullion. This is because the United States did not generally promote mechanisms or vehicles that facilitated bar ownership.

In the early 1980s, a number of firms emerged to offer gold bar accounts. Investors could buy and sell kilo bars through these firms, which acted as both clearing and storage facilities. As with many quickly developing investment offerings, some gold investment houses ended up defrauding customers. One such example was North American Coin and Currency, which was operated out of Phoenix, Arizona. The founder apparently emptied the vaults and disappeared after improprieties were discovered. This is why certified depositories are a good idea for any physical ownership.

Subsequently, gold bars gained respectability as companies like the United Bank of Switzerland and Republic National Bank offered customers gold bar accounts with storage insurance services. Gold bar faded as prices declined through the 1980s and 1990s. Gold bar accounts performed miserably and the volume imploded over two decades. Popularity did not reemerge until after 9/11 and the significant U.S. dollar decline. As crude oil reached $50, interest in gold accelerated. In particular, institutional investors began to consider gold as an asset of last resort.

Patterns of hoarding and dishoarding continue to vary. Factors that seem to affect the process include political change, monetary stability, alternative investments, and wealth. As an example, Saudi Arabia experienced relatively low accumulations from 1985 through 1988, averaging about four tons per year. As tensions arose over Iraq's invasion of Kuwait, accumulation leaped to more than 20 tons in the latter half of 1989. During the next three years from 1990 into 1992, the amount averaged more than 25 tons per year. Then, demand plunged below pre-1989 levels with less than 2.5 tons in 1993 and a modest 5.6 tons in 1994. The same uncertainty over the Gulf War was reflected in the accumulations of other Middle East countries.

Contrary to popular belief, Middle East accumulation grew proportionately with oil prices. This suggests the correlation between oil and gold is more investment oriented than a reflection of individual wealth. Jewelry accumulation is not the dominant Middle Eastern focus as oil wealth builds. Conversion into gold represents an important pattern. According to the figures, Middle East bar hoarding peaked in 1992, after the successful completion of Operation Desert Storm. I say "successful completion" cautiously since the war with Iraq was extended into George W. Bush's administration. Like father, like son.

Referencing Figure 6.6, we see that gold (top) began mirroring crude oil (middle) from approximately October 2001 through the last quarter of 2004. Both gold and crude oil exhibited similar peaks and troughs. For some analysts, gold was simply taking on the U.S. dollar's complexion since gold was generally quoted in dollars. By the same token, crude oil is quoted in U.S. dollars. Thus, when U.S. dollar parity declines, both gold and oil should proportionately reflect the decline. Yet Figure 6.6 clearly shows a divergence from September 1998 through September 2000 when crude oil and the U.S. dollar moved higher together.

Notice that in 1998 the U.S. Dollar Index (DX) remained in a relatively flat trading range as crude oil declined along with gold. This demonstrates the fickle dynamic among gold, crude oil, and dollar parity that often causes a logical nightmare for traders. "I know how it's supposed to work, but it ain't working!" Such is the cry of metals traders who seek an absolute relationship among gold values, dollar parity, and crude prices.

While early in its development, the link among U.S. dollar parity, gold prices, and oil values has been sporadic and unreliable. This is why pattern trading is so difficult over longer interim periods. We simply cannot tell the probability of a trend based on our relatively small data accumulation and the patterns generated. Perhaps it is too optimistic a quest. It may

FIGURE 6.6 We see the expected pattern for gold and the U.S. dollar whereby gold's upward movement comes with a weak U.S. dollar, while gold's decline comes on dollar strength. Oil can have distinctly contra parity movements as we see from September 1998 through November 2001 when oil rises even as the U.S. Dollar Index (DX) gains strength. (*Source:* eSignal.com)

simply be sufficient to use correlated periods for gold and oil as a reference rather than an absolute forecast. Unquestionably, the fact that gold is priced in floating dollars distorts the real trend. While gold was rising in 2003 dollars, it was flat to declining in euros. This pattern carried into 2004 as well.

During Operation Iraqi Freedom, U.S. and British forces recovered over $600 million in gold bar accumulated by Saddam Hussein over an unknown period. However, tons more were believed to have been transported to Malaysia, Indonesia, and other safe havens for undisclosed Islamic assets. These bars were probably not accounted for in published statistics. In fact, considerable underground gold bar movement is likely to be undisclosed and, therefore, undetected.

Although not generally announced to the public, several post-9/11 surveillance operations focused on gold movement as a means for identifying terrorist cells. Large cash gold dispositions were linked to cash accumulations for weapons purchases or subversive operations. A large cash gold sale unrelated to central bank divestiture became a warning beacon that money was on the move for some purpose.

Overall, we see an affinity for gold in the Middle East. This may be due to tradition, or it may be a sign that OPEC members can lose faith in the "full faith and credit" of the U.S. government. Although this is a debate that must, by nature, extend beyond this book's publication date, a pragmatic conclusion is that there can be some disproportionate U.S. dollar parity relationship that would force OPEC to reconsider using the dollar as a pricing benchmark. Unfortunately, there is no historical perspective we can reliably reference because the last serious reference to nondollar pricing took place in the late 1970s. This was the period of extraordinary inflation and dollar uncertainty. OPEC suggested using a "basket of currencies" as an alternative to the greenback. The Hunt brothers preferred the concept of silver certificates. In the end, the dollar maintained its incumbency.

There are two possibilities that might sway oil producers away from U.S. dollar pricing. The first is a total collapse of the U.S. dollar that would make oil unreasonably cheap when priced in dollars. The second might be political discontent if the United States is viewed as overly powerful. From the dissolution of the Bretton Woods Accord through the turn of the millennium, the United States was generally viewed as the world's security blanket. In particular, its status as the only remaining superpower provided an initial sense of comfort that the most powerful economy also controlled the most powerful military.

Perceptions quickly change. A friend today can easily be viewed as a threat tomorrow. The lack of participation in Operation Iraqi Freedom by Germany and France was indicative of a breach in the U.S. global status. The unilateral move to disarm an unarmed dictator and hold the spoils hostage did not sit well with the two largest European Union members that control the euro. This is not a history lesson, but more an example of a situation that creates a shift in economic-political status.

If and when the euro is used to price oil, we may see a more closely aligned gold price parity. This creates an incentive to inventory gold as a buffer. The most logical form for this buffer is gold bar. Thus, any break in oil-for-dollars pricing can have a long-term positive influence on gold bar accumulation. The degree to which such accumulations remove gold from the market can determine prices moving forward. This also implies more permanent removal from the supply equation and, hence, less of a danger of being reintroduced.

Figure 6.7 plots Middle Eastern gold bar hoarding over more than two decades. We see a substantial amount of accumulation. A ton of gold represents 32,151 troy ounces. Even at the relatively low prices for gold from 1980 forward, at $300 per ounce, a ton is worth $9,645,300. For every 50

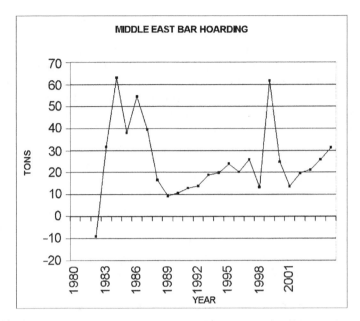

FIGURE 6.7 Middle Eastern gold hoarding has been declining since the 1980s, but still represents a substantial dollar value each year. (*Source:* GFMS, Ltd., Gold Institute, World Gold Council)

tons, the value is almost a half billion dollars. This means Middle Eastern accumulation accounted for several billion dollars in net purchases.

Of the Middle Eastern states, Saudi Arabia accounted for more than 50 percent of the total region's accumulation. While the values are impressive, we should consider that at $30 per barrel of oil, the 8 to 11 million barrels per day capacity of this desert nation amounts to $330 million daily. That means a billion dollars in gross revenue can be generated in about three and a half days. One hundred tons of gold can be purchased with less than a week's oil production.

This should put the oil-for-gold potential into perspective. If 2003 world production was approximately 4,000 tons, the value at $325 was $10.5 million multiplied by 4,000 tons. World production would have a $40 billion value compared with Saudi Arabia's oil output at 8 million barrels per day with a $30 per barrel value reaching $876 billion. In other words, Saudi Arabia could buy world gold production more than 20 times over.

At the accelerated rate of 11 million daily barrels claimed in the fourth quarter of 2004, the Saudi production was worth $550 million per day as oil prices exceeded $50 per barrel. This is why gold advocates scream that gold's price could explode in an investment instant. If, heaven forbid, the Saudis decided to convert a small portion of oil revenues into gold, the price could easily be propelled to $1,000 per ounce and beyond. When examining the Saudi economy, we see very little diversity. In effect, Saudi Arabia had very limited capacity to grow beyond oil as of 2005. This lack of diversity is not unique to Saudi Arabia. It is characteristic of all Middle East OPEC members and represents one of the destabilizing elements of the region.

If oil is on a collision course with technological innovation, conservation, and new capacity, OPEC economies could be destabilized. This may sound humorous when considering the perceived lack of stability that has existed since ancient times. However, destabilization in a modern setting is particularly dangerous. Unless Middle East oil producers adopt expanded and diversified economic models similar to Israel, oil will play the only role in economic prosperity. Consider the possibility that new technology can actually reduce the global rate of oil consumption. The world has technology to lift automotive fuel efficiency by 50 percent, with pending technology that might produce a two-fold jump in fleet mileage. Alone, this could create a huge Middle East depression without accounting for large production capacity growth. This is why Lebanon must regain status as the "play land" on the Mediterranean Sea. This is why Saudi Arabia must break away from fundamentalism and produce goods and services outside of oil. This is why Iraq's unique position between the two most important water resources must be exploited, from hydroelectric facilities to the fertile crescent of Middle East agriculture.

If a transformation is not forthcoming in the years ahead, the Middle East gold demand can easily turn into Middle East gold supply. We do not know the amount of Middle East gold that could become freely available. As mentioned earlier, gold hoarding is a double-edged sword that can represent supply and demand.

Accumulation habits in the Far East are equally pronounced. Although not necessarily linked to conflict, Japanese gold investment is hypersensitive to economic developments. Japanese investors view gold as a symbol of stability and status. Because Japan is a small island nation, real estate is scarce and at an extreme premium. Precious metals and other hard assets act as supplements to land ownership. Thus, Japan has been the largest accumulator of private gold and platinum hoards. Figure 6.8 shows estimated Japanese accumulations from 1980 through 2003.

While we can identify a 15-year downward sloping trend line, we must be careful not to form any absolute conclusions. When amounts are compared against average gold prices during the same period, we see this hoarding does not necessarily have a significant price correlation in U.S.

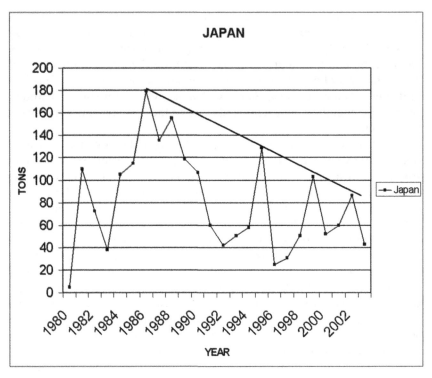

FIGURE 6.8 Japanese gold bar hoarding from 1980 through 2003 illustrates a rising trend from 1980 through 1986 and a declining trend thereafter. (*Source:* GFMS, Ltd. All rights reserved)

dollars. From 1979 through 1986, the Japanese yen exhibited a modest downtrend against the U.S. dollar as observed in Figure 6.9. This calculated strategy permitted Japan to sustain a highly competitive price advantage against U.S. goods. In particular, cars and electronics gained a reputation for being better quality at a better price. Once established, Japan was able to allow the yen to gain more aggressively against the greenback.

The phenomenon of "Japan Inc." took hold from the mid-1980s moving forward as Japan's economy exhibited the strongest growth spurts in modern history. Japan was accumulating huge dollar surpluses that were being poured into U.S. investments. There were concerns that Japan was buying the United States wholesale.

Gold reached its record highs in U.S. dollars in 1979–1980. Notice that the high price did not discourage Japanese accumulation even as the yen declined against the dollar. This refutes any theory that price sensitivity

FIGURE 6.9 The Japanese yen declined in U.S. dollars from 1979 through 1985 before embarking on a substantial inverse trend that tripled parity by 1985. (*Source:* eSignal.com)

will drive investment demand. To the contrary, as prices rise, we know demand is increasing. To the best of my knowledge, no one has been able to define the point at which gold's real price discourages investment. It is not always a function of high price because gold is viewed as a safe haven that, by nature, is worth more as other assets falter. What we see is that Japan's newfound wealth and economic status drove gold accumulations through the mid-1980's.

Japanese bar hoarding patterns suggest a decline in hard-asset investing as gold prices slumped and alternative investments flourished. In addition, the yen became a more attractive investment vehicle because it was rapidly and substantially gaining against the dollar, which was gold's pricing benchmark. The logic is simple: Why invest in a declining parity when an appreciating parity is available?

Culturally, Japan has become the most Westernized nation in the Pacific Rim. As such, its cultural attachment to gold has become less pronounced. This suggests Japan will accumulate and distribute gold in accordance with economic ebbs and flows. An underlying concern some gold analysts share is the potential for divesting if Japan experiences an economic boom that encourages a move into paper assets. This concern must be measured against the underlying accumulation pattern that hints at a baseline of approximately 20 to 40 tons per year.

In contrast, I believe the majority of the Far East maintains a cultural bond with gold. In particular, the emergence of Vietnam as a viable economy after the war demonstrates how a small country with very little world economic impact can become a moderate accumulator. From virtually no accumulation, this small country has emerged as a global player in gold bar accumulation. Consider the comparison of China versus Vietnam illustrated in Figure 6.10.

An emerging economic giant like China had a huge swing in identified gold bar accumulation from 1994 through 2004. In contrast, a small economy like Vietnam held steady between 28 and 36 tons per year over the same period. There are obvious reasons why Vietnam would place

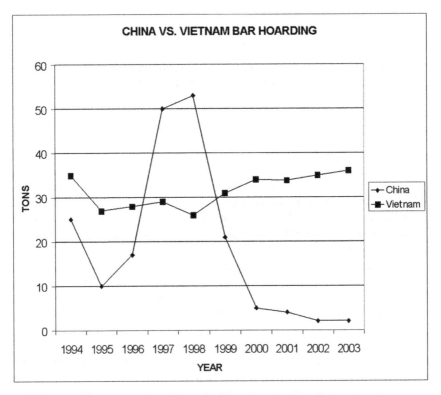

FIGURE 6.10 China exhibited a burst in gold bar accumulation in the late 1990s, but the economic boom created more commitment to capital investments. Vietnam maintained a steady accumulation over the same 10 years. (*Source:* GFMS, Ltd. All rights reserved)

its trust in gold rather than the local currency. Its economy remained uncertain through the post–Vietnam War adjustments, and the banking system lacked the stringent regulation found in other progressive Far East countries.

There are theories that the Vietnam accumulation as well as accumulations and distributions through Thailand represent an undisclosed flow among several nations and, in particular, China. All bar hoarding statistics are subject to significant variation because they are based on identifiable bar movements. Official gold bar accumulation falls in a small number of recognized categories. However, gold is cast in unofficial forms as well. China's abrupt decline in official accumulation to less than 10 tons per year in the beginning of the new millennium appears highly suspicious.

Unlike Western nations, which have held the majority of bars as central bank assets, the Far East accumulates bars in private accounts. Political and economic sensitivities that can drive private gold into the market are very different from motivations for central banks. As the Far East economies turn progressively Western, I feel gold bar accumulation will remain steady to higher. The interesting aspect of this accumulation is the fact that it is new and private, as opposed to old and government controlled. Why is this a potentially important consideration?

Since the unification of Western Europe into a common market, there has been pressure for central banks to divest gold hoards. Indeed, when we analyze supply, we see that considerable new supply is, in fact, old distribution as alluded to in the beginning of this chapter. Who is buying the central bank distribution? Based on the jewelry statistics and fabrication trends coupled with the other categories of gold consumption, we must conclude that private accounts are picking up the excess. When the numbers do not match, the difference is probably an undisclosed or unaccounted for accumulation.

This suggests a strong undercurrent of gold demand that is missing from mainstream media and reports. It cannot be *proven* and, therefore, is excluded. Certainly, there is the possibility of private gold divesting. It must be in the back of our minds when evaluating the big prospective picture. However, an interesting computer simulation conducted in 1990 suggested that gold's price would sink to $150 based on anticipated central bank sales. Gold did not dramatically drop in response to the actual sales, raising the question, "Where did the demand come from?" The metal was accumulated and incorporated into the global private hoard.

This brings up the emerging gold derivatives market mentioned in Chapter 4's discussion of new investing strategies. Having traded and analyzed commodity markets since my early years in college, I am intimately familiar with gold futures, options, forwards, and certificates. Derivatives are paper representations of the physical market. However, there are no constraints upon the amount of hyperextension derivatives can impose on the physical market. Gold futures carry margin requirements between 1 percent and 10 percent of the total contract value, which is measured in ounces and kilograms.

The reason gold futures are so important in evaluating demand is because futures prices are far more dynamic than the London gold fix and represent the most liquid segment of gold trade. The COMEX division of the New York Mercantile Exchange listed gold open interest at more than 296,000 contracts of 100 ounces each in mid-October 2004. That amounted to approximately 921 tons. Open interest is the number of contracts existing between buyers and sellers. Of this amount, more than 50,000 contracts traded regularly each day. That represents about 155 tons. This is only the New York market. The London bullion market exceeded COMEX by more than 50 percent. Equally impressive ratios are traded through the Japanese markets. Although less than 2 percent of contracts are delivered, this paper representation of an underlying physical asset has a major influence on prices. In fact, in many instances futures are believed to drive the cash markets.

At any moment, as much as one-third of annual gold demand is represented by the New York futures market alone. The institutional participants span gold producers, fabricators, and investment funds. In the post-9/11 environment, gold began to assume a renewed glitter. Funds began taking a serious look at something called nonparametric risks. These are risks that are not within the identified parameters of risk evaluation. No one expected an attack upon the United States or the resulting response leading to the war in Iraq. The risk of such an event fell outside the scope of known risk factors; however, gold's assumed response would be to move higher in real terms.

In reality, gold did not spike higher as world tensions increased. Rather, the U.S. dollar fell and the parity difference was reflected in gold's price. However, global scandals have impacted world currency markets and, concurrently, gold parities. For more than 200 years, Barings Bank was a pillar among U.K. financial institutions. From July 1992 through February 1995, a currency trader managed to lose approximately 850 million pounds. The result was an immediate decline in dollar/pound parity as Barings was forced out of existence. In 2000, a similar scandal rocked Allfirst Bank.

When the United States faced the meltdown of Enron and subsequent scandals at WorldCom and Tyco International, serious questions about the integrity of large corporations, and the financial information on which investment decisions were being based, came to the forefront. Even when companies survived, an underlying uneasiness mounted. The giant German conglomerate Metallgesellschaft lost more than $1 billion trading energy derivatives, while Ford Motor Company confessed to an equally large loss speculating in palladium!

One might conclude that lessons have been learned from these back-to-back incidents, but a New York attorney general named Eliot Spitzer turned the investment industry on its ear by prosecuting scandals ranging from improper after-hours mutual fund trading to bid fixing among major insurance companies. His tenacious pursuit of wrongdoers gave rise to the term "Spitzer risk." Money managers were moved to consider securities called exchange-traded funds (ETFs) as an alternative to mutual funds. Enter the concept of gold as a hedge against an entire spectrum of nonparametric risks.

There is nothing new about using gold to hedge uncertainty, as explained earlier. But the cycle of favor and disfavor with gold should be weighed against the developing economic environment. Are we in a destabilizing cycle or a stabilizing trend? Was gold favored during the eight years under U.S. President Clinton or not? Did gold come back into favor after the war on terror erupted?

From 2001 through 2004, speculative hedge funds increased assets by approximately 50 percent per year. The top 10 hedge funds showed assets increased from approximately $26 billion in 2002 to $40 billion in 2003 and almost $60 billion by 2004. This was attributed to weak performances in equities and bonds as investors disparately sought alternatives to bring back double-digit returns seen in the techno-bubble formation prior to the bursting after March 2000.

Among the investments targeted for speculation by hedge funds were precious metals. Although gold was not the exclusive focus, it was the major focus. Volatility and uncertainty provided fat option premiums and extensive speculative opportunities. When considering the size of speculative capital pools relative to margin requirements, as well as the scope of the gold derivatives market, we must conclude that a massive speculative thrust is well within the realm of possibility. Further, the probability of a sustained speculative uptrend becomes more pronounced as hedge funds increase assets.

Even before the chaos invoked by 9/11, fund traders were shifting toward commodity-based investing. The renowned money manager Jim Rogers formulated his own commodity index and predicted China's long-term influence upon raw commodity prices more than four years before the China Syndrome was identified and widely publicized. The point is made for participating in the speculative influences organized

funds can have upon gold. Since the delivery standard for most exchange-traded gold is gold bar, the derivative portion of gold's market is
linked to this category.

Alongside gold bar hoarding is the accumulation of official gold
coinage. This category should not be confused with numismatic collec-
tioning. Official gold coinage is relatively new. Essentially, it represents
gold coin of the realm minted for investment purposes. Unlike prior
coinage with face values based on a fixed official gold price, today's
coinage is minted in specific weights and fluctuates in value with the price
of gold, silver, and platinum. Official coinage has the added safety feature
of face value. Thus, a $20 gold coin cannot fall in value below $20.

Coinage has generally been associated with small investor participation. Quantities have been variably small and are not believed to wield a
significant influence on overall demand. Indeed, at the end of the twentieth century, total world coinage production dropped from just over 150
tons to approximately 76 tons. Numbers began to increase within the first
decade of the new century, but remained sharply lower than fabrication
during the 1980s, which seemed to be a residual of the huge moves made
by metals at the end of the 1970s. Figure 6.11 plots official gold coinage
from 1980 through 2003.

When reviewing many of the available gold reports, a distinct feature
and potential drawback is the limited historical analysis. There tends to
be a concentration on the current year and the possibilities for the next
year. Yet, very little material covers the historical potentials. We can understand why investors would have an interest in gold coins and bars
when prices are rising and there is a fundamental view that demand will
continue increasing. We can comprehend why investors might turn away
from gold when its performance is weak and paper assets are strong. Still,
there are subtle forces deserving exploration.

Two major events appear conspicuously missing from an analysis of
investment accumulation. One was the introduction of a totally new paper
currency in the United States beginning in 1996 with the introduction of
$100 bills. The distinctive feature was a new large presidential portrait
and special dual-color imprints designed to thwart counterfeiting. Coincidentally or not, as the new notes were introduced, the amount of currency
in circulation began to rise. By the release of the new $20, paper in circu-
lation had jumped by almost one-third.

The new paper notes represented the first time a government pur-
posely cast aspersion upon the integrity of its currency. In effect, the Treasury was touting the new bills because the old bills could be more easily
counterfeited. The result was a de facto recall of old money. The U.S. Mint
was destroying the old currency as quickly as it could issue new. At the
same time, President Clinton maintained some of the highest tax rates in

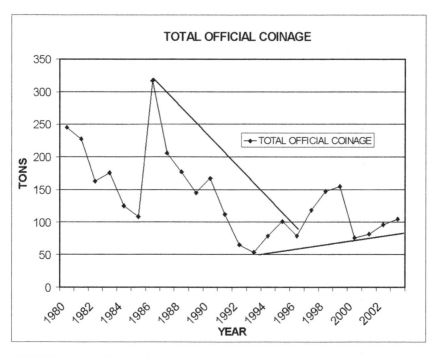

FIGURE 6.11 Official gold coin fabrication had a momentary jump in the mid-1980s, followed by a steady decline into the early 1990s. A recovery attributed to economic prosperity maintained growth until the recession beginning in 2000. Uncertainty over terrorism may have regenerated interest after 2001. (*Sources:* GFMS, Ltd.—All rights reserved; U.S. Mint)

U.S. history. Was there a connection between the burst in U.S. consumerism and the unpredicted U.S. budget surplus?

Notice in Figure 6.11 that gold coin accumulation made a sharp jump in 1996 and continued to climb until 2000. The theory that investors would step away from gold and into paper during the economic boom from 1995 through 1999 contrasted against increasing gold coin fabrication and accumulation. Perhaps old paper was being converted into gold as well as consumer goods.

The pattern is more pronounced when looking at the statistics within the United States. Between 1996 and 1997, gold coin fabrication jumped from about 11 tons to more than 26 tons. In 1998 it reached 57 tons and peaked the following year at more than 60 tons. After the recession began in March 2000, the number declined to a paltry 5.4 tons. Since U.S. paper currency is the dominant secondary currency where local notes are less stable, the move from old currency to new represented a global event. The United States actually exported several billion dollars in new notes to Russia to make sure there was no adverse impact as the old currency was withdrawn.

In 2000, the euro currency was introduced. Again, there was a jump in gold coinage fabrication and, more importantly, overall European accumulation of old and new inventory. The European Union experienced an uptick in economic spending and currency circulation. However, the euro was a more comprehensive and immediate exchange of old bills for new. The opportunity to accumulate gold was compressed into a shorter period when compared with the U.S. conversion.

I bring this up because paper currency is the antithesis of gold. The 1996 introduction of new U.S. currency was the first change in approximately seven decades. The idea has always been to portray a safe and stable paper currency. Suddenly, paper currency was changed twice in less than a full decade—when the U.S. began releasing new notes with multiple background colors in 2003. The slogan of "Safer, Smarter, More Secure" brought home the message and may have incrementally raised interest in securing some amount of gold as insurance against a flaw in the slogan's logic.

Another development in accounting for gold coinage was the rise of Turkish production and the popularity of their coins among Muslims who exchanged them as gifts. From virtual obscurity in the 1980s, Turkey surged to the forefront of coinage in leaps from 2002 through 2004. Figure 6.12 plots official coinage for Turkey, the United States, and South Africa. From its position as the dominant producer, South Africa declined to near obscurity from the 1980s through 2003.

Anyone who has owned newly minted gold coins is likely to be aware of the contrast between the coppery color of the Krugerrand and the more familiar golden hue of the U.S. Golden Eagle, Canadian Maple Leaf, Chinese Panda, and Australian Nugget. Investors moved toward the .9999 purity advertised by Canada, Australia, and China. This may be why South African fabrication was so substantially diminished.

The U.S. fabrication has been untamed. The official release of U.S. gold is responsible for varying amounts allocated to coinage. Overall, the U.S. Golden Eagle has enjoyed increasing popularity and is likely to share a rising proportion of gold released from U.S. gold reserves.

In contrast to official coinage, medals and medallions do not generally offer a face value and can range from commemorative offerings to Olympic prizes and corporate gifts. Medallions have been associated with gold price sensitivity because of an assumption that they are gifts and luxury items. However, fabrication patterns from 1980 through 2003 show rel-

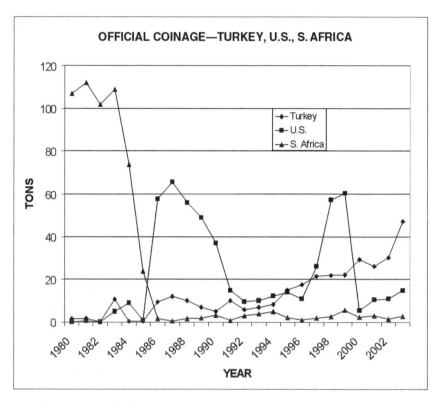

FIGURE 6.12 South Africa's notable decline from the premier manufacturer to a minor player is attributed to the rise of competitive coins and the decline in the Krugerrand's popularity as the coin of choice. A strong preference for the U.S. dollar and Canadian dollar face values encroached upon the Krugerrand's territory. Turkey's promotion of coins to the Middle East has been linked to increasing fabrication. (*Source:* GFMS, Ltd. All rights reserved)

ative stability between 20 and 30 tons. There was higher popularity from 1980 through 1984, but the overall trend has been flat.

When gold is affordable in real terms, people buy. As prices increase, investment takes precedence over casual accumulation. Casual accumulation could easily conflict with investment demand because higher prices may switch interest from one to the other. I point this out because my earlier discussions about the booming 1979–1980 market covered increasing investor participation with increasing prices. In that particular instance, all forms of gold appeared attractive and it is difficult to identify casual accumulation. It is the later data that suggests reluctance to buy when prices are too high.

Among the growth areas are medallions like the Turkish Zynet, which celebrates the Islamic circumcision ceremony. According to the Gold Fields Mineral Services, Ltd. (now GFMS Limited) *1996 Report,* production of these medallions increased 160 percent from 1995 through 1996 to 13.6 tons. A middle-class family might receive 50 grams, whereas a wealthy son could get two or three kilograms. This is similar to gold exchanged at Chinese and Indian weddings. Not all Islamic sects commemorate circumcision with gold. Yet the world's Islamic population is large and rapidly growing. It is fair to assume that this tradition, as well as customs in other countries, can engender and sustain reasonable medallion sector growth. However, the statistics on which this assumption is based are recent and within the context of growing global wealth. The Zynet is attributed with the overall popularity and growth in Turkish official coinage fabrication.

Such major emphasis is now placed on demand from the Pacific Rim, China, India, Turkey, and central Asia that it is worth touching on global perspectives. While not necessarily politicized, wealthy nations are concerned about issues like global warming and the environment as well as limited natural resources. The altruistic nature of these concerns (i.e., saving the environment) may, in some respects, represent a smoke screen for blocking industrial progress in the Third World. Understand that many scientific projections call for serious environmental deterioration and economic stress if the world, as a whole, adopts living standards similar to those of North America and Western Europe. The "green" movement may be a "me" movement because saving the Brazilian rain forest benefits the world more than Brazil. How is it fine for the United States to decry Brazil's development as long as the United States' standard of living and wasteful ways remain unchecked?

I bring this up because any book about markets and global conditions is bound to be off target if conditions change. A book about gold during the 1920s would assume a gold standard. As of this writing, the strong divergence between wealthy and developing nations remains. Within a few decades, the global economic complexion could be completely different. You must keep an open mind when approaching any market. One of the most significant problems facing investors is change. If anything is likely to cause conflict over the next few centuries, it will be resource scarcity. Simply put, there is not enough of anything to support a world living standard as lavish as those of the United States, Japan, and Western Europe. Who will dictate which countries can have and which cannot? This will be particularly important as you look for accumulation trends in precious metals markets.

Dentistry

Once again, wealth is the primary determinant in trends associated with gold's dental fabrication. Two additional developments helped increase dental gold demand since the late 1980s. First, Europe and North America responded to the supposition that silver/mercury amalgam poses a health hazard. It is possible that mercury used to bind amalgam can slowly leach out. This process might accelerate if gold and silver are present in the same mouth. Then, the demographic bulge in those needing restorative dentistry progressed along with the wealth curve from 1985 through 2000. Gold thrifting reduced the amount of metal required for restorations, thus keeping prices under control. This made gold more attractive as the material of choice.

Replacement of silver/mercury amalgam with gold is a process that should diminish as new materials are selected for the replacement restoration and the amount of decay in the three largest consuming regions declines with fluoridation and advanced hygiene. Based on demand from 1980 through 2003, it appears that dentistry is not a major growth category. (See Figure 6.13.) Unless less developed nations find an attraction toward gold-decorated teeth, the population opting for gold inlays, onlays, and foil faces growing resistance.

For the immediate future (2005–2010), palladium is likely to play a role in offsetting gold dental fabrication demand as long as the price ratio favors palladium. This is not a relationship that should be relied upon based on palladium's extraordinary 1995 bull move or its propensity to move out of supply and demand balance. Dental restoration technology suggests that growth in gold fabrication will meet increasing resistance as alternative reconstruction materials become available. By 1990, dentists were experimenting with trademarked composite materials like Dicore and Concept that consisted of glass, ceramics, and resins. These materials are designed to match natural teeth in all respects including color, strength, temperature reactivity, and conductivity.

Prior to 1990, composites were mostly used cosmetically for front teeth. Nonmetallic restoration materials and techniques are finally able to support molars with an estimated effective life exceeding 20 years. Recall earlier analysis that referenced the information age as a major factor encroaching upon precious metals in areas ranging from price discovery and marketing to chemical process engineering and electronics. Even in dentistry, our increasing sophistication in AutoCAD and process control has created machines that read three-dimensional photographs of a tooth preparation and automatically mill a precision inlay or onlay that substitutes for a gold or palladium/gold casting. The machines operate as minilabs that can create a complete restoration in less than 20 minutes.

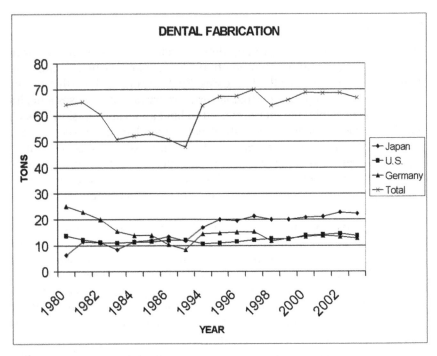

FIGURE 6.13 Dental fabrication moved to an overall steady state during the 1990 and into the new century. Germany, the United States, and Japan represent the major world consumers. Although the slopes for all three appear flat, the bias may take a downward turn as seen between 2002 and 2003. (*Source:* GFMS, Ltd. All rights reserved)

Patients no longer receive a temporary filling in anticipation of several weeks of lab work nor must they endure more than one office visit. The restoration can be accomplished from start to finish in a single session lasting approximately two hours or less.

This trend toward alternative materials will continue, and gold fillings may be virtually eliminated by the mid-twenty-first century. Even as this book goes to press, there are distinct signs that gold is losing momentum within the dental sector. This projects to recapturing between 60 and 70 tons of annual fabrication. When compared with total demand that exceeds 4,000 tons, this represents only 1.6 percent of annual consumption based on 2003 estimates. However, the impact of declining dental use is likely to be offset by unrelated emerging technologies.

To be sure, health-care progress among emerging economies in South America, Africa, India, Eastern Europe, the CIS, and the Far East could offer a temporary boost to dental fabrication in the near term. The debate is not whether substitutes will be used, by when and to what extent. This technological trend is already in place.

Electronics

Massive growth in computer sales and related semiconductors has been the basis for expanding gold consumption in the electronics sector. In addition, telephone and telecommunications switches add to demand. As global modernization continues, this consumption trend should continue upward with occasional interruptions associated with economic hiccups. Yet, as explosive as electronics and telecommunications industries have been, gold consumption in this sector has been somewhat less spectacular. Better plating and bonding techniques have reduced the amount of gold used for contacts and bonded components. Electronic profit margins tend to run razor thin, creating a highly price-sensitive sector. Alternatives like nickel/silver alloy and palladium have made inroads. Circuits previously incorporating gold are now configured with less expensive materials. In addition, circuit boards are smaller, with more functions on single chips and chip sets. The result has been stable growth in electronics gold consumption from 1980 through 2004.

Based on trends in mobile communications, personal computers, and automotive electronics, I feel confident electronic consumption will double before 2015. Digital cameras as well as experiments in gold-based superconductors lead me to believe investors will experience steady 2 percent to 3 percent annual growth beyond the year 2000. There is also a high probability the space and military industries will increase consumption in conjunction with new projects. A straight-line projection of the trend line established from 1982 provides a technical basis for this conclusion. (See Figure 6.14.)

Gold's ductility and resistance to oxidation make it essential for critical applications. This is why companies like Toyota boast about using gold in the air bag circuitry of their Lexus automobiles. Of course, the amount used for air bag contacts is extremely small. The more important applications are in switching mechanisms and plug contacts.

Decorative Applications

The use of gold plating and decorative material doubled in the 10 years from 1986 through 1995 and again into 2000. From approximately 64 tons in 1986, the estimated consumption rose to nearly 120 tons into 1996. There was an unusual increase in gold leaf used for signs and building decorations beginning in 1994. Some analysts attribute this rise to restoration of historical sites in China and other Far East countries. As long as

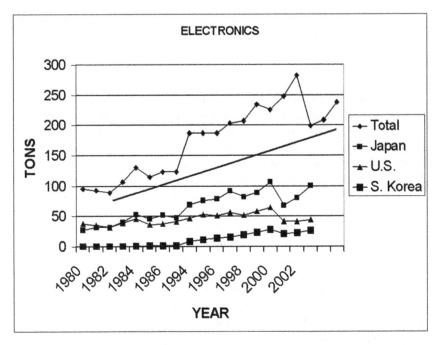

FIGURE 6.14 Gold consumption in electronics has been increasing from 1980 forward. (*Source:* GFMS, Ltd. All rights reserved)

the price remains under approximately $450 per ounce, gold can be effectively used as industrial decorative material. Gold leaf can be as thin as one-hundredth of an inch. By 1997 decorative applications were 114 tons; however, decorative demand declined to approximately 80 tons by 2004.

When gold rises above $400 per ounce, gold substitutes are used in noncritical applications. In 2004, a series of gold mesh accessories that included undergarments, handbags, and billfolds exemplified gold's versatility and spawned elitist interest in gold threads/yarns. A multimillion-dollar diamond-studded bra caught the eye of gold bugs who were informed that the material was white gold. It is difficult to determine whether the interest was focused upon the gold or the model! Either way, the implication was that gold adornment or decorative applications would hold steady despite a rising price.

Other Applications

The gold industry breaks out other applications with a primary emphasis on plating. Gold is used to enhance reflective properties of window glass, is a reflective coating for hardware used in corrosive environments, and can be used for medical implants and in medicines. In reality, the scientific community is just waking up to applications for gold that could have profound long-term effects on demand and pricing.

Although much of the work with gold in new technologies is proprietary, the most significant potential applications have received some public recognition. Electro-reactive polymers hold the promise of new lightweight batteries and sensors (not to be confused with electro-active polymers). Highly proprietary experiments with gold and gold salts hint that this metal could unlock room-temperature superconductivity. Gold is not the best conductor. Copper and silver have less electrical resistance. However, the stability of gold and its interaction under various controlled conditions imply a host of undiscovered electrical and electronic applications as of this writing.

Despite its known nobility and, hence, lack of reactivity, gold has rapidly emerging efficacy as a low-temperature catalyst for carbon monoxide (CO) and nitrogen oxides (NO_x). This application has widespread implications because it applies to existing energy plants like gasoline and diesel engines and new motor systems based on fuel cell technologies. In combination with palladium, gold can increase efficiencies in catalytic converters while helping to thrift platinum group metals. This establishes a balance between platinum and palladium consumption for this application.

Analysts correctly point out that platinum and palladium loadings are relatively small. With annual auto and truck catalysts commanding 3.18 million ounces of platinum and 3.67 ounces of palladium in 2003, a similar amount of gold might be just enough to offset the decline in dental fabrication moving forward. Indeed, the processes for introducing gold auto catalysts are likely to ramp up very slowly through 2025. Caution is advised because modern technologies have been assimilated at an accelerating rate. The rise of digital imaging to a dominating role in new consumer photography demonstrates the speed with which new technologies take hold.

The first joint-venture hydrogen fueling station between oil companies and the U.S. Department of Energy appeared in late 2004. A single station does not predict a rapid implementation of such stations during the twenty-first century. But it is a beginning. Gold catalytic applications include H_2 purification for hydrogen fuel cells used to produce electricity. In addition, this technology applies to composite or complex hydrogen fuel stocks like methanol, methane, and even white gasoline. These liquid fuels must be "reformed" into hydrogen for fuel cell consumption. Gold may play a critical role in this process.

As of this writing, there was only an experimental amount of gold consumed in these catalytic processes. But, the projections based on these applications hold the promise of a new and significant demand sector. Figure 6.15 makes a projection of gold catalyst fabrication through 2030. It paints a conservative picture based on particular growth assumptions related specifically to the automotive sector and fuel cell technologies.

Other chemical applications include "expoxidation" of chemicals called olefins, gas detection devices suitable for antiterrorist applications and process plant safety controls, and air and water purification. These areas can add an equal amount of demand projected forward over the next several decades. In fact, some optimists believe chemical processing technologies will come on stream faster than auto catalyst and fuel cell applications because the infrastructure penetration cycle is believed to be lower.

In the previous iteration of this book released in 1998, I mentioned that gold's cost-to-benefit ratio might stand in the way of widespread gold consumption in new areas like superconductors or gold plasma lasers and optical luminescence. Problematically, superconductive gold wires could require huge quantities that in all likelihood would price gold out of the market. Still, it is worth keeping an eye out for new uses. Over the years, I have received many inquiries about such applications because material was not readily available in the public domain. Even industry ex-

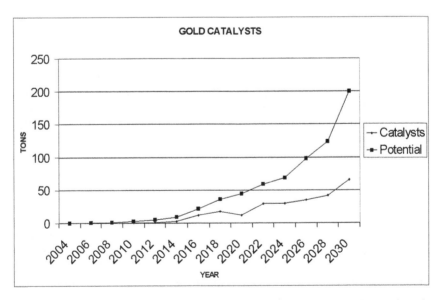

FIGURE 6.15 Gold catalyst fabrication is projected on a conservative path and potential path leading to consumption between 60 and 200 tons by 2030. (*Source:* EQUIDEX, Inc.)

perts suspect some science fiction. My inclusion of these potential applications was derived from requests to invest in projects proclaiming experimental potential and commercial promise. To the extent I am able to give mention, it seems that the potential is of interest even if the science never fully materializes. A futuristic view adds intrigue and excitement in my opinion.

I have been pleased by the more public fulfillment of some of the previously mentioned technologies. In particular, gold optical properties may lead to curvilinear lenses and materials that apply to storage media, hollow light-tube optical fibers, heating and cooling systems, and photoluminescent products. These technologies have the potential to draw down modest to moderate quantities of gold during the twenty-first century.

DEMAND IN GENERAL

All sectors combined give clear signals of increasing gold consumption through the twenty-first century. Economic patterns point to rising demand possibly accelerating within the first decade of the new millennium. Assuming a normal economic environment and progress against the war on terror, jewelry should lead the growth curve while investment will represent the balancing wheel. The assumption of steady and controlled growth in demand depends on the demonetized gold status. Demand can instantly change if governments return to this metal as monetary backing or dump reserves. This is a threat that will not fully dissipate until central banks adopt a uniform and consistent gold policy. Thus, we live with a significant wild card.

As previously discussed, the wild card has too many implications for any intellectual exercise. Will our gold be taken away? Will new generations ever embrace this metal as money? The supply side holds some answers to these questions, but not a solution you can invest in!

SUPPLY

Gold supplies fall into two categories: newly mined and aboveground inventories. The nature of these categories is somewhat unusual because it relates to gold's unique personality as an investment or store of value. We may analyze other markets in a similar fashion when we refer to existing home sales and new home sales. Other precious and base metals have aboveground supplies like scrap and stored inventories. By far, stored gold represents the most striking two-tiered supply situation. Thus, central bank demand must be measured against central bank sales. Private bar hoards are a source of supply as well as demand. In the macro sense, aboveground supplies depend on newly mined gold. This is why some analysts view existing gold as less important than new production. Yet, we know the impact disinvestment can have on prices. Because investing or speculating is the underlying theme of this text, the enormous global gold stash is a paramount consideration.

Gold scrap represents a segment of aboveground inventory and creates a price-sensitive variable that adds or subtracts from supplies. When prices trend higher, scrap is more vigorously recovered. Low prices discourage reprocessing to recover scrap. Gold scrap comes from diverse sources ranging from jewelry to recycled electronic components.

The trend in new gold production is solidly up and has been for more than three decades. Beginning with the price boom of the late 1980s, gold discoveries and mining technology have combined to increase gold production by approximately 300 percent. From 1980 through 1990, the United States increased gold production from 30 tons to 294 tons. In other words, U.S. output was 980 percent more in 1990 than in 1980. From 1990 through 1995, production moved from 294 tons to 330 tons. Although this was only a 12 percent increase in the following five years, we should keep in mind that the 36-ton increase is more than the entire U.S. 1980 output. This is similar to arguments about stock market corrections in reverse. The 500-point crash of October 1987 would be small in year 2000 terms, since the Dow Jones Industrial Index more than quadrupled from about 2,500 to 11,500. Western production moved from 960 tons in 1980 to 1,755 tons by 1990, an 85 percent increase. Over the next five years, output increased by 135 tons, or 7.7 percent. By 2003, total world mining output was estimated by GFMS Limited to be 2,593 tons. In just over two decades, new gold production rocketed by 270 percent.

This growth brings to mind comments made during the debate over gold as a monetary standard. President Richard Nixon's Gold Commission issued a statement saying that new gold production would have to increase by more than three times for gold to become viable as currency. According to geological and technological experts of that time, such an expansion in new gold supplies was impossible. Behold two decades later, identifiable gold production is up by more than four times since Nixon closed the gold window.

Figure 6.16 charts gold mine production from 1980 through 2003. The impressive acceleration in production through the 1980s and 1990s is significantly attributed to advances in extraction technology and increasing by-product production. First, "heap leaching" enabled companies to economically remove gold from low-grade ores and surface soils. As an exam-

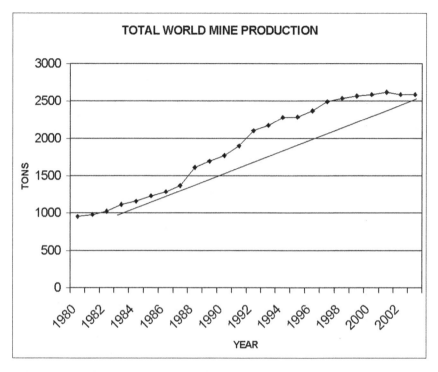

FIGURE 6.16 The 20-year trend for mine production has been decisively up. (*Source:* GFMS, Ltd. All rights reserved)

ple, this development alone elevated South Carolina from a virtual non-producing state to the ninth largest gold-producing state in the United States by 1992. As newer technology has been applied to existing properties, output has expanded at unexpected rates. In the late 1980s, industry literature suggested that production technology had reached some practical limits. The conclusion was that any significant new production would depend exclusively upon new discoveries. Historical precedents and continuing technological developments proved this assumption incorrect. First, by 1993, mining companies had barely scratched the surface of cutting-edge mining and extraction innovations. The emphasis during the 1980s was primarily enhancing efficiencies of known oxidation/reduction methods. Global production remained a mix of high-tech chemical processing and low-tech manual crushing using mercury binding for isolation and removal.

In 1996, approximately 35 percent of global gold production was attributed to refractory deposits. Without becoming too technical, gold is bound in pyretic deposits containing hazardous materials like arsenic and arsenopyrite. Conventional extraction methods call for expensive "roasting" processes that present environmental problems and challenges. Substantial progress has been made in heap leaching oxidized gold ore. Autoclaving continues to increase yields from low-grade ores at decreasing costs.

On the horizon were *Thiobacillus ferrooxidans*, bacteria that actually eat low-grade ores, leaving behind more easily processed gold-containing counterparts. These new bugs actually digest the unwanted materials away from the gold. The added advantage to using bugs is the lack of hazardous by-products. Any arsenic remaining after digestion is rendered inert. The process does not use highly poisonous cyanide leaching. More remarkably, bacterial oxidation is efficient and provides reductions in both capital and operating costs. In 1994, Newmont Mining received a patent for its specialized version of bio-oxidation. Since then bio-leaching has been improved through a variety of genetic upgrades and ore pretreatments.

At the beginning of the twenty-first century, microbiologists were discovering an entirely new science of bioprocessing ranging from creating electronic circuits to molecular memory modules. Microscopic organisms called extremophiles appear to metabolize metals in ways similar to our use of oxygen. Derek Lovley of the University of Massachusetts in Amherst discovered that certain microorganisms' breath dissolved metals ranging from cadmium to gold and silver. This discovery led to an interest in whether certain organisms living around deep-ocean hydrothermal vents could convert soluble gold into precipitated solid metal.

Early experiments were not promising because microbic efficiency was lacking. Too many organisms were required in a highly controlled environment to produce minimal gold. Yet, this same technology was being successfully applied to a widely diversified processes ranging from containing oil spills to harvesting chemicals and processing waste. This science is as old as wine. In fact, fermentation has played a major role in developing specialized bio-extraction technology.

Chaim Weizmann was a chemist who developed a vital fermentation process that helped the Allies win World War I. Weizmann's contribution to Britain's war effort was recognized by the Balfour Declaration, upon which the State of Israel was founded. History aside, part of the Weizmann process involved training "bugs" to convert substances into desired end products. Today, scientists at the Weizmann Institute continue working on bioprocessing using microorganisms. It represents one of many institutions on the cutting edge of this endeavor.

I bring this up because genetic engineering holds the promise of increasingly efficient bioprocessing. Based on global samples, geologists estimate there are 25 billion ounces of gold dissolved in oceans. Billions more may be found in carlin type gold ores which hold particles of 0.1 ~ 0.01 μm in size and are disseminated in rock minerals, like pyrite, illite, and montmorillite. This micro-sized gold cannot be seen under a standard microscope. It is sometimes called "invisible gold" or "micro-sized disseminating gold." As of this writing, extracting gold from seawater or carlin type ores remained uneconomical.

Yet economies are a function of gold's price and technological advancement. Given modern breakthroughs in biotechnology, I believe efficient gold extraction processes for seawater and generalized deposits are possible. Further, lower grade ores could be processed at decreasing costs. The catch 22 is gold's possible price plunge if production outpaces demand. I have faith in the market system. There will be an appropriate balance. It will be interesting to see how quickly this processing technology develops, if at all.

There are several varieties of ores, each requiring a specific processing approach. During the 1980s, surface mining gained momentum because capital costs and risks associated with deep-shaft mining favored this alternative. Moving through the new millennium, robotic mining and computer modeling are likely to shift the industry back to deep hard-rock mining. One of the largest expenses associated with shaft mines is environmental control. Deeper mines have higher temperatures and environmental challenges. When miners work, air-conditioning alone adds large expenses. Water containment presents further problems. Sophisticated remote control and computer systems reduce requirements for human rock removal and transportation. Equally important, monitoring equipment more accurately detects rock formation stability to anticipate possible "rockbursting." This is an explosive event resulting from stressing structures adjacent to ore removal sites.

In conjunction with these developments, geologists have new tools for evaluating gold-bearing potential. Satellite imaging, magnometers, subsurface signatures, and an improving understanding about how the earth formed reveals an increasing number of possible gold mines with untold potential. We know that the earth's crust moves on huge tectonic plates. The continents as we currently know them were once a single landmass during the pre-Vendian era. As tectonic movement progressed, large portions of the earth's crust shifted locations and elevations. Minerals were redistributed to form pockets or concentrations that carry very specific electromagnetic signatures. The geophysical study of "terrane tectonics" has revealed more precise data about how and when these deposits were formed, where they are likely to be located, and how to search for them.

For those interested, "magnetotellurics" is a process for detecting certain rock formations with high probabilities of containing certain minerals. The method is used in oil and mining industries to efficiently and accurately map promising exploration sites. Simply put, the earth's crust exhibits particular electrical resistance based on the structure and material. By measuring current flow through a structure, scientists are able to derive a subsurface profile that yields a probability distribution for mineral deposits. In combination with three-dimensional subsurface tomography, mineral exploration has entered an entirely new phase of complexity and efficiency.

Other emerging technologies include electro-active/reactive filtration systems that show promise for low-cost extraction of gold and other metals from very low-grade deposits. The inventors claim commercial-scale plants for extracting gold from seawater can produce gold at a cost as low as $50 per ounce. This would be an amazing evolution in the gold market that could pave a return to a gold monetary standard. Is the world ready for plentiful gold? Demographic warnings imply vast amounts of gold could not appear at a better time!

It is a bold leap, but I believe the combination of technologies will yield enormous new gold discoveries at an increasing rate. The unknown or critical variable will always be the price of gold relative to the cost of extraction. However, even based on current commercial technology, I anticipate a renewed upward steepening of the supply trend line. The slowdown in growth toward the end of the 1990s should reverse and steady growth should be maintained for at least several decades.

Perhaps the most significant factor in determining year-over-year supply is the geopolitical environment. Entering the new millennium, most major gold-producing regions remained under a veil of economic, political, and demographic instability.

Between 1988 and 2003, only two countries managed to maintain status on the top 10 gold producer lists. These were the top two, South Africa and the United States. There is a question whether the United States was actually second in 1987, because unofficial estimates for Russian production ranged from 150 tons to as much as 270. As seen in Figure 6.17 and Figure 6.18, the countries among the top 10 changed in rank and name. South Africa's dominance at more than 600 tons in the late 1980s diminished to 400 tons by 2003.

The rankings immediately reveal that the entire complexion of world gold production has changed. Not only are the dominant players dynamic, but also the quantities are more uniform. This indicates a pattern of global expansion and equalization. Whereas the difference between

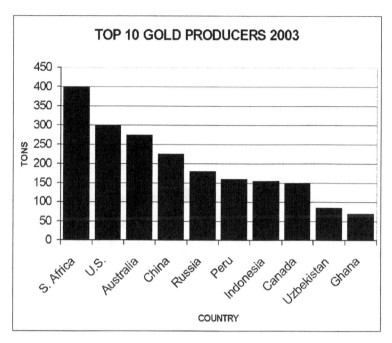

FIGURE 6.17 2003 Top 10 rank by country. (*Sources:* GFMS, Ltd.—All rights reserved; U.S. Bureau of Mines)

South Africa as number 1 and Venezuela as number 10 in 1987 was 591 tons or 97 percent, the difference in 2003 between 1 and 10 was 330 tons or 82 percent. The difference between 1 and 2 was substantially less in 2003 than in 1987.

Notice the change in names as well as rank. In 1987, the top 10 produced the majority of gold. Approximately 15 years later, countries that did not even fall within the top 20 are producing as much as fourth-ranked Australia produced in 1987. This pattern of diversified production will continue moving forward and the list is likely to change dramatically based on geological discoveries and economic development.

This is particularly important when considering the influence production dislocations have had in the past. Most notably, labor unrest, strikes, and political turmoil have had major impacts upon production. As gold output spreads among an increasing number of regions, the impact of single incidents will dissipate in proportion to the affected production. Certainly, a shutdown of South African mines over a labor dispute will have a large impact. The loss of Cuban output would be insignificant.

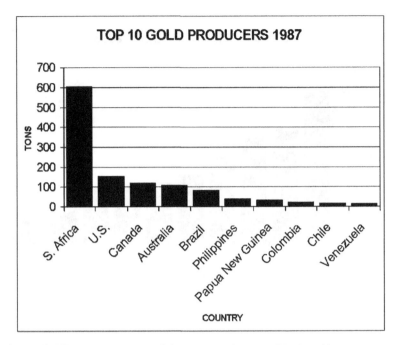

FIGURE 6.18   1987 Top 10 rank by country. (*Source:* GFMS, Ltd.)

As the twentieth century drew to a close, the AIDS epidemic presented a threat to the continuity of African labor. With an estimated 60 million AIDS victims on the horizon and a large percentage of the South African labor force in jeopardy, AIDS was more than a human tragedy. It represented a time bomb ticking toward the economic downfall of many African nations. Gold production relies on a steady supply of healthy, young male labor. Therefore, AIDS can easily become a factor that reduces African potential.

Even if mines reduce labor requirements through automation, the near future does not promise a sufficient reduction to avoid colliding with an AIDS-related labor shortage. Further, South Africa is not exclusive to the AIDS threat. As of 2004, several demographic experts proclaimed AIDS to a pandemic equal to, or more serious than, the Spanish flu and Black Plague combined.

The AIDS projections show a geometric spread in China, India, Russia, Latin America, and the Pacific Rim. There is no room for complacency among Western powers when considering the massively negative effect world population decimation can have upon the global economy and political stability. AIDS has the ability to wipe out more than half the developing world's populations.

Equally unpleasant threats loom in the form of SARS, terrorism, global conflict, and more. This is not a book on ecopolitical disaster. However, it is important for anyone investing in physical metals to track demographic patterns as related to consumption and the means for production.

Along other lines, geological surveys indicate that production can accelerate in the United States, Canada, South America, Indonesia, Australia, China, India, and Russia. In proportion, South Africa's output will grow at a proportionately smaller rate or decline into the twenty-first century. Experience tells us that surveys are not always reliable because technology can alter perspectives and potentials. Reports indicate the type of deposits found in South Africa will become less economically attractive—hence a projected decline in South African output. This means it is possible that the United States will assume the number one rank if Russia does not capitalize on its vast resources. I caution that the United States is shackled with the same constraints on ore quality as South Africa and, more importantly, environmental restrictions that can severely limit expansion. The United States is not mine-friendly and does not have an abundant source of low-cost labor.

When considering the difference in labor and technology, I am not sure I agree that South African gold deposits are destined to become less attractive. For more than a century, South Africa has enjoyed some of the highest-yielding ores. Its geological structure still presents vast areas that will be successfully developed. South Africa has access to more affordable labor and is not burdened with the same rules and regulations as the United States. It is not simply the quantity or quality of ore that determines the production leader. It is capital, labor, political stability, and the investment climate, not to mention gold's price performance.

Figure 6.19 illustrates the growth pattern from 1980 through 2003 by major region. For the most part, producers were able to expand output from the 1980s forward. The most remarkable departure from this trend is South Africa's steady decrease in output. In contrast, China, Indonesia, the Commonwealth of Independent States (Russia), and Peru are increasing output. The promise of Brazil was dulled.

Alone, the chart only gives a historical snapshot. The essential ingredient for proper analysis is the addition of a broad fundamental assessment. Based on geology, I believe there are huge untapped resources in South America, the Pacific Rim, Australia, and Canada. At the end of the twentieth century, geologists intensified their search for particular rock

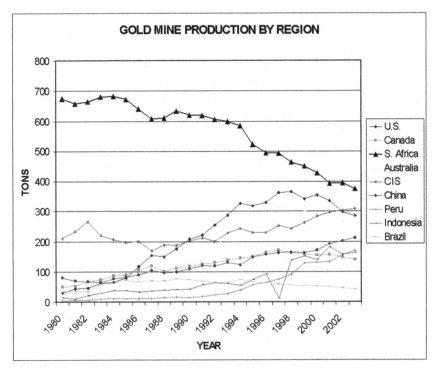

FIGURE 6.19 While the number one producer has seen yields declining since 1980, other producers are increasing production as they develop gold properties. Composite gains have offset South African declines. (*Source:* GFMS, Ltd. All rights reserved)

formations called kimberlites that are associated with diamonds and minerals like gold. One of the largest kimberlite fields is located in northern Canada.

The "Canadian Shield" refers to rock formations extending north from the U.S. border. Until the 1990s, this area remained essentially unexplored even though common sense dictated that the geology favored diamonds. Indeed, a massive diamond field was discovered in Canada's northern territories. The find is believed to rival deposits in South Africa. As of this writing, Canada was just beginning to explore the gold potentials of these regions.

Indonesia became home to the Grasberg mine, one of the largest in the world. From 55 tons in 1994, Indonesia's production grew to 183 tons in 2001. Peru boasts enormously rich copper resources. With copper comes gold. The Yanacocha mine ranks at the top of the list with Grasberg. This illustrates the shift from South Africa to new untapped areas.

My research shows impressive potential along the copper-rich western ridge of South America encompassing Chile as well as Peru. This region will increase contributions through the first half of the new millennium. Pacific Rim resources were barely touched in the late 1990s as this book was first written. In less than a decade, this region has become the leader in new capacities.

Of course, the Commonwealth of Independent States wields outstanding credentials. As the economy continues to Westernize, it is safe to assume the CIS members will account for a major portion of total global production.

Total mine production demonstrates a relatively smooth upward trend. Based on regression analysis extrapolation, mining companies may increase production by 25 percent and more each decade. Statistics cannot necessarily measure resources in the ground or future economic viability for production expansion. Therefore, assumptions based on straight-line or even curvilinear projections require caution. Three decades of experience provide a sound foundation for expecting gold mining to increase along the path illustrated by Figure 6.16, at the very least.

THE PRICE-TO-COST RATIO

Enthusiasm for higher prices is inexorably linked to a steady climb in production. Therefore, projections must be tempered or even scrapped based on the price-to-cost ratio. As mentioned, everything from discovering new mines to processing ore has become more efficient and cost-effective. But, we can expect costs of labor, reclamation, and capital to rise with global economic expansion.

In broad strokes, the cost of gold derives from:

- Land, plant, equipment
- Ore quality
- Capital costs including prevailing interest rates
- Labor
- Land reclamation and pollution control
- Energy
- Exploration and development
- Secondary refining
- Land leases

- Taxes
- Marketing
- General overheads
- Hedging

Given the diverse categories contributing to costs, it is difficult to discern a specific trend. For example, in 1986 costs ranged from approximately $150 per ounce to as high as $280 per ounce. On average, South Africa was at the low end at $188 per ounce while the Philippines was at the higher end with $216 per ounce. The average gold price was approximately $370 per ounce. The price-to-cost ratio ranged from 2.46 to 1.48.

In 2003, cash costs ranged from a $180 low to a $291 high. The world average was $222 while the average gold price was $363. The price-to-cost ratio ranged from 2.01 to 1.25 with a 1.64 average. Despite almost two decades of inflation, it is striking to note that both the costs and average price of gold in 1987 and 2003 were extremely close. Of course, there were unusual circumstances from 2002 through 2004 as interest rates made four-decade lows. The cost of capital (financing) is not likely to be consistently low and, therefore, we can expect a portion of gold's cost to vary with interest rates.

We do see proof of advanced technology since it is apparent that gold mining expenses have not been inflating. Even with the stripping out of higher-grade ores, the industry has maintained a relatively static cost structure. This becomes an important factor when considering gold stocks, as we will cover in Chapter 10. The efficiency of the gold mining industry bodes well for stock performance *even in a period of declining prices*.

Given new high-tech exploration and the propensity toward discovering high-grade deposits, costs should remain contained for a reasonable period moving forward. However, when the price-to-cost ratio dips below 1.1, we can expect industry restructuring and the shedding of marginal production. If we assume a steady state for costs, the likely cause of a low ratio would be a low price.

In contrast, a high ratio promotes marginal production. When gold moves above $500 per ounce, mining and processing can move as high as $450 and maintain the 1.1 ratio. For simplicity, a spread between costs and price needs to be more than $50 to encourage industry growth. Having seen gold swing as low as $250 and as high as $440 as the new century began, industry management is conditioned to pursue a very conservative growth path. Yes, there will be competition to acquire new and existing properties, but the level of aggressiveness is not likely to become frantic until (and unless) gold reaches $550 to $600 per ounce.

If gold reaches a high ratio, the larger quantities must be absorbed. It is fair to presume that a good portion will be hoarded as bars that can eventually feed supply. This is a somewhat unique dynamic that can lead to increasing amplitude in a natural business cycle.

OFFICIAL RESERVES

I previously touched on official gold reserves as adding to potential supplies. Global politics associated with modern economic structures proposes gold will be abandoned as central bank reserve assets. The Maastricht Treaty disavows gold as an official reserve asset. Indeed, the trend since President Nixon closed the gold window has been toward divestment. There have been exceptions where some governments have accumulated new inventory. Emerging economies still use gold to bolster monetary reserves, as seen by countries like Vietnam.

According to the International Monetary Fund (IMF), total world central bank reserves as of 2002–2003 were approximately 32,358 tons. Undoubtedly, this was a large amount for the market to contend with if it were to be sold in bulk. However, under an agreement between central banks called the Central Bank Gold Agreement (CBGA), official sales are limited to a predetermined amount per year. The purpose is to permit orderly and nondisruptive divesting over time.

Interestingly, the largest official hoard is not in Switzerland as so many believe. As of this writing, the United States remained the largest official holder of inventories at more than 8,000 tons. Germany came in at number two with almost 3,500 tons. Figure 6.20 shows the top 10 central bank official reserves. With all of the assumptions about Switzerland having the largest gold hoard, it ranked a distant sixth behind the United States. The United Kingdom did not make the top ranks.

Historically, Figure 6.21 shows the pattern of gold hoarding from 1948 through 2003. We see that total world hoarding has not significantly changed despite central bank sales. Contrary to popular belief, the United States did not divest substantial amounts after legalizing gold in 1975. The majority of U.S. reserves were taken down through the open policy at the gold window that Nixon closed. Countries that maintained a trade surplus with the United States exchanged dollars at the gold window for bullion. Notice that from the 1957 peak in U.S. reserves, Germany began accumulating at the expense of the United States.

There are several nations that appear reluctant to part with their gold at the turn of the century. Portugal, Spain, Japan, and Germany show steady and even an upward pop in the chart derived from IMF data seen in

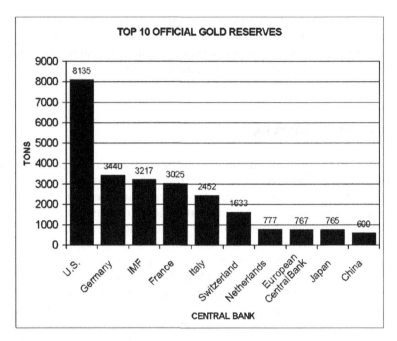

FIGURE 6.20   Top 10 official central bank gold reserves show the United States with 2.36 times the amount of the next largest holder. (*Source:* GFMS, Ltd. All rights reserved)

Figure 6.22. No doubt the CBGA will have a forced impact upon member reserves and the trend is toward a decline in central bank holdings. The key element to this pattern of divesting is that it has not driven down the price of gold on a proportional basis.

This means that private demand has absorbed public auctions. To this extent, gold is filtering from government control into the private sector. This is a very important consideration because the gold industry and its associated analysts view official sector sales as supply. In reality, it is simply a shift of ownership. True, the 500 tons of gold proposed for sale in the CBGA will add to the amount "for sale." It is a supply-side consideration. But as mentioned earlier, today's divesting represents someone's accumulation with the exception of amounts consumed in fabrication.

The first rendition of this book stated:

> *Central banks will never dump gold reserves. If any liquidation process is to take place, sales will be clandestine during long periods. It would be self-defeating to cause a decline in the value of*

reserve assets through improperly executed sales. Assuming world economic systems permanently abandon gold, the size of reserves and pattern of sales through 1995 suggest these assets will be depleted within a 25-year span. This places a zero date around 2020.

The impact on prices cannot be determined because economists cannot project economic conditions forward that many years. In fact, experts have difficulty forecasting more than a few months with any certainty. A steady liquidation would mean a stable economic environment. The conclusion is that gold will lose value or parity if reserves are added into the flow of new production. Experts do know that total reserves are finite. At some stage, sales can exhaust these stored supplies if no future accumulation policy develops.

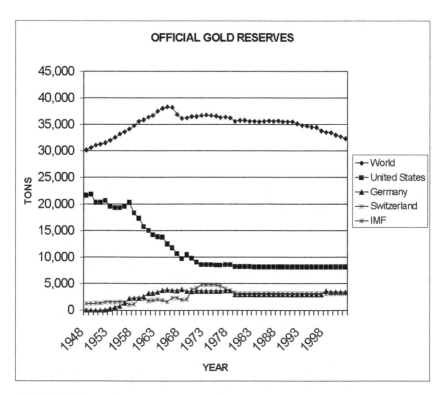

FIGURE 6.21 Official gold reserves from 1948 through 2003. (*Source:* International Money Fund)

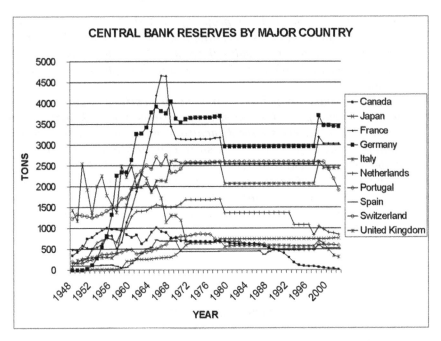

FIGURE 6.22 Gold reserves by major country from 1948 through 2003. (*Source:* International Money Fund)

My analysis predated the CBGA, which takes the sales from uncertainty to more certainty, and from clandestine to public. However, the assessment remains remarkably intact considering that the rate of sales does point to minimal holding by countries participating in the divesting process through 2020. There are only 15 participants in the CBGA. Many more countries can construct substantially different gold policies moving forward.

Realizing that gold's stability is important, central banks have taken a conservative approach toward converting gold into other assets. With new mine production progressing toward 3,000 tons per year, sector sales of 500 tons are less than 20 percent of new production. When examining demand, sector sales should be considered a stabilizing component moving forward.

Gold advocates argue that sector sales distort the real gold price. This is like saying the sale of wheat from reserves distorts grain prices. Sector sales are part of the gold equation. They neither enhance nor detract from price transparency. Central bank holdings are also leased and operated as a regulating mechanism much the same way as central banks regulate money supply through open market operations.

Without the reserve sector, gold prices would be likely to gyrate widely and the industry could find itself facing considerably more risk. If gold exploration is to be supported, gold prices must not rise and fall below practical values in a chaotic manner. The reserve sector serves as a buffer that will prove its value over time.

THE HEDGE BOOK

Hedging has been considered a source of supply when, in practice, it is a commitment of sale. Producers are in the *business* of making gold. While it is not a creation, gold is, in a sense, manufactured like any other product. Companies know their costs and profit margins for products. Gold producers are not necessarily interested in speculating on gold prices. If they have an opportunity to hedge value and lock in a good profit margin, prudence dictates taking such action.

Hedging provides an indication of supply moving forward at the hedged price. When prices are firmly in an uptrend, hedged positions can fall because companies *do speculate* at particular levels. This brings us back to the concept of the price-to-cost ratio. When this ratio exceeds 2.0, there is a disincentive to hedge because the margin of price over cost is high enough to assure a healthy profit. As we will see, companies do not necessarily do better when gold prices go up. In particular, a hedged position can lose proportionally more than the increase in price provides if the hedge is poorly executed or gold's price moves too quickly to take countermeasures.

This is why a company's hedge policy is so important to investors seeking to participate in gold via stock ownership.

THE BIG PICTURE

The prevailing trend points to increasing gold supplies that appear able to keep pace with demand at a decreasing rate. In the absence of monetary or political crises, gold will remain a commodity balanced between supply and demand. As the premier monetary metal, gold has been displaced by monetary technology that includes rapid information transfer and processing as well as synthetic valuation vehicles like futures, options, and derivatives. Nations can always move back to asset-backed currencies. However, this is not likely with the present pace of global economic expansion.

Religious and cultural attachments to gold are likely to be diluted by modernization. Old traditions give way to new thinking more quickly in our information age. Will Chinese families accumulate gold as they become wealthier, or will they prefer televisions and personal computers? In short, gold, as a symbol, is being challenged in the West and revised in the East.

The fundamental appeal of gold will never be completely expunged. There will be a practical value to this precious metal. Even with technology and discovery tipping scales toward more economical production and, perhaps, lower selling prices, there are many industrial applications that can easily turn gold more toward a consumable rather than a storable.

We assume that gold has always represented a crisis hedge in modern times, but this relationship between disaster and gold was not supported during the 1980s and through the 1990s. Even after the 9/11 attacks, gold remained subdued in comparison with the expectation of a pronounced reaction. Yet, increasing nonparametric risks that can range from terror attacks to Wall Street scandals has placed a new emphasis on gold as the ultimate hedge that has been so reassuring. Combined with derivative transactions, gold is reemerging as an asset class. Gold's divorce from investors may have been only a separation moving forward into more uncertain monetary times with far more accelerated global development. Therefore, gold may, indeed, have a place in the modern portfolio.

CHAPTER 7

Silver
Fundamentals

S ilver's unique qualifications as a major industrial metal as well as a potential monetary standard provide a more diversified foundation than other metals. Silver's historically affordable price has made it an attractive alternative to members of the precious metals group. We frequently hear silver referenced as "poor man's gold." In reality, silver's industrial applications are sufficiently different from those of gold to make the label a misnomer. Still, it is the high degree of price correlation that permits the association between silver and gold to stick. Regardless of inflation, silver's applications extend to photography and imaging, electronics, welding, mirrors, medicines, water treatment, jewelry, tableware, batteries, glass coating, and medallions. Silver remains the best electrical conductor among metals. It has exceptional thermal conductivity. Silver can achieve the ultimate level of polish and, therefore, reflectivity.

The fastest-growing industrial applications involve electronics, batteries, catalysts, and biostatic treatments. The largest single use has been associated with photographic imaging. Until recently, no viable silver alternatives existed for applications relying on its unique properties. However, during the 1990s, technological innovations began to impinge on silver's territorial imperative.

Silver received increasing negative publicity during the 1990s into the new millennium. I must confess that I was responsible for some of the waning enthusiasm. As early as 1988, I appeared on NBC's *Today* show to talk about the new paper money and silver. My props included silver bars, a roll of film, and a video camera. My talking point was that "filmless photography" was going to have a negative impact on silver consumption. It seemed that each week brought some new technological innovation that encroached upon silver's high-consumption sectors. For example, just when there was an industrial resurgence in silver-based mirrors, science began delivering monomolecular "dielectric mirrors" that represent the most highly reflective surfaces known. These special mirrors are spectrum-sensitive and can reflect almost 100 percent of the specified light. Although the use of dielectric mirrors for large-scale reflective surfaces was still experimental at the turn of the century, there is little doubt these scientific marvels may have the potential to cut back silver consumption in the industrial mirror sector.

There is a huge difference between potential and reality. Although dielectric mirrors hold many promises, manufacturing processes require long lead times. If and when mirrors substitute this new technology, the news will lead a decline in silver consumption by a moderately long time, by trading standards. We would see reports of upcoming technology and, hence, anticipate a decline in silver consumption. However, it is important to work this possibility into any long-term silver strategy. In particular, any plan to buy and hold physical metal over an extended period should consider the chance silver mirroring will be replaced or augmented.

As mentioned, silver is one of the most effective and oldest known bactericides, algicides, and sporicides. One of the first medicines commonly administered to newborns is a silver nitrate paste that is applied to the eyes to prevent infection. Silver has an extremely low toxicity and allergic reactivity. Therefore, it is ideally suited as a substitute for antibiotics and sterilization reagents. In the late 1980s, there was a push to reintroduce silver as a more versatile bactericide. Even before the widespread fear of a bioterrorist attack, the medical field was seeking ways to combat new and natural microbic threats like antibiotic-resistant staphylococcal and streptococcal infections. Hospitals were increasingly vulnerable to resistant infectious bacteria and fungi. Silver offers a promising solution. Extremely low concentrations of silver in ionic or colloidal solutions have been proven very effective in sterilizing surfaces. Unlike some chemicals with high toxicity or noxious fumes, silver is environmentally friendly. According to most experiments, bugs cannot develop a resistance to silver because the mechanism silver employs to destroy bacteria is different from other antibacterial applications.

Silver's antibacterial properties have led to applications in water treatment, air purification, food preservation, and more. In fact, silver technology was judged the most effective for large-volume water purification because it does not require an energy source. In areas like India, Pakistan, China, South America, and Africa, clean water is a priority. Often, areas in need of water sterilization do not have access to standard electricity. Silver purification units can operate as stand-alone machines.

The flip side to the potential growth area is the development of sterilization processes using ultrasonic sound, ultraviolet light, and X-rays. By the mid-1990s, several companies were introducing irradiated foods with a theoretically indefinite shelf life. This same process was making progress in water purification systems. Because new applications have been based on the antibacterial properties of silver, alternative bactericides are important considerations. In India, two water purification systems have been considered for residential use in small villages. One is a silver filtration system; the other uses ultraviolet light. As mentioned, the major advantage of using silver is its independence from an external energy source. However, this edge could be lost as energy distribution systems rapidly emerge in undeveloped countries.

The booming electronics industry may hold the greatest potential for silver demand. Here, too, the white metal races against technological innovation. Small silver oxide batteries used for watches, cameras, hearing aids/medical devices, and other applications represent a huge growth area. Unfortunately, electro-plastics that may produce equally potent lightweight batteries are being researched. Further, these plastic devices appear to be rechargeable and environmentally friendly.

As of 2000, the most extensive use of silver came from three categories: jewelry/silverware, photographic, and electrical/electronic. (See Figure 7.1.) This represents a significant change over a relatively short period. In 1997, photography held the dominant role. Imaging remains a major category encompassing 28 percent of annual consumption, yet it has dropped from holding as much as 40 percent.

From 1977 through 1988, total world silver consumption was declining to flat. This pattern changed as wealth within developing countries increased moving into the 1990s. Fierce competition developed between major film and photographic paper producers like Fuji and Kodak. At the same time, both giants agreed on a new film standard in an effort to hold off digital imaging.

Figure 7.1 plots silver consumption by major category. We see the boom of the 1990s reflected in an increase in total consumption. The economic slowdown following the stock market decline of March 2000 is illustrated as we see the immediate dip back to 1999 levels.

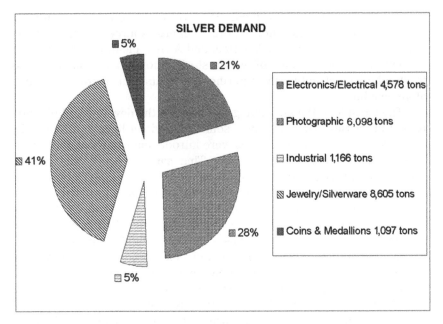

FIGURE 7.1 World silver consumption by major category as of 2003. (*Source:* GFMS, Ltd. All rights reserved)

JEWELRY AND SILVERWARE

From my perspective, the growth area that caught my attention was jewelry and silverware. When introducing the demographic patterns that can lead to changing demand, I assumed that the tradition of bringing out the silver had tarnished. Silverware is not what it used to be, and my conclusion still stands unchallenged by the numbers. But, bridal registries for silver in the United States have not declined. Department stores have registered increases during the very period I expected we would see continuing declines. I continue to believe high-quality stainless steel flatware will impede silverware's popularity, but my view is admittedly overly subjective.

Silverware sales have shown a decline, yet the decrease has been more than offset by surging jewelry demand. If silver were a living organism, we might conclude that jewelry and silverware demand have achieved homeostasis—an equilibrium that keeps silver stable. Silver jewelry has enjoyed steady growth over several decades. In the transition from the twentieth century to the twenty-first century, jewelry consumption moved up by approximately 27 percent against a modest decline in silverware. Silver's unique color, light weight, comfort, subtle patina, and malleability have added to the appeal of rings, bangles, pendants, hair accessories, earrings, watches, and other knickknacks. Silver has come of age. Its relatively low price-to-utility ratio makes silver an ideal middle ground between pure costume jewelry and very expensive platinum and gold.

As of this writing, silver adornments were enjoying surging popularity in Asia. The contrast of white reflective metal against the Asian skin tone produces a more appealing contrast than gold, which tends to blend. Of course, platinum is the preferred high-end metal. But it is the mass market that produces mass demand. This is not to say that there is a raging bull market for silver jewelry. It is to say that the popularity of silver jewelry is growing and has the potential to add 1 percent to 3 percent per year, based on the pattern from 1990 through 2004.

The trend toward silver jewelry began in the 1990s. Unlike traditional gold and gemstone jewelry, silver's popularity may represent a fashion event that may not endure the vicissitudes of time. Thus, relying on extended growth in either silverware or jewelry represents a higher degree of risk than extrapolating expected growth from an industrial application that requires silver.

Since India occupies the number-one position in jewelry fabrication (see Figure 7.2), it stands to reason that increasing prosperity will support consumption growth. It is interesting to note that the initial U.S. stock market failure was negatively correlated with India's silver appetite. In fact, fabrication leaped above 100 million ounces for the first time.

While the recession following March 2000 probably slowed silver jewelry and silverware consumption, the damage appears to have been minimal. When trying to discern fundamental logic, one finds that none definitively exists. The category of silverware has been expanded to include items unrelated to cutlery, bowls, and goblets. Silver personal items like hairbrushes, hand mirrors, picture frames, key chains, and plaques are additions to silverware. Even with this expansion of the definition, the general consensus is that demand for silverware will tarnish.

ELECTRONICS AND ELECTRICAL

A bright side is found in the electronics sector that is directly linked to the health of high-tech. Specifically, computer chips, circuits, and contacts are

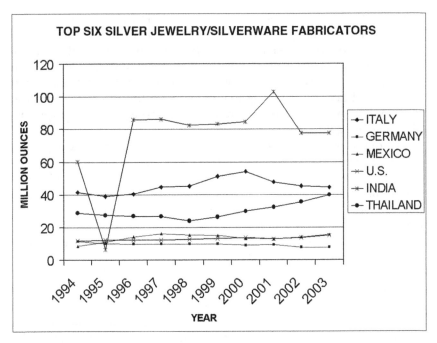

FIGURE 7.2   The top six jewelry and silverware fabricating countries all displayed mixed trends after rising into the new millennium. Italy showed a large jump in production as it converted some of its gold jewelry production into silver. (*Source:* GFMS, Ltd., Silver Institute, Commodity Yearbook)

using increasing amounts of silver solders and pastes. That's the good news. The restraining news is that industry is increasing process efficiency and reducing the amounts of silver required for each chip, contact, and circuit. This thrifting process has reduced the amount of silver used per unit by as much as 30 percent over just five years from 1995 to 2000. Although there should be a practical limit to thrifting, "micronization" is shrinking the size of circuits at a geometric rate. Moore's Law foresees doubling the number of transistors per square inch on integrated computer circuits every year. Since Gordon Moore's statement in 1965, the law has generally held through 2004. On a straight-line basis, one might conclude that the amount of silver per circuit will remain static as size shrinks and power grows. The key to more consumption is the use of more circuits.

The boom in information technology and its close cousin, automated process control, can encourage us. When we think of process control, we may conjure up an image of machines making machines or parts. This is a cliché. Process control encompasses everything from remotely starting your car to starting a bath with a telephone call. It involves lighting, heating/air-conditioning systems, cooking, cleaning, telephones, televisions, and other devices that can be run using processes. Silver pastes are used to create a variety of components. Multilayer ceramic capacitors (MLCCs) are using an increasing amount of silver as manufacturers attempt to save on palladium. Research and development on these components is a high priority.

If we examine the trends in cell phones, portable music players (MP3), personal digital assistants (PDAs), optical storage devices, and more, it is easy to conclude the trend is forever higher. Unless some monumental nonmetallic breakthrough is on the horizon, silver will play an increasing role in overall electronic industry expansion. Prospects for chips are good.

Silver brazing and solders are used in electronics and large component welding found in automobiles. This area will grow with general economic expansion, but is sensitive to economic cycles that adversely affect demand for finished products. As economic expansion continues in China, India, the CIS (Russia), and South America, we can feel assured this consumption will grow proportionately. I caution that any growth will be over an extended period. We cannot expect to suddenly see demand for silver brazing and soldering double or triple in a year. The patterns indicate an imbalance between growth in electronics and welding versus contraction in photography. Still, it is important to keep in mind that there is an offset.

In the 10 years from 1994 through 2004, industrial consumption rose from 758 million ounces to 860 million, a 13 percent increase. This was by no means a straight line. Within that period, demand peaked at 910 million ounces just before the recession began in 2000. That represented a 20 percent increase over six years, or about 3.3 percent per year. Understanding that the high-tech bubble burst in 2000 and the effects lasted through 2004, we can assume that normal expansion is somewhere between 1.5 percent and 3.5 percent. (See Figure 7.3.)

The unknown portion of the equation is the speed of economic expansion in China, India, and other industrializing nations. Given the demographics, it is very possible a 3.5 percent growth will be extremely understated. According to some estimates, China will rely on portable telephonic technology more than wired. This means more handheld sets requiring increasing amounts of silver.

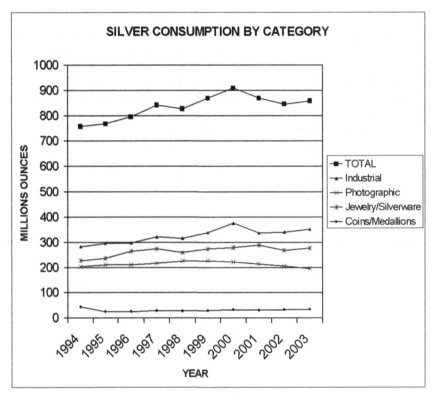

FIGURE 7.3 World consumption from 1994 through 2004 reveals relatively flat patterns for all categories with the exception of photography that shows a divergence from other uses. (*Source:* GFMS, Ltd. All rights reserved)

PHOTOGRAPHY

As of 1996, approximately 43 percent of new production was consumed by photographic processes that included consumer and industrial photography, medical and industrial X-rays, lithographic printing, and other film-based imaging. In 2003, the percentage dropped by 10 percentage points to 33 percent. With one-third of all new mine production dedicated to this area, we can assume photographic applications remain critical in the price equation. It seems truly amazing that little attention was focused on the future of film as digital imaging accelerated. Although new imaging technologies were virtually exploding on the scene in the 1990s, investors and analysts ignored the potential impact on silver demand until 2000.

As a comparison, there was once a discussion among audiophiles concerning the future of the compact disc (CD) when it was initially introduced. The consensus was that the CD would never gain mainstream acceptance because it was more expensive than vinyl records, and the installed base of record players was too extensive for any new technology to gain a foothold. The CD was forecast as an esoteric technology that would be embraced by only the most discriminating ear and enhanced pocketbook. Of course, the CD took over the music market within half a decade. By 1994, it was almost impossible to buy vinyl records in a record store or a turntable at a stereo center! I bring this up because digital and other filmless photography assumes the same track.

Consider that the home movie camera became virtually extinct within the single decade of the 1980s. This was the initial indication that silver's largest demand sector was facing trouble. The first cameras were analogue. However, the jump to digital recording was rapid. By the early 1990s, digital still-shot cameras with computer interfaces were introduced within comparable price ranges to high-quality 35mm cameras. By 1997, there were more than 30 popular digital cameras with retail prices ranging from $199 to $15,000.

As I had predicted in 1997, within five more years digital snapshots became sufficiently popular to inspire drugstores, mass retailers, and photo developing businesses to install digital readers with instant developing. This trend is irreversible. Although the initial impact of filmless developing was to boost photographic paper, the eventual move to high-resolution ink-based printing was on the horizon.

Figure 7.4 shows a breakout of silver film by use. Combined, consumer film and paper represented 30 percent of photographic usage in 2004. This accounted for 59 million ounces. There was a 4 percent decline in these categories that had a pronounced impact upon total consumption. There is insufficient data to derive a purely statistical conclusion; however, the trend in digital technology suggests an accelerating decline in both film and paper. Based on a comparison of digital relative to conventional film cameras sold from 1998 through 2004, it is fair to say that the crossover whereby digital exceeds film will occur within the first half of the twenty-first century. As of 2004, approximately 52 million digital cameras were sold. While industry sources reported approximately 3 billion film units for the same period, the majority were one-time use or disposable cameras. Essentially, one-time use film cameras are like a single roll of film.

Based on internal marketing projections, digital still-shot cameras are likely to replace film units before 2050. We can anticipate as much as 60 million more ounces of free stocks once this conversion is complete. However, radiology is another candidate for rapid conversion to digital.

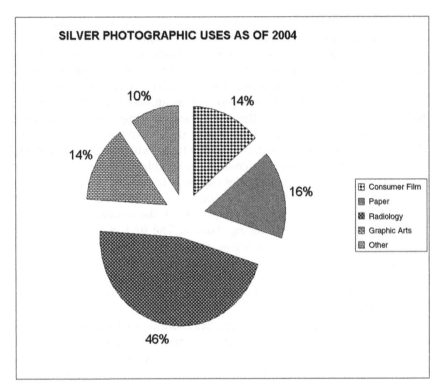

SILVER PHOTOGRAPHIC USES AS OF 2004

FIGURE 7.4 Photographic use is comprised of five categories that encompass silver halide film, silver photo paper, radiology (X-ray) film, lithography plates (graphic arts), and other imaging applications. (*Source:* GFMS, Ltd. All rights reserved)

Radiology encompasses medical and industrial X-ray, which uses high-density, large-format black-and-white imaging. When economically advantageous, a reasonable portion of old X-ray film is recycled, as are the chemicals that develop the photographic plates. Thus, radiology is a give-and-take sector.

Like consumer photography, X-ray images can be digitally captured and stored. Images can be displayed on a high-resolution screen using computer enhancement. Color is now an available option.

Low-radiation X-ray was introduced for dental and medical applications by companies like Schick Technologies, Inc. with its CDR imaging system. Instead of film, units record X-rays onto disk files and display pictures on-screen. If printouts are required, output devices produce negatives or positives. No silver or developing is used in these processes.

Magnetic resonance imaging (MRI) and positron emission tomography (PET) augment and sometimes displace conventional medical X-ray. These alternative technologies can both run silver free. Even with conventional X-ray, images can be digitally captured with lower radiation requirements and recorded onto electronic media. A printable acetate film substitutes for silver-based X-rays. These newer images have the advantages of being more easily stored, transmitted, and computer enhanced.

X-ray extends into construction, mineral exploration, materials development, aviation, and more. These industrial applications have used the same type of silver-based film as the medical field. However, densities are frequently much higher. As with progress in medicine, digital industrial X-ray has the capacity to supplant silver. Thus, radiology, as a sector, is likely to follow consumer photography down.

The graphic arts or printing industry has used conventional film to create lithographic plates. Hours were spent cutting and stripping film negatives to produce the completed and color-separated lithographic plates. The digital alternative process converts images from computer files directly into printing plates. Further, electrostatic and ink jet technologies allow high-speed and high-volume full-color printing with no plates. The Silver Institute predicted a slow migration toward nonfilm technologies. This was based on the assumption that printers would not spend the required funds to upgrade. However, print industry sources indicated the pace of conversion and equipment upgrade has accelerated faster than anticipated because direct imaging significantly improved quality while cutting costs. Like the PC itself, ancillary technologies have been steadily declining in price while offering greater power and flexibility.

By the late 1990s, Kodak introduced Advantix film, which combined conventional silver-based technology with a magnetic strip for encoding processing instructions. Inside sources stated that this new film was a stopgap measure to protect huge revenue streams associated with film development. Everything from paper to chemicals represented a massive investment and income source for Kodak, Agfa, Fuji, and others. The installed base of developing machines and one-hour photo stores is truly threatened by the advance of digital imaging.

Although a quality differential seemed to justify using film over digital imaging, arguments favoring filmless technology are overwhelming:

- Environmentally, digital imaging is clean, with no developing processes, no chemicals, and no significant expertise required. Conventional photography uses sizable amounts of fresh water and involves toxic materials.

- Digital resolutions as low as 640 × 720 pixels can exceed the maximum line screen used for newspaper and magazine printing in pictures that are 5 × 7 inches and smaller. With resolutions exceeding 3 million pixels, pictures can retain clarity as large as 23 × 29 inches—poster size.
- The cost per million pixels is coming down while the quality has been rising. Pixel density is only one of many criteria used to determine image quality. Color saturation and definition, gray scale, contrast, and resolution all contribute to the final result. High-resolution digital imaging has reached the necessary overall quality to challenge conventional film.

Modern spy satellites allegedly have the ability to read license plates from miles away in space! The use of more photosensitive receptors and better image compression technology holds the promise of progressively higher-quality computer images.

The implication of declining photographic consumption is a 30 percent boost in available supplies for other applications as long as all else remains the same. Examining Figure 7.2, we can discern an equidistant divergence between photography and jewelry combined with industrial consumption. The problem is that the acceleration in digital imaging appears to be more pronounced than the rise in jewelry, silverware, and electronics. Further, an economic slowdown is likely to have a more significant impact on industrial consumption. Silver can find itself in significant trouble if demand for silver-based goods wanes.

Photographic consumption remained virtually flat from 1990 through 2002. Even during the economic boom from 1996 through 2000, photography peaked in 1999 at 228 million ounces. By 2003, usage dipped to 196 million ounces, which is a 14 percent decline. From 2002 to 2003 consumption fell almost 5 percent. When compared with the increase in industrial usage, the numbers appear to be in balance. However, the acceleration in digital imaging is likely to have a greater impact because of the proportional amount of metal used in photography versus electronic devices.

When I began writing about the impact of digital imaging, my compatriot analysts rebutted that China and India would fill the gap as they became more affluent and consumed more film. Timing is everything. By the time demand for consumer photography takes hold in populations of China, India, and the Third World, film may already be obsolete. Growth in film-based photography predicted by the silver industry did not seem feasible.

There is little doubt that the trend toward the end of the twentieth century was toward increasing industrial consumption. If fact, nothing within the statistics indicated a decline in usage relative to earlier discussions about technological displacement. Although digital imaging was on the scene before the new millennium, it did not seem to have a significant effect on rising demand. Yet that perception is somewhat deceiving. What is missing from the equation and evaluation? First, while demand was rising, the slope of the curve was adversely impacted by alternative technologies. Equally important is the fact that growth was a function of increasing global wealth. The speed of wealth accumulation was greater than the introduction of alternatives to silver. Therefore, the statistics should not be viewed independently from other fundamental developments. Thus, on yet another front, silver's emerging industrial infrastructure appears challenged.

BARS, COINS, AND MEDALLIONS

Like gold, silver has a large investor following. As the only other metal that has been widely used as a monetary standard, silver has retained its status as a store of value and, therefore, an investment vehicle. In reality, any nonperishable commodity has the same potential. One might buy a warehouse full of copper and speculate that the price will go up. Of course, silver, gold, platinum, palladium, diamonds, and other gemstones have the advantage of packing high value in a small package. It is more convenient to hold a small bag of diamonds than a warehouse full of iron.

Silver bullion gained popularity during the late 1970s and early 1980s. Spawned by the spectacular price spike in 1979–1980, silver bars were accumulated by investors and accounted for more than one-third of speculation in physical metal. To put silver into perspective, *The Commodity Yearbook* published by the Commodity Research Bureau in 1961 listed 1.74 billion ounces of bullion held by the U.S. Treasury. There were 125 million ounces stored as silver dollars. Approximately twice as much silver was stored as silver dollars in 1948 and only 1.53 billion ounces held by the Treasury in bullion. In 1961, spot silver traded at approximately 90 cents an ounce. The trend was moving away from coin and toward stored bullion. In 2003, government stocks were a meager 206 million ounces, down from 289 million ounces the year before. From 1960 through 2000, a massive amount of silver was converted from official reserves into a private hoard. Since private interests do not report holding, it is impossible to derive an accurate assessment of the total hoard.

This plays into the same dynamic as gold. At any moment, the demand for bars, coins, and medallions can turn into supply. Today's accumulation can become tomorrow's distribution. Total identifiable bar holdings have been declining as a result of government divesting. At the same time, private purchasing can be surmised by tracking the ebb and flow of European, Far Eastern, and North American inventories. These numbers are partially reflected in warehouse holdings for the major commodity exchanges like the COMEX division of the New York Mercantile Exchange.

Unfortunately, there is insufficient history to draw any conclusions about when silver will move into or out of the private hoard. The one experience when silver moved rapidly into the supply came when prices moved above $35 per ounce in 1979–1980. At the top, lines formed to trade in Mom's old silver set; bags of coins were hauled from closets. The public finally saw a price that was too good to pass up.

When silver trades at or near the original purchase price, investors or hoarders don't feel an urge to liquidate. It is a strange dynamic because it defies basic investment principles. You don't hold a nonperforming asset when there are alternatives like stocks and bonds. But like gold, silver provides a sense of security. Those who bought at $5 per ounce have an attitude that the most they can lose is 20 percent to 25 percent. The upside could be $100. So, it does not matter that the same upside could have been achieved by an annuity yielding 7 percent over the same period the silver has been hoarded!

Coins offer very reasonable access to owning physical metal. The most common size is the one-ounce official coin of the realm that is face-valued at $1 for the U.S. Silver Eagle and $5 for the Canadian Maple Leaf. As previously mentioned, the advantage to buying coin of the realm is that it never declines below its face value—unless, of course, the country goes bankrupt.

U.S. Silver Eagle dollars have a face value of $1 regardless of the silver price. They are .999 fine silver.

Thus, silver currency is perceived to be more sound than paper currency backed by the U.S. Treasury or any other national treasury. Tracking silver coin and medallion fabrication is a mixed bag. As we see in Figure 7.5, Total world fabrication plunged from 1994 through 1996. The paper investment boom was partially responsible as investors abandoned hard assets in favor of stocks. In addition, government mints slowed their distribution of metal from inventories.

Subsequently, there was a moderate upward trend beginning in 1996 forward. The United States and Germany were the largest official coin producers for the 10 years from 1994 through 2004. The very same nations clashed over draining U.S. gold at the gold window.

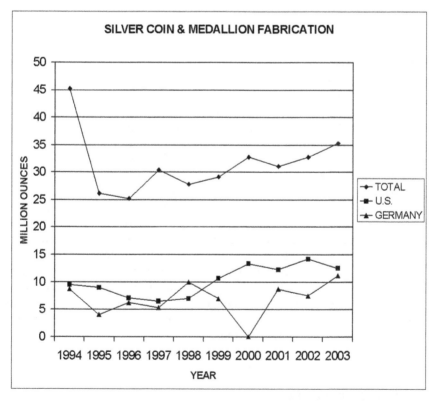

FIGURE 7.5 Silver coin and medallion fabrication statistics show official annual releases. The trend appears to be rising from the mid-1990s forward, but there is no way to determine if the interim trend represents a longer-term pattern. (*Source:* GFMS, Ltd. All rights reserved)

Fabrication is not necessarily an indication of consumption. Once made, these coins are literally in circulation. It is difficult, if not impossible, to track the actual flow of silver coinage from person to person or entity to entity. There are compilations of coin store and wholesaler sales, but demand in the secondary market cannot be measured with the accuracy of compiling official annual mintage.

Depending on inflation and monetary realignment, silver coins will enjoy a burst of popularity and can influence silver prices. Looking at the percentage of total silver dedicated to coinage and medallions, I cannot see this sector as having any dominant price influence. However, it is worth noting that a private currency backed by silver and gold exists concurrently with U.S. Federal Reserve notes. The Liberty Dollar is a legal private issue currency that can be used to transact business with anyone willing to accept such currency. These "dollars" are privately backed by physical silver and gold. The hard manifestations are coins (medallions), whereas certificates represent deposited silver or gold.

While there was no indication that private currency was a factor in determining silver prices, please understand that there is a powerful underlying consensus that we should or *must* return to a physical monetary standard. There are web sites providing statistics on annual physical commitments to Liberty Dollar currency.

Overall, it is safe to assume silver coinage will maintain an upward secular trend. If only to keep pace with casual demand, we can anticipate rising annual fabrication. Of course, if silver declines below $4, incentive to own coins may evaporate. However, a dip in production costs might encourage physical accumulation around $2.50 and lower.

Why move back to silver coinage? After all, composite coins work fine. In addition, earlier chapters mentioned the possibility of plastic coins in the future that can be encoded with tracking information. Silver coins offer no advantage other than perceived value. Silver is a known and accepted form of exchange. It can restore or maintain confidence in a nation's money supply. Confidence is the foundation of all monetary systems. Without trust, there is no viable money. Even with no reason to question confidence, it may be advantageous to foreclose any possible loss of faith by instituting silver coinage. Thus, silver could be a preemptive strike against a confidence crisis.

SILVER CATALYSTS

Like platinum, palladium, and gold, silver has several catalytic properties that add to industrial demand. The most familiar catalytic application involves producing plastic feedstocks out of ethylene. Approximately 700 to 750 tons of silver are used to oxidize ethylene into ethylene oxide and to produce formaldehyde. As plastics and synthetic fiber demand increases, so will the amount of silver for this application. Since silver is not consumed in the process, much of the base supply remains intact or recycled into and from scrap.

Silver operates as an oxidation intermediary. This process opens the door to a host of important applications including fuel cells. As these areas expand, silver consumption will obviously increase. Progress may appear slow, yet there is hope for those entwined in a personal stash of silver bullion or coin.

Eventually, silver photovoltaic cells will gain popularity as we seek ways to supplement energy production. Silver solar cells are becoming increasingly efficient and therefore more desirable as a renewable energy source. The silver-based photoelectric generation is not simply renewable; it is continuous and inexhaustible!

DIGITAL SILVER

Silver's unique photosensitive properties may extend beyond imaging into the digital domain. The very technology that can spell disaster for demand today could become tomorrow's salvation. There are "chemical memory" devices based on silver, including today's smart cards that store data, and even dynamic memory that uses ionic characteristics to represent binary values. Those who are up on the technology may be aware of computing systems based on light circuits rather than electronics. So-called photonic computers may become a reality, and silver is a major consideration for bridging the gap between light and electricity. The potential growth for computing applications could rival film in two respects. First, silver storage devices may be used to record images. Unlike film, which is recycled, silver computing and storage components are likely to have much longer useful lives. This implies that less scrap will be available. Second, silver storage chips may be used in everything from portable phones to music players.

It seems ironic that silver might return to provide images after being displaced. However, any revolution in silver technology will take time. Do not forget that production may not keep up with demand. With this in mind, let's examine the various sources for the white metal.

SUPPLY

From a production standpoint, silver has gone through a significant transformation. Prior to the 1960s, dedicated mines dominated silver production. Today's major supplies come as by-product from other mining operations. Therefore, silver output is highly dependent on demand for base metals like copper, nickel, zinc, lead, and tin. In addition, silver is produced as a by-product of gold, platinum, and palladium. This means silver is directly linked to macroeconomics affecting base metal markets. Surging demand for housing, automobiles, and durables could skyrocket base metal demand and values while depressing silver, gold, platinum, and palladium. The implied inflation of roaring economies may actually develop an inverse relationship to silver prices if silver's industrial applications are static or declining.

Effectively, it's a new dynamic requiring an entirely new perspective to become a successful precious metals investor/trader. Under old rules, silver operated in accordance with normal supply/demand/price correlations. High prices stimulated more production from primary sources. Low prices encouraged cutbacks in mining operations. When silver was unable to sustain lofty levels following explosive 1979–1980 price trends, market dynamics completely changed. Considerable dedicated silver production became uneconomical. Yet, by-product output was unaffected. Understand that when silver is produced as a by-product, supply fundamentals are no longer independent. Therefore, the silver price will not necessarily impact this production.

Certainly, if silver advances above $20 per ounce, there is a question of whether the by-product is driving the primary market or vice versa. At some price level, silver production could migrate back toward more expensive primary mines. However, this scenario seems less likely when investors evaluate technological and economic developments. As mentioned, stimulating fundamental demand requires new and substantial applications. The price elasticity of these applications must support a high price.

While interviewing hundreds, or perhaps more than a thousand, avid silver traders/investors over the years, I have been surprised by the lack of attention paid to production costs. Surprisingly, costs have been declining substantially in real terms because mines are producing with increasing efficiency and the true cost of by-product supplies has become marginal. According to the GFMS Limited *World Silver Survey 2004*, cash costs for a subset of primary silver mines were $2.12 per ounce. When compared to costs in 1980–1981, we see that low-grade ore and tailings were processed at costs exceeding $8 per ounce. Of course, the incentive driving 1980–1981 production was the belief that $40 silver would be around for a while.

After a quarter century of inflation, 2004 silver costs were half of those in 1980. In real terms, the decline reflects less than 50 cents per ounce. This is not a fair comparison because it does not compare the selling price with the production price in current price parity. Still, it is apparent that the trend in costs has been pointing down. Moreover, some mines report *negative* production costs. How is this possible?

Accounting plays an extremely important role in determining the cost of producing silver. When gold prices shot up in 2003, consequential gold output from silver production more than offset the cost of silver. Because gold was accounted for on a contributory basis, gold revenues were applied as an offset against silver rather than a gross revenue stream with independent accounting. Thus, the cost of silver turned negative based on the ancillary profits from gold and other metals. Taken a step further, when silver derives from a base metal like lead or zinc, silver may be treated as a reduction in the cost of the primary metal. Thus, silver itself has no cost allocation. By the same token, the actual cost of lead is distorted by the amount of silver revenue used as an offset.

This can become particularly intriguing when silver prices rise to levels that invert the revenue curves. If silver were to increase to $100 per ounce because of a new application (i.e. demand side), silver revenue might actually exceed that of the lead or zinc. Historically, silver appears to have tracked its base metal counterparts. As traders or investors, we would not be concerned if silver were the leading metal. We would be concerned if silver became a sacrificial metal. The first hint of this potential came in the mid-1990s when copper reached above $1.40 per pound. During that rally, silver remained rangebound between $4.50 and $6.00. There were indications that copper producers were dumping silver simply to make whatever marginal income was available. Figure 7.6 plots monthly copper prices against silver.

We see the obvious correlations and can identify divergence from 1994 through 1996. Based on the overall correlation, we might jump to the conclusion that silver and copper move together or at least in tandem. Any divergence seems brief and, therefore, is an exception to the rule. This takes price action out of the fundamental context. We have not seen a sufficient surge in copper demand relative to silver that would produce the necessary price differential to make silver a throwaway metal. At $2 per pound, copper might be hauled out of declining ore grades at an increasing rate. In turn, silver might flood the market, depressing prices.

As of 2004–2005 most primary silver production could survive with prices as low as $2.90. This would reduce primary production to a breakeven. Nonetheless, mines would continue to operate because a breakeven holds the prospect for something better whereas shutting

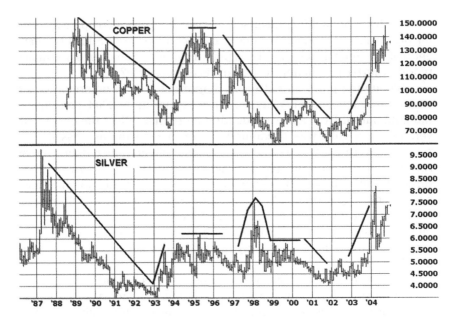

FIGURE 7.6 Copper and silver prices from 1986 through 2004 appear in step, with the exception of the mid-1990s and 1998. (*Source:* eSignal.com)

down ends all potential. This is not a unique concept. We frequently see sales below cost in retail because it is better to get something than nothing. Seasonal expirations frequently inspire retailers to move out the old at any price to make room for the new. This is true for silver. There is a cost of ownership that can cut into profits. It can be better to unload silver than to hold in anticipation of price appreciation. Mining operations tend to avoid speculation. This is more the case if the company has high debt service. Lenders want to see revenue, not merely hopes or aspirations.

The majority of global mine production comes from eight major producing regions. Based on production figures compiled by GFMS Limited for the Silver Institute as well as surveys of top-producing mining entities, Mexico was leading silver output, with approximately 94 million troy ounces in 2003. Mexico's status was the same in 1995 with 75 million ounces. Next in line was Peru, with 89 million ounces in 2003. Peru was number two in 1995 as well, with 60 million ounces.

Australia took the number three position with 60 million ounces in 2003; however, 10 years earlier Australia was number eight with only 30 million ounces. China moved into the number four position with 46 million ounces, but the proximity of China, Poland, Chile, the United States, and Canada around the 40-million-ounce mark makes the relative positions highly mobile.

When considering the major producing nations, it is easy to see why analysts assert that silver supplies are highly susceptible to disruptions. Political, economic, and labor stability in more than half the major producing nations has been questionable. Strikes and monetary adjustments have been responsible for several impressive price reactions. Some may recall the Third World debt crisis that placed considerable pressure upon Peru, Chile, and Mexico. Liquidity has also affected Russia, Poland, and China. However, the progress toward more democratic government and capitalistic economies was changing the perception of supply stability during the 1990s. Diversification is the pattern to observe. The greater the production diversity, the less any one producer can impact supply.

Diversity is not only by region, but also by companies within region. For example, Kazakhstan produced approximately 23 million ounces in 2003 of which 19.5 million ounces came from one company, Kazakhmys. Industrias Peñoles produced half Mexico's entire 2003 and 2004 production. Such concentration may generate efficiency, but also extreme exposure to strikes, political unrest, and financial instability.

Total mine production has been decisively rising. Figure 7.7 plots world mine output from 1994 through 2003. Price sensitivity adversely affected silver in the early 1990s when prices turned sharply lower. However, statistics may be skewed because much of the data reflects *shipments* and not necessarily *actual production*. Inventories held by producers could have accounted for moderate production that was marketed when prices became more favorable during 1995 and 1996, and certainly in 1998. Since silver can constitute a cost item rather than a revenue item, hoarding by producers is not uncommon. Inventory can be stored or lent to fabricators.

It seems fair to assume silver supply will grow based on the brief period from 1994 through 2004. World production accelerated during this period when compared with the longer-term perspective illustrated in Figure 7.8. We see that when silver was fixed through 1948, production remained in a narrow band. Treasuries were primary buyers. With an official purchase price, it is difficult to find incentive to build capacity. Notice that when silver was freed from price bondage, it was able to expand supply based on price motivations. Ah, the free market!

MINE PRODUCTION

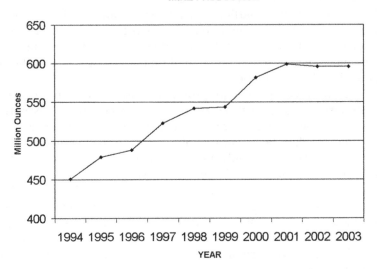

FIGURE 7.7 Silver mine production shows an upward trend with the exception of the recession years beginning in 2000. (*Source:* GFMS, Ltd. All rights reserved)

The secular trend is keeping pace with economic growth. However, it is not keeping pace with demand when we compare Figure 7.8 with Figure 7.3. This is one of the key arguments silver advocates make when debating eventual price direction. It is true that the market relies on scrap and divesting to make up for mining deficiencies. This is a valid conclusion, but mines are very responsive when prices are right. Since more than two-thirds of new silver comes from nonsilver mining, the world appears to have plenty of additional capacity.

Silver is obtained from the ores of argentite, cerarygrite, pyrargyrite, stephanite, and proustite. It is a component in base metal mining that includes lead, tin, copper, and zinc, and in precious metal extractions with gold, platinum, palladium, rhodium, and related elements. Silver-bearing ores are widely distributed throughout the world. The transition from dedicated mining to a combination of primary and secondary production has shifted the emphasis and alleviated some of the concern over regional instability.

From 1980 forward, silver mining and processing enjoyed a great deal of research and development. The supply side benefited from progress that was specific to silver and also general to other metals. Solvent extraction was responsible for substantially reducing capital costs for copper mining by as much as 50 percent and smelting overheads by an equal

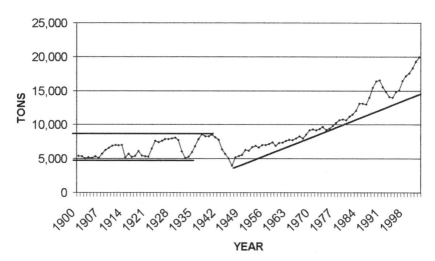

FIGURE 7.8 World mine production for the twentieth century through 2004 reveals a seven-year cycle between 5,000 tons and 8,000 tons until there was an incentive to increase production after gold was removed from public ownership in the United States and elsewhere. (*Source:* GFMS, Ltd. All rights reserved)

amount. By some estimates, copper extraction using more modern facilities dropped to 50 cents per pound by the mid-1990s. This process also reduced the cost of secondary metal extraction. Like gold, silver benefits from advanced discovery techniques and more efficient processing. As mentioned in the previous chapter, there are minute quantities of various metals dispersed within carlin type ores. Technology is finding ways to extract metal from increasingly difficult resources with rising efficiency and cost-effectiveness.

Samples of ocean volcanic vents reveal extremely rich mineral contents. For the moment, mining companies have not tapped this potential because there are questions of ownership, environment, and cost. Yet, as the world's appetite for minerals grows beyond land-based resources, there will be a global dialogue concerning the ocean floors. Based on my research, it is not likely that the world will run out of minerals. While many experts claim the "easy stuff" will be exhausted, that prediction was made in the 1960s for the year 2000, and it was way off the mark.

Within half a century, primary silver production was reduced from 70 percent to approximately one-third of total annual mine output. This is a progressive development as global base metal consumption grows in step with economic expansion. Figure 7.9 illustrates the breakdown of proportional silver production by major mining category as of 2004.

Before there was significant by-product production, silver mines primarily supplied treasuries and major industrial users. In all likelihood, rapid global industrial expansion is responsible for the transition away from silver as a monetary standard. There was an important crossover where industrial demand outstripped treasury requirements. Had by-product production been available after World War II, there might have been some equilibrium between supply and the two-pronged demand of treasuries and industries.

As mentioned, increasing demand for copper, lead, tin, and zinc will, by default, increase the amount of silver. This is an important fundamental consideration because much of the traditional thinking about silver's relationship with inflation remains. Consider that the market has reacted in tandem with rising commodity prices. However, investors were stung several times during the mid-1990s when silver rallies failed to be sustained despite bouts of inflation fear. This lack of traditional inflation correlation is directly linked to increasing base metal output. By examining global trends, it is clear industrial metal supplies are expanding.

Industry projections call for annual increases of approximately 6 percent through 2010 and beyond. Keep in mind that this projection is compounded. Consider that 1995 world production was approximately 14,570 metric tons. The 1999 estimate climbed to almost 17,000. When analyzing

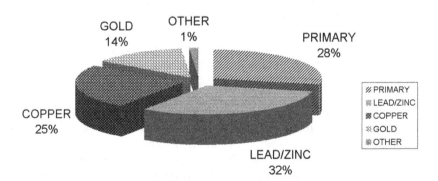

SILVER PRODUCTION BY CATEGORY

GOLD 14% OTHER 1% PRIMARY 28%

COPPER 25%

LEAD/ZINC 32%

PRIMARY
LEAD/ZINC
COPPER
GOLD
OTHER

FIGURE 7.9 New silver production by category shows a majority is a by-product of base metal mining. (*Source:* GFMS, Ltd. All rights reserved)

the production trend, it is essential to break out individual components. For example, lead mining began experiencing a structural decline in the late 1990s carrying forward into the new century. Unlike a cyclical decline associated with either economic or industrial trends, a structural decline involves an industry transition. Lead batteries account for the majority of lead that is consumed each year. Batteries also account for most of the recycled lead. The second most significant application, albeit much smaller, is in pigments and compounds. Most of us are familiar with the controversy over lead paint and its toxicity. Although lead has been removed from the household market, it remains a major component in commercial coatings.

Approximately 3 million tons of new lead is mined each year while an equal amount is recovered from scrap. Global economic trends imply that lead consumption will grow; however, a series of new technologies may reduce demand in the largest consumption category. Highly efficient batteries that do not rely on the classic lead-acid design were beginning to penetrate the market at the beginning of the millennium. In addition, miniaturized fuel cells were making their way into the device market (i.e., cell phones, potable computers, PDAs, etc.), and scaled-up versions were being tested in automobiles and trucks. The most promising fuel cells use methanol as a portable and replenishable feedstock; however, gasoline can be reformed to work as well. The advantage of using a fuel cell power source is the high efficiency and elimination of expensive recharging components like alternators, capacitors, belts, and regulators.

Thus, the future of lead remains positive, but at a declining rate. This suggests that the demand for new mines may continue to decrease with a negative impact on ancillary silver production. By most estimates, lead is the most fruitful of the base metals for silver. Therefore, trends in lead mining will be extremely important to the silver supply equation. More than 50 percent of the world's lead came from three countries at the beginning of the twenty-first century: China, Australia, and the United States. The most common lead ore is galena or lead sulphide, which is reasonably well distributed in South America and parts of the Commonwealth of Independent States (CIS). Where there is the potential for new and efficient lead extraction, there is the potential for new silver production.

The supply/demand relationship for lead was tightening as of 2000 forward based on the decline in new mine production. There is no lead futures contract traded on the COMEX, and therefore no speculative opportunity. If the trends identified in the beginning of the twenty-first century continue, I suspect lead prices will rise sufficiently to bring about new mine development in areas like the CIS, Peru, Chile, and Australia.

Tin is another metal worth watching to glean potential trends in secondary silver supplies. Tin is obtained from the mineral cassiterite, which is also well distributed throughout the earth. Large concentrations were mined in Western Europe prior to the collapse in prices that took place in the mid-1980s. The differential between union labor costs and tin's lower selling prices shut dome mining operations, which helped prop up prices. More recently, Brazil, Bolivia, China, Indonesia, Thailand, Malaysia, and Peru are the top producers and hold the most potential moving forward. The CIS is likely to become a player, too. Almost 50 percent of annual zinc production is used in galvanizing steel. This is a process of layering a thin zinc coating that acts as an oxidation shield and reduces the need for more expensive antioxidation alloying. Galvanized steel is used in construction, marine applications, and vehicle manufacturing—all growth areas.

China accelerated into the leading producer in 2000, accounting for more than 18 percent of new mine production. Zinc enjoyed a 25 percent increase in mine production through the 1990s and the trend appears likely to continue. Unlike lead, zinc's primary application does not appear threatened by new technology. Large new projects exist in Western Europe and, most notably, Ireland. Australia was on a fast track as well. Projects like Sun Metals' Townsville smelter/refinery in Queensland, Australia, and Anglo American's Lisheen mine in County Clare, Ireland, are two examples of mines that should contribute to silver supplies.

According to the Bureau of Mines, approximately 66 percent of the world's silver reserves are linked to copper and lead/zinc ores. Based on 1997 production estimates, these reserves amount to 12 billion ounces. This is why future silver production could become somewhat independent of silver's price. Copper's spread between costs and selling prices during the 1990s into the 2000s created a motivation to increase capacity from 1991 forward. Resulting silver flooded the market and was partially responsible for depressed prices.

While keeping a watchful eye on lead, zinc, and tin, we should not diminish the role of primary production. Toward the end of the 1990s, production technology had improved to the point where several mining companies found it economical to reopen primary facilities. As an example, the Coeur and Galena mines in the United States were given new life in 1996 through a joint venture between Coeur d'Alene and Asarco. In 1997, the Green's Creek mine in Alaska reopened with projected output between 10 and 15 million ounces per year. This trend is likely to continue with estimated extraction costs after capital depreciation between $1.50 and $2.25 per ounce. It is not difficult to grasp the economics if silver can maintain an average selling price between $4.50 and $5.50.

Efficiency was the lesson from the energy crisis of the early 1970s. The trend toward becoming "lean and mean" continued with respect to labor, management, and process technology. In particular, heavy industry developed more nimble facilities with greater production flexibility. This carried over into the mining industry, which is notorious for long capital-accumulation lead times. Building a new mine is an extremely expensive and time-consuming project. There is extreme sensitivity to price changes because profit margins can become thin or negative between the time a company breaks ground and the mine becomes productive. However, the design of modern mines allows greater output variability with less financial exposure.

THE SILVER HOARD

The silver hoard is also referred to as "aboveground stocks." However, we must be careful in making a distinction between all aboveground stocks that include available scrap and specifically hoarded inventory that is generally associated with bullion held in government and private vaults.

The amount of silver held by central banks is no longer as significant moving forward from 2000. Identified government reserves fell from approximately 760 million ounces in 1994 to just 200 million in 2003. The United States has been regularly selling reserves, with less than 28 million ounces available in 1996. The market has absorbed central banks' sales without significant reactions. Unlike gold investors, silver investors do not focus as much on government supplies. Of course, a mass dumping would negatively impact prices. But, with less than a year's production stored, this would be a temporary factor.

There are four major unknowns concerning official government reserves. By far the largest is China, which combines government stocks with government-controlled supplies. As of this writing, there was no divorce between silver processing and sales and government control. China's stockpile has been accumulated over decades with no access to reliable numbers. From 1994 forward, China's participation in government sales suggested a considerable stash, but by 2000 the flow of silver pointed to a reasonable drawdown that was substantially supplemented by scrap reprocessing. Russia, too, has unknown official reserves. While Russia claims more transparency, many silver traders suspect a large amount of silver remained within Russian control in 2000. Finally, the loan of government stocks does not give an accurate read on the amount of official silver available for sale. Silver on loan is already in the supply chain and, therefore, should not be double counted.

Finally, silver was a broad reserve asset that is not addressed as specifically as gold in mandates to divest. Silver accounting and accountability have been lax in comparison with gold, and many countries that have reasonable amounts available for sale have not yet found the incentive to unload. At $20 per ounce, there is a remarkable impetus to profit from reserves. At $40, the urge becomes almost irresistible unless there is some catastrophic driving force like collapse in paper assets. It is fair to conclude that the official hoard will be mobilized over time to the point where it no longer plays a price-determining role. The contradiction to this assumption would be a net accumulating trend by governments. Such does not appear likely.

Alongside government reserves are private holdings. Here, estimates are vaguely derived, at best. Silver has been widely accumulated without interruption because it was never officially banned from private ownership. While companies and institutions have use aggregating methodology to trace private inventory movements, there is no accurate way to identify where private silver may exist and when it was acquired.

Experience has shown that silver hoards migrate into the market when prices reach above $8. This was explicitly seen in 1979–1980 when silver reached above $40 per ounce. Then, even silverware made its way to the smelter. More recently, the spike of the mid-1990s brought silver to market as well as the price hike in 2003–2004. Like government stocks, private investors seem to have sensitivity to the $8 and above level. While an $8 price may not be sufficient to tempt all hoarders to market, correlations suggest this is a price point worth watching.

Two statistics allow investors to track readily available supplies. The most popular in the United States is the COMEX warehouse receipt stocks. The European equivalents are the dealer estimates and receipts for delivery on the London Metals Exchange (LME). The rule is that these numbers expand as prices rise and fall as prices decline. I believe this is not a reliable indicator because timing tends to be imprecise and there has not been an extended price appreciation in silver since the great boom of 1979–1980. The fact that silver has remained in a range around $5 for so long tells us that the ebb and flow of exchange and dealer stocks cannot define a secular trend.

However, traders may find clues to immediate price variation in swings among exchange and dealer stocks. A shortfall will, indeed, pressure prices. A glut will depress prices. If we see a decline in stocks as prices rise, we can conclude that a squeeze is in play. As mentioned, speculative accumulation can drive prices against supply and demand logic. If you are in the market as a trader, this makes a difference.

As private investors claim government inventories, the propensity for manipulation grows. Governments do not usually manipulate markets, with the exception of interest rates. (They call it regulation.) Private investors can purposefully move to alter prices by removing supply and flooding supply. Since silver offers a two-tiered market for physical metal derivatives, there is an incentive for creating price movement.

The theory on manipulated speculation is, itself, intellectual speculation. The concept is that leverage in the derivative markets like futures and options creates a multiplier. With modest funds, a would-be manipulator can build a long or short paper position. Then the removal or flooding of physical metals moves the market to create a greater profit (or loss) in the paper position than the physical holdings. Keep in mind that this is the theory and not a proven strategy!

In addition to silver bar, coins represent that double-edged category of both supply and demand. Coins are accumulated on the demand side. Yet, for every coin accumulated, there is a coin waiting to be sold. Thus, as the supply of coins builds, there is a question about when the supply might be mobilized. Over time, the global coin inventory can represent a huge overhang. Like bullion, coins may have sensitivity to prices above $8.

There is an unsolved paradox in the coin equation. As prices rise, interest in silver coins moves up in tandem. Elasticity works in reverse like the so-called luxury principle that states demand *increases* with price. The perception is that rising silver prices make coins good investments. While professional traders may feel an urge to sell above $8, private coin buyers might ask for a considerably higher price.

There are throngs of investors who hold coins purchased in the late 1970s and through the 1980s. Coins are handed down in sacks from generation to generation—in some cases, without paying tax. Silver coins provide a feeling of safety and security. But, every man or woman has his or her price. At $20 and higher, some coins reenter the supply chain.

In much the same way governments promote stamp collecting, silver coin hoarding is considered a one-way street. I recall being told by a philatelic enthusiast that the U.S. Postal Service would "go broke" if collectors decided to use their massive collections of regular commemorative issues. The comparison is not exact, but provides an appropriate metaphor. Coins are bought and held, aren't they?

CONCLUSION

There has been a great deal of publicity about a pending silver shortage. From 1993 through 1996, statistics suggested that consumption was strongly outpacing supply. My own investigation found this analysis to be flawed. Much of the hype was based on assumed increases in consumption and declines in output, which were events that did not materialize. Even before the digital evolution, forecasts for massive increases in silver halide film were offset by technological advances in film coatings that reduced silver saturation by 10 percent to 15 percent. Silver oxide batteries had to compete with nickel cadmium (nicad). The expected growth in silver demand has a major digital obstacle.

The twenty-first century represents a transition for silver. Growth in nonimaging applications is not likely to keep up with the decline in silver halide film. There will be less demand moving forward and, by definition, more available supply. Consider that during the brief time to research this book, new discoveries in Indonesia, the Philippines, Brazil, Australia, Canada, Colombia, Bolivia, Mexico, and the United States actually changed projected production by more than 8 percent. Silver is good business. Based on the average price of extraction using a deflated U.S. dollar, silver is profitable at $3 per ounce.

Regardless of the general consensus and the ease with which hucksters can tout silver, I do not see a bright interim price picture for the white metal. From the perspectives of the late 1990s, silver production will continue to rise as a function of increasing base metal output while demand will encounter serious resistance. Electronic and electrical demand is moderate compared with film and there could be substitutes for several promising silver technologies like batteries, water purification, and reflective surfaces.

Once the "poor man's gold," silver has lost much of its long-term investment luster. If prices fall sufficiently, silver may be used for coinage simply to absorb excess quantities. It is sad to conclude that digital technology will displace this precious metal. Of all the metals explored in this book, silver's outlook appears the most uncertain. There are valid arguments for renewed interest and it is wise to keep an eye on technological advances. Silver values will hinge on the furtherance of digital imaging with improved quality and wider acceptance. As with any forecast, time will tell!

However, silver bulls have a valid argument that the decline in silver film will lead to a decline in film recovery. Based on mine output and demand, we have deficit production. At some stage, the deficit will outweigh the shift in technology regardless of how much digital technology displaces film consumption. With this in mind, speculative participation can drive a major upward move.

It would be foolish and irresponsible to ignore this argument. The question is, "When?" From the statistics, the crossover is beyond 2015. Within the period, there are too many variables to make an accurate prediction that demand will outstrip supply.

Two sides of the silver coin make a market. For each buyer there is a seller. Each has his or her reasoning. Our job is to identify the stronger side and participate in the right direction.

CHAPTER 8

Platinum
Fundamentals

Platinum is an extremely important industrial metal. Its unique chemical properties make it indispensable for a multitude of processes encompassing everything from automotive industries, glass manufacturing, chemicals, and refining to fertilizer manufacturing. The primary feature is its ability to promote chemical reactions as a catalyst. Most of us are familiar with automotive catalytic converters that reduce hydrocarbon emissions and associated air pollution. However, platinum catalysts extend far beyond this widely recognized application. As an industrial precious metal, platinum has few substitutes. Although palladium and nickel have stepped into platinum's shoes for certain technologies, I believe it is highly unlikely this metal will be displaced to any extent within the foreseeable future.

Platinum is an extremely hard metal with a high melting point. It is not reactive by itself and, therefore, is extremely stable. Platinum is an excellent electrical conductor, ductile, and relatively malleable. Its usage meshes with other precious metals in jewelry, dentistry, electronics, coinage/medallions, and bar hoarding. Thus, platinum demand has a well-diversified base.

DEMAND

Platinum is a very rare metal. This characteristic combines with its versatility to make it one of the most valuable nonnuclear metals. The adoption of clean air standards around the world helped boost platinum demand through a potentially difficult period from 1993 forward. In addition, explosive growth of computer sales supported platinum's demand curve despite palladium's encroachment on automotive and truck catalysts. Demand falls within eight major categories:

1. Automotive
2. Petroleum refining/processing
3. Chemical processing
4. Electrical/electronics
5. Glass
6. Jewelry
7. Dentistry/other
8. Investment

Figure 8.1 illustrates how platinum demand was divided among its applications in 2003. Over time, usage ratios have been moderately stable. However, there was a significant boost in jewelry and automotive use through the 1990s as this metal became increasingly fashionable in the Far East while automotive expansion added to catalyst demand. From 1996 through 1999, palladium came more into favor and platinum auto catalyst

PLATINUM DEMAND BY CATEGORY

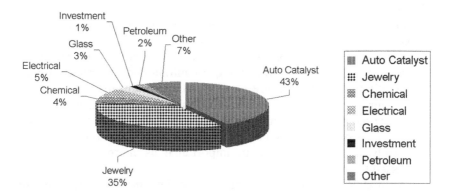

FIGURE 8.1 Platinum use by major category in 2003 reflects a relatively stable ratio with the exception of investment demand that became nominal in 2003–2004 after prices significantly inflated. (*Source:* Johnson Matthey)

demand declined. Toward the beginning of the new millennium, there was concern that platinum catalytic converters might decline as lean-burn engine technologies came to market. Because approximately 35 percent to 40 percent of annual allocation is for catalytic converters, any decline in this category would have a serious price impact.

Automotive Use

The primary application in the automotive sector is for antipollution devices. These include catalytic converters, oxygen and ozone detectors, and even the tips of hot-burning spark plugs. As world populations mobilize, there will be a steady growth in related platinum usage, including other sectors like petroleum refining and chemical processing. As of this writing, platinum was being combined with palladium and rhodium in a three-way converter designed to reduce hydrocarbon, nitrogen dioxide, and other tailpipe emissions. Obviously, increasing demand in the automotive sector will be directly related to increasing car and truck sales.

One of the most useful current data sources for platinum group metals is Johnson Matthey of the United Kingdom. Having attended their Platinum Breakfasts on a regular basis and received their beautifully constructed reports, I can thank them for adding a pound or two to my figure while informing me of the latest trends. Much to my surprise, the automotive and truck industries exhibit remarkable flexibility in making the transition from platinum to palladium and back again. From 1990 forward, substantial progress was made in reducing platinum group metal loadings in car and truck catalysts. At the same time, the ratio of metals was altered to meet specific pollution control goals that extended from nitrogen dioxide (NO_2) emissions to unspent hydrocarbons.

I bring this up because we tend not to see this on a quarter-by-quarter basis. Rather, we find changes on a biannual cycle. From the time prices in one metal or the other soar, it takes about 24 months to adjust. This is lightning speed for an industry as huge as automobile and truck manufacturing. It is simply amazing how price sensitivity motivates!

As our discussion of platinum supply shows, considerable quantities are recovered as scrap because catalysts are not consumed in the converters. Scrap recovery has been an extremely important component of overall supply and will increase in importance as more converters are processed for recycling.

As of 2004, catalytic converters were still needed to compensate for inefficient combustion. Depending on weather, tuning, fuel characteristics, ignition, compression ratio, and cylinder design, some gasoline or diesel fuel will remain unburned after each stroke cycle. These unused hydrocarbons are converted to carbon dioxide and water by the catalyst. Incorrect fuel-to-air mixtures are responsible for oxidized gases like nitrogen dioxide. This can be broken into its components of nitrogen and oxygen. Carbon monoxide results from incomplete combustion and represents a deadly gas because it binds with hemoglobin in blood like oxygen, but acts like carbon dioxide. Ozone is also a target of converters.

Because catalysts may be needed to correct combustion deficiencies, it stands to reason that they could be eliminated if technology could improve engine efficiency. During the 1980s, transportation companies were experimenting with approaches that could significantly increase engine efficiency. These systems use computer chips to precisely mix fuel and air while exactly timing the ignition. Through intricate control of the combustion process, computerized engines accomplish two objectives: higher horsepower and fuel efficiency with little or no pollution. By 1994, experimental technology had evolved to include small storage devices that recorded driving conditions like temperature, altitude, humidity, road grade, and driving habits. This information was incorporated into an efficiency algorithm to calculate ideal engine settings. The ultimate objective is to maximize efficiency.

Interestingly, high-efficiency gasoline engines that were touted as the solution during the 1980s had not come to commercial fruition as of 2004. Instead, the automotive industry embraced hybrid technology that combines fuel-efficient gasoline engines with electric motors to achieve higher mileage and, hence, lower emissions per mile traveled. As mentioned earlier, Toyota introduced the hybrid Prius in the late 1990s, and by the time 2004 rolled in, the Prius had become the most sought after car in U.S. history, with a waiting list extending more than 10 months. For 2005–2006, Toyota introduced the hybrid Lexus SUV and Toyota Highlander SUV that boasted 40-plus miles to the gallon under optimum conditions with road tests (normal driving) at well over 30 miles per gallon. Honda had its introduction of the hybrid Civic and Insight with mileage claims of 50 and 66 miles per gallon respectively.

The 2006 Honda fleet included the Accord with more than 260 horsepower and fuel economy ranging from 30 to 37 miles per gallon. This trend extends to Ford's hybrid Escape SUV and a full line of sedans and trucks. It is true that many hybrid engines require less platinum and palladium, but catalytic converters are still needed. Thus, hybrid cars only serve to lessen rather than eliminate auto catalyst demand.

In contrast, lean-burn or clean-burn cars and trucks truly increase efficiency to the point where catalysts are not necessary. In theory, such engines will be available by 2015, if not sooner. The technology is more complicated than laboratory tests might imply. Since there are so many pollutants produced by hydrocarbon-fueled vehicles, balancing the tailpipe output is difficult without using some catalyst. This is why the platinum industry feels confident catalyst demand will grow. Yet, these advances may have the same impact on platinum demand as digital imaging can have on silver.

Platinum Fuel Cells

There is a platinum lining to the transportation story. Platinum fuel cells provide an alternative to internal combustion–powered vehicles. The cell converts chemical energy (usually hydrogen and oxygen) directly into electricity, heat, and water. The key to advancing the technology is cell size and efficiency. The costs of manufacturing and running fuel cells were seen as too high to be commercially feasible even in 2000. Among the drawbacks are the lack of hydrogen fueling stations, difficulties storing hydrogen, platinum prices, and price instability.

Just three years after hearing discouraging fuel cell projections, various manufacturers demonstrated cells that worked on "reformed" fuels ranging from gasoline to methanol and methane. Reformers clean and convert petroleum-based fuels into usable fuel cell components. Thus, the pace of new technological development put fuel cells back on an accelerated track. A practical platinum-based fuel cell could emerge at any moment to have two effects. First, it would substitute for conventional power sources. More important to investors, it would render parts of the automotive analysis obsolete.

Approximately 17,000 ounces of platinum were dedicated to fuel cell development in 1996—up 7,000 ounces since 1993. By 2003–2004, estimates ranged from 20,000 to 30,000 ounces. This would suggest that fuel cell use is relatively static. The lack of growth is attributed to the lack of commercialization. Very few commercial fuel cells were in place by 2004. Most were fixed stations used to provide backup power and heating for small mission-critical buildings like hospitals. During a crucial time in the development curve, platinum prices reached above $900 per ounce to disrupt progress in bringing the cost equation down to a desirable $1,000 per kilowatt-hour (kWh). Vehicle manufacturers demonstrated more than 25 prototype models with marginal cost-to-efficiency ratios at $1,500/kWh. The industry admits the required number is closer to $1,000/kWh.

Every week, news about breakthroughs reaches the Internet. As of this writing, prospects for $500/kWh cells appeared bright, but these rely on decreasing platinum content (thrifting). Advances in coating technology are destined to reduce platinum contents to very low levels. For example, one process uses an evaporation method to deposit thin platinum films onto substrates. Another process called epitaxy actually deposits molecular metal that is less than 1,000 atoms thick onto a surface. If such coatings accomplish their designed purpose, an ounce of platinum will go a long way in producing efficient and plentiful fuel cells.

Phosphoric acid fuel cells (PAFCs) and proton exchange membrane fuel cells (PEMFCs) are being designed in Japan, the United States, and Europe at capacities ranging from 50 to 2,500 kilowatts. Output is sufficient to power passenger vehicles, buildings, or even small communities. Units have the advantage of being a source of electricity and heat. There are safety and control issues, yet these cells appear to be the most likely to absorb quantities of platinum on an increasing commercial scale. It may take several decades before platinum consumption for fuel cells rivals the auto catalyst. Progress in this area leads me to believe there is excellent potential. The time frame associated with the advance of this technology and the potential decline in auto catalysts hints that long-term trends will be subtle and could take half a lifetime to trade from beginning to end!

Although emphasis was placed on PAFC and PEMFC technologies, other fuel cell designs exist that do not use platinum as the cathode element. These include molten carbonate fuel cells (MCFCs) and solid oxide fuel cells (SOFCs). The MCFC uses nickel and, thus, has the potential to achieve the same results as platinum-based cells without the higher costs. However, MCFCs are large and have high operating temperatures. Efficiency is good, but the design appears more suited for stationary installations. Still, a reduction of the stationary power plant market would represent a significant dent in platinum demand from fuel cell applications.

The SOFC raced to the forefront between 2000 and 2004 with major strides in miniaturization and efficiency. These cells have significant advantages and, again, do not rely on platinum. Initial problems centered on very high operating temperatures. NASA sponsored research to solve heat and efficiency problems with good success. By 2004, SOFCs held the promise of replacing batteries in portable devices and powering vehicles using conventional fuels without reformers. The are also known as alcohol cells, the most common fuel being methanol. However, these cells are effective using methane (cooking and heating) gas.

Like all technologies, initial commercialization begins slowly. Once in place, the modern acceleration path is extremely progressive. Digital photography and audio CDs are perfect examples of introduction-to-commercialization times. The greatest obstacle to fuel cell vehicles has been hydrogen (H_2) storage and distribution. If SOFCs can use available distribution systems for gasoline, diesel, and natural gas, the move to nonplatinum cells will dominate.

There are no precise projections for platinum-based fuel cell consumption because we cannot determine the ultimate direction this technology will take. Based on corporate forecasts, patent filings, and press releases, my best guess holds consumption under 40,000 ounces per year until approximately 2011. Thereafter, the curve accelerates based on more rapid and widespread commercialization. (See Figure 8.2.) When compared with more than 3 million ounces dedicated to auto catalysts in 2004, it does not appear likely fuel cells will displace or fill in for changes in catalytic applications anytime soon.

This is an important consideration for anyone taking a longer-term view of platinum's potential. A watchful eye is recommended for technologies that may reduce platinum catalysts in cars and trucks. The first hint of any alternative to the platinum or three-way catalyst that uses platinum, palladium, and rhodium threatens as much as 25 percent of total consumption as of 2003. Since fuel cells offer the most obvious replacement, we see a disproportionate potential for a decline in auto catalysts without uptake from projected fuel cell consumption.

Figure 8.3 tracks gross auto catalyst platinum demand from 1989 through 2003. Consumption is directly linked to economic conditions

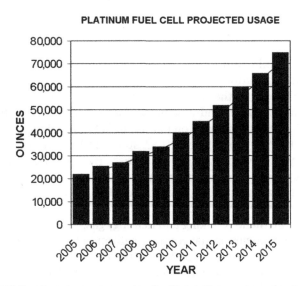

PLATINUM FUEL CELL PROJECTED USAGE

FIGURE 8.2 Platinum consumption for fuel cells is projected to be relatively straight line with an acceleration after 2010. (*Sources:* Johnson Matthey and EQUIDEX, Inc.)

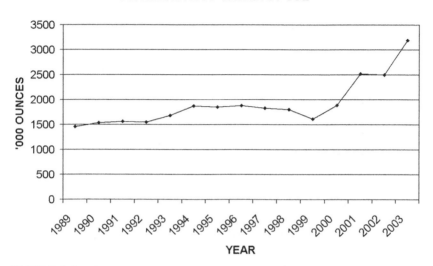

PLATINUM AUTO CATALYST USE

FIGURE 8.3 Platinum consumption in auto and truck catalysts remained flat from 1988 through 1999. Changes in emission standards in the United States and Europe forced platinum demand higher from 2000 forward. (*Source:* Johnson Matthey)

that encourage greater or fewer car and truck sales and emission standards. There is secular growth inherent in Third World industrialization and former Eastern bloc industrialization that will pick up the pace in overall car manufacturing regardless of intermittent economic trends. More importantly, China and India have emerged as huge potential platinum consumers based on newly adopted emission standards and a steep growth curve.

A change in the slope of the auto catalyst consumption curve beginning in 1989 can be attributed in part to the advancement of palladium. As previously mentioned, the growth in palladium use offset platinum to an extent; however, changes in emission standards, coupled with a trend toward diesel power in Europe, skewed loadings back toward platinum in 1999. Vehicle purchase patterns imply we can expect this pattern to continue. Yet, this same assumption was made before palladium catalysts had been perfected as a substitute for platinum loadings around 1990. Regardless of the ping-pong match between platinum and palladium loadings, it is not likely that there will be a total substitution of one metal for the other. Palladium is not as efficient as platinum for certain catalytic functions. Most palladium-based converters continue using platinum and rhodium. Recall the discussion of spreads between platinum and palladium prices. Investors can expect platinum's price premium to deteriorate if the tendency to use more palladium than platinum is reconstituted.

For those inclined to track pollution standards, the United States created definitions for a national low emission vehicle (NLEV) standard in 1999 and extended this to a transitional low emission vehicle (TLEV) and ultralow emission vehicle (ULEV) standard. Hybrid gasoline vehicles met the ULEV requirements from 2001 forward. These standards operate in conjunction with a U.S. federal Tier I standard passed under the Clean Air Act of 1990.

In 2004, the U.S. Environmental Protection Agency began implementing a Tier II standard that applied uniform standards for particular emissions across all vehicles, regardless of category (i.e., SUV, midsize sedan, compact, economy). In addition, Tier II had guidelines for specific models and various emission components. Tier II requirements dictate the type of catalytic converter necessary to conform. Although platinum and palladium loadings can be tweaked, the more stringent the pollution control, the more rigid the catalyst design must be.

Europe's equivalent standard is called Euro 5 and calls for equally strict standards moving from 2005 through 2007. However, Europe's automotive and light truck fleet has a much greater skew toward diesel-fueled vehicles. Tier II, Euro 5, and concurrent rocketing platinum prices combine to create a powerful incentive to reduce platinum loadings. The prior meteoric rise and fall of palladium presents an equally disturbing challenge and incentive to reduce dependence on these rare metals.

The United States has resisted joining the Kyoto Protocol, but industrialized and developing nations have formed an environmental consensus that will reduce emissions believed to harm the atmosphere. Even if there is no definitive proof that manmade greenhouse gases are affecting the atmosphere, the possibility is enough to motivate nations into actions that hold a future for platinum group metals. Any further emission standards will likely impact platinum and palladium.

Environmental regulation inevitably sets the stage for platinum consumption. However, general economic conditions will dictate the level of sales and, hence, the actual demand for metal on a more near-term basis. A booming economy that spawns increasing car sales should be viewed as a positive for platinum as long as thrifting does not offset per-unit sales with reduced per-unit platinum. As we can see, the balance is delicate.

Perhaps the most important theme throughout this book is that times are changing. Even if technology introduction is slow, market reactions are swift. When Toyota announced its intention to use palladium converters in some exported models in the mid-1990s, platinum immediately reacted lower while palladium made new life-of-contract highs. Markets are usually anticipatory. Once there is an expectation for technological change, it can be permanently discounted in price relationships. Remember that relationships do not always dictate gross price movements. When technology plays such a major role and is rapidly changing, do not expect long-term price stability.

Jewelry

One of the most significant applications setting platinum apart from other platinum-group metals is its use in jewelry as a pure or near-pure element. Platinum's extreme hardness and durability, coupled with a rich silver-blue hue, make it an extremely attractive metal. Its resistance to oxidation has elevated platinum above other white metals as the queen. For precious stone settings, platinum maintains an edge over gold because of its strength and its neutral color. When the stone is the emphasis, platinum's color does not detract from the focus. Yet, platinum's reflective properties can enhance appearance. The traditional price premium compared with gold also adds to its attraction as jewelry. Although there are moments when gold sells over platinum's price, the consensus is that platinum is (and will remain) the more valuable commodity.

A keen aspect of growth in platinum jewelry is related to skin tone. The most impressive expansion in jewelry demand comes from Japan, China, and other Asian regions. Platinum has more contrast against the Asian complexion. This same characteristic began to push demand in India and Africa as well as among ethnic groups in the United States and Canada. Clearly, Japan has displayed the greatest admiration for platinum jewelry. Consider that Japan consumed approximately 1.5 million ounces of platinum as jewelry in 1996 whereas Western Europe accounted for only 123,000 ounces. The North America total came in around 62,000 ounces. Considering that total world jewelry fabrication was approximately 1,840,000 ounces in 1996, Japan's 1.5 million ounces represented about 82 percent. This suggests that platinum prices will be highly sensitive to economic conditions in Japan. Any change in Japanese consumption patterns should be carefully observed.

Indeed, Japan exhibited a sharp decline in platinum jewelry consumption with the turn of the new millennium. From 2000 through 2004, Japan's jewelry demand dropped below 1 million ounces. A combination of cautious discretionary purchases and rising prices contributed to more conservative buying patterns. Jewelers found profit margins thin as retail prices remained static, while platinum bullion increased by several hundred percent. Normally, we might think this decrease would have a negative price impact. Yet, platinum moved to its highest levels since 1980 in 2003 as consumption dropped to 665,000 ounces. Johnson Matthey observes that Japanese 2003 jewelry consumption dropped to its lowest levels since 1980. Is it a coincidence that 1980 and 2003–2004 both represented huge price spikes?

Figure 8.4 plots platinum jewelry consumption for the world, Japan, and "other." In this instance, "other" represents non–North American and non–Western European consumption, taking into consideration regions like China and India. The general trend for 1989 through 1999 was higher. We can attribute some of the decline to the recession that began in 2000. High prices may have also discouraged purchases. The chart is not a projection, but rather a reflection of consumption relative to economic conditions and pricing.

From 1970 through 1985, platinum was associated with settings for precious stones, most notably diamonds. However, platinum's durability has made it an increasingly popular material for high-end fashion watches. Platinum watches have been manufactured since the early

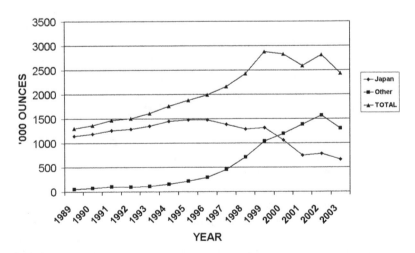

PLATINUM JEWELRY CONSUMPTION

FIGURE 8.4 Total jewelry demand peaked in 1999 and then flattened. While Japan experienced a significant decline, China, India, and other non–North American and non–Western European regions (represented by "Other" line) picked up the difference. (*Source:* Johnson Matthey)

1900s, but its hardness and high melting point made platinum difficult to work. Even in modern facilities, platinum takes a quick toll on tools and dies. After the huge 1980 price surge, there was a tangent desire for platinum timepieces on the wrist. This trend has carried forward. In the early 1990s, the New York Mercantile Exchange co-hosted a remarkable display of platinum watches in New York City. The most expensive platinum and diamond watch fetched a price toward $1 million. The everyday Vacheron Constantin's "Perpetual Skeleton" self-winding chronometer was a meager $73,900! To qualify for a platinum hallmark, a watch can contain only a small amount of alloy (usually copper)—just 50 parts per thousand. From any perspective, platinum watches are not likely to make a potent dent in supplies. The expense alone limits the extent of the market. Investors can take comfort in the knowledge that if there is major growth in this narrow area, the world might be on a fast track to enormous wealth!

Jewelry trends suggest growth stability and moderate sensitivity to economic variations. There is no direct substitute for platinum in jewelry, only alternatives. Because of the high-end nature of platinum settings, bracelets, necklaces, and watches, price elasticity is assumed not to be a factor, although the severe downturn in Japan's fortunes demonstrates that every society has a point of general economic constraint.

The steady growth in jewelry consumption up to the 2000 recession, and a presumption that global wealth will encourage this trend, plays heavily in the price equation. Some experts question the industry's ability for production to keep up with demand. It will be important to see a decline in industrial consumption for platinum to maintain price stability. Of course, there could be a point where the metal's industrial value outweighs fashion. However, if platinum becomes too expensive, demand will ease. Where there is a need, there is usually a solution. Shortages cannot be tolerated when needs are essential.

Chemical Processing

As a catalyst, platinum is important for producing various fundamental chemicals. Most widely recognized is its use as a catalyst in producing silicones. It is also essential for producing nitric acid and nitrogen compounds, fertilizer components, and synthetic fibers. Chemical use is fractional compared with auto catalysts and jewelry, as are the other consumption sectors. Yet, platinum's unique characteristics and the lack of an adequate substitute make its use for chemical processing an essential consideration. Specifically, members of the platinum industry are closely observing global agriculture for indications of increasing demand for fertilizer and urea. Increasing global wealth points to greater demand for synthetic fibers. Some materials used to make boat sails require platinum catalysts to synthesize on the front end of the process, while platinum dies are used to extrude threads at the back end. The chemical paraxylene is produced using platinum catalysts. This is a feedstock for terephthalic acid, a precursor for several synthetic fibers.

As an aside, just when studies showed the possibility of major fertilizer requirements into the first half of the twenty-first century, experiments with petrochemical aerosols appeared to give some plants an ability to absorb nitrogen from the air or increase root absorption. For example, the use of methanol sprays during periods of high-intensity sunlight increased the size and yield of certain melons, corn, wheat, and grapes. The exact mechanism by which plants benefit from this procedure is not clearly understood today. A potential conflict exists between the benefits of petrochemical yield enhancement sprays and environmental protection. A cornerstone of the Clean Air Act in the United States is the reduction of volatile organic compounds (VOCs) from soils, water, and air. Therefore, environmentalists might view methanol spraying with a jaundiced eye. Once again, I call attention to technologies that might have an effect on platinum trends. To be aware is to be prepared.

Figure 8.5 displays the interim trend in demand for chemical usage. There is an argument for an upward trend in industrial uses based on the short period from 1989 through 2003. The propensity for modest swings reflects linkage to a highly volatile industrial sector. Anyone familiar with chemicals, synthetic fibers, and fertilizer can understand why platinum uses reflect such fluctuations. The observation tells us growth in platinum's chemical applications may be relatively slow when compared against other usage. However, industrial expansion in China, India, and the CIS could accentuate the upward slope. While not indicated in Figure 8.5, projections for acceleration call for more than 1 million ounces by 2010. This begins to rival more extensive applications.

Electrical/Electronic

Platinum is used for a wide variety of electronic applications. Most demand potential comes from computers and related products. Platinum alloys are used to improve magnetic coatings for disks. Super high-density optical storage systems incorporate platinum coatings for read/write surfaces. Microscopic platinum films are used to form platinum silicide wafers that are incorporated in highly sensitive light- and heat-detection devices. These devices are displacing cadmium and mercury because they are less expensive, more reliable, more accurate, and environmentally friendly.

Platinum is extensively used in thermocoupling devices for measuring

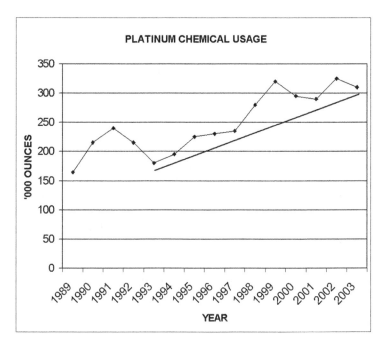

FIGURE 8.5 Platinum's chemical usage displays a consistent upward slope from 1993 through 2003. (*Source:* Johnson Matthey)

temperatures in production processes for glass, metals, and electronic circuits. As process technology expands in size and scope, platinum-based control mechanisms should enjoy steady growth. While minute quantities are used in each device, the number of units can become substantial over the next few decades.

Platinum remains a component of the highly controversial cold fusion process. Although palladium is the primary metal touted for this energy-producing anomaly, the experiments announced by Professors Stanley Pons and Martin Fleischmann used platinum wire. As an adjunct, platinum demand could surge if cold fusion becomes a commercial reality.

Platinum contacts are critical in certain high-voltage and high-temperature environments. I already mentioned the use in long-life automotive spark plugs. Mission-critical switches also incorporate platinum points. Again, quantities for each unit are tiny, but the number of switches can be enormous. Expect electronic and electrical platinum consumption to increase at a steady pace over time. It is doubtful whether technology will develop effective platinum substitutes for electronics and electrical applications in the near future.

Figure 8.6 gives a perspective on electrical and electronic demand. The powerful increase since 1993 is indicative of a strong personal computer and electronics market. Patterns in the electronic sector point to constant innovation and development. This supports the prospect for growth. Based on the technical slope of the curve along with industry evaluations, investors can expect between 2 percent and 5 percent annual expansion. At such a rate, electronic applications could play a more important pricing role within a short time.

Like other usage categories, electrical and electronic applications were adversely impacted by the recession that began in March 2000. Since it was the high-tech bubble that initially burst, it stands to reason that electronics would be more affected. As we see, consumption dropped from just over 450,000 ounces to approximately 315,000 from 2000 to 2003. This 30 percent drop is dramatic, but we see how quickly demand began recovering by 2003.

Among the new technologies that promised to absorb more platinum in the electrical/electronic category were MP3 players, digital cameras,

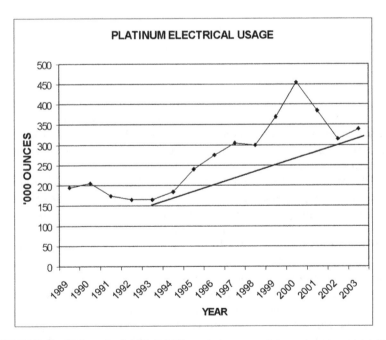

FIGURE 8.6 Platinum's electrical/electronic consumption was on an upward slope from 1993 through 2000. Although the recession took a brief toll, the trend resumed in 2002. (*Source:* Johnson Matthey)

and digital video recorders. However, this book extends beyond the novelty of these devices. Apple Computer's introduction of the iPod and mini-iPod represents an example of how miniaturized, high-density hard drives are making their way into mainstream consumer products. The same disk technology was proposed for storing digital photos in an iPod-like camera and video camcorder.

As more digital devices incorporate disk storage, platinum demand should proportionately grow. By 2020, annual electronic demand could easily approach 1 million ounces. This is why new platinum supplies are critical for balancing the longer-term price equation.

Glass

Platinum is used in dies and process technology for manufacturing high-quality fibers and glass extrusions as well as fiberglass for insulation and reinforced plastics. This sector is sensitive to economic trends in housing, boating, and electronics. The demand for fiberglass insulation moves in conjunction with housing construction, while fiberglass reinforcement is heavily used for boats, light planes, and even lawn furniture. Figure 8.7 displays demand in this area.

The United States luxury tax was blamed for a severe depression in the boating industry that was reflected in weak fiberglass reinforcement demand. Boats use fiberglass roving in conjunction with epoxy and polyester plastic resins for hull, deck, and interior construction. Obviously, the consolidation in the boat manufacturing business slowed demand for fiberglass and associated platinum use.

The pickup in platinum demand in the early 1990s was linked to growth in communications fibers, as well as high-resolution cathode ray and liquid crystal displays. Huge demand for portable displays in notebook computers, personal digital assistants (PDAs), cellular phones, beepers, flat panel televisions, digital camera displays, and other devices requiring high-grade glass reversed the downtrend in platinum use in glass manufacturing. Global economic expansion increased demand for conventional fiber insulation, and several automakers have adopted glass-reinforced parts, including bumpers, side panels, and even chassis springs.

The housing boom from 1995 through the beginning of the new millennium increased fiberglass insulation demand. This trend has been linked to economic health, interest rates, and demographics. The large bulge in Generation Y over Generation X suggests a strong demand for single-family homes moving beyond 2020. Of course, the ability to buy new housing will be economically dependent.

Although glass accounted for a small portion of annual consumption,

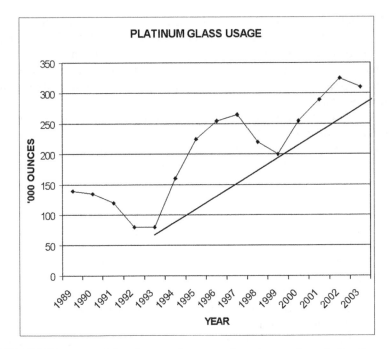

FIGURE 8.7 Demand for glass product manufacturing weakened after the luxury tax and economic conditions reduced spending on boats and other recreational vehicles using fiberglass construction. The trend pointed higher during the boom from 1993 until the 2000 recession. (*Source:* Johnson Matthey)

it still represents a growth area. Every bit helps when potential investors consider that advances in thrifting catalytic converters or lean-burn engines could reduce demand in the largest consumption category—33 percent to 40 percent of annual usage.

Petroleum and Other Uses

The petroleum industry uses platinum mesh or gauze in cracking processes to refine crude oil and certain feedstocks. Platinum catalysts play a critical role in primary refining and for isomerization octane enhancement. Toward the end of the 1990s, approximately 33 percent of the industrialized nations incorporated platinum/palladium-based isomerization processes, compared with less than 15 percent for Third World refineries. The global movement toward environmental protection will push these numbers higher. Based on a straight-line analysis, experts anticipate demand reaching between 400,000 and 600,000 ounces as North America and Western Europe move toward full capacity. Thereafter, expect another 100,000 to 300,000 ounces in demand as other regions catch up.

Consumption in this sector can become static because a healthy amount of platinum can be recovered and recycled. Refineries have a rotating inventory of new and used catalytic material. As capacity grows, platinum reserves have a proportional increase. In some respects, the recyclable nature of platinum makes it similar to gold; it's not consumed. There is a certain loss factor associated with reprocessing. However, careful recapturing procedures have made recycling extremely efficient and effective. The petroleum sector could reach a steady state whereby recycled supplies meet most demand requirements. Under such conditions, only incremental amounts of platinum would be needed to supplement losses or accommodate additional capacity. Figure 8.8 plots platinum use in the petroleum industry.

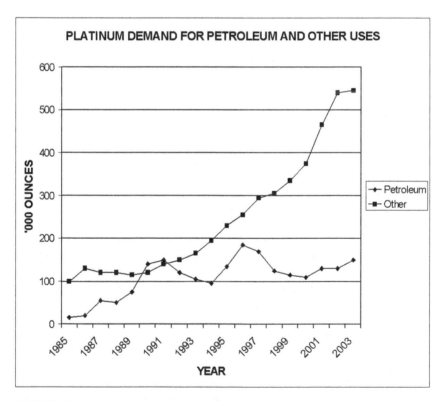

FIGURE 8.8 Petroleum sector demand has remained static from 1985 through 2003 between 100,000 and 200,000 ounces per year. Growth in other areas has had an accelerating rise from 1990 forward. (*Source:* Johnson Matthey)

With all of the discussion about clean air and zero emissions, platinum's industrial future appears brighter than that of silver and gold. Although there is a major threat from computerized engine systems, it is unlikely we will eliminate fossil fuels anytime soon. Demand in this sector seems assured—for now.

Investment

As with most precious metals, the swing factor is investment demand. However, unlike gold and silver, platinum has a far more limited supply with a much greater proportion dedicated to vital commercial processes. This means investor interest can have two motivations:

1. The general economic atmosphere can encourage hoarding. This coincides with inflation, confidence, and investor moods.
2. There are the potential market squeeze situations that arise from labor strikes, mine closings, global politics, and related developments. When traders perceive a squeeze, speculation increases. This makes investment demand difficult to assess over the long term. A squeeze today can easily lead to dumping tomorrow.

The overall pattern moving forward into the new millennium followed a trend away from hard-asset accumulation. Most growth was narrowly concentrated in Japan, which has an appetite for coins, small bars, and large bars. Other world markets are attracted to coins and small bars. For the Japanese, platinum represents a method of hard-asset saving because it is frequently used as a transfer vehicle against the yen. Although parity differentials can be played in currency markets, physical metal provides a measure of safety while value is in transition. In addition, there have been unusual arbitrage situations when the cash market and U.S. futures have been at odds with Japanese pricing relative to the dollar.

Dollar parity has become particularly important because we have 40 percent swings against the yen and euro. Consider that a large portion of platinum's 2003–2004 upward movement was dulled when measured in euros or yen. A strong yen can be an incentive for Japanese accumulation; however, this logic was not revealed in the numbers from 2000 through 2004.

Figure 8.9 graphs investment demand from 1989 through 2003. Wide swings are indicative of a speculative vehicle with no definitive accumulation pattern. As with any hoarding, demand can easily lead to sup-

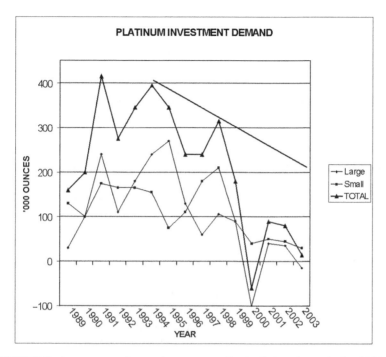

FIGURE 8.9 Investment demand was generally declining through the 1990s into the new millennium. However, the pattern appears erratic. (*Source:* Johnson Matthey)

ply as investment changes to divestment. There are no firm numbers for the amount of platinum held as private investment hoards. If we sum large and small investor accumulations from 1989 through 2000, we have a net accumulation of 3,235,000 ounces. This means that over approximately 12 years, private investors have acquired and currently hold less than a year's annual production based on 2004 figures. Unlike silver and gold, platinum has not been accumulated by central banks as a reserve asset. The entire hoard should be considered to be in private hands with the exception of some strategic reserves needed for military and related purposes.

It is impossible to determine the amount of platinum held in private vaults. Based on patterns measured through the 1970s and 1980s, we can safely assume that there is more than 18 months of production readily available for reintroduction as supply if the investment hoard were to be liquidated. Another 24 months may be found in strategic reserves held by Russia, the United States, Western European countries, Japan, and China.

It is equally impossible to predict the behavior of investors from one year to the next. In fact, even day-to-day forecasts are seemingly impossible. However, any increase or decrease in investment demand impacts prices and all other applications. If investors move prices too high, industrial processes fall victim to diseconomies. This forces a search for alternatives or relief from the entire application. One of the strongest incentives to perfect palladium catalytic converters came from the large price difference. Palladium holds an advantage all the way up to a two-to-one ratio based on 1996 technology and a platinum price of approximately $450 per ounce. When palladium prices soared in 2000 through 2001, platinum almost instantly regained the attention and emphasis from the auto catalyst market.

There are two investment categories: those who buy small quantities in one-ounce bars and coins and those who purchase large quantities in kilo bars or 50-ounce contract deliveries. While erratic, the trend since 1991 was down all the way through 2003. The higher cost of owning platinum coupled with a considerably less liquid futures market in the United States and abroad keeps platinum investment subdued.

In general, platinum's investment demand follows the precious metals sector. When there is strong demand for hard assets, platinum is a central element. When paper assets and real estate offer more potent returns, only die-hard metal advocates find platinum and its relative, palladium, attractive.

As we will see from supply analysis, the platinum supply/demand balance has been delicate and is likely to continue on narrow margins of deficit and surplus. For this reason, I have been keenly observing speculative accumulation to detect any hint of an investor-driven squeeze. In 2003, total futures contract volume and open interest extrapolated to over 4 million ounces of average demand. When platinum reached $700 during the first quarter of 2003, investors were responsible for liquidations that drove prices back below $600. Forecasts by leading industry groups called for an $800 high as supplies tightened going into 2004. The breakout above $900 was not expected and was probably driven by speculative agglomeration. With margins of 1 percent to 10 percent, investors could corner an entire annual platinum supply for between $50 and $500 million in futures margin. Either amount is small in comparison to the billions of dollars controlled by speculative hedge funds.

Therefore, the demand picture painted by Figure 8.9 should not be taken literally. There is only a suggestion of a secular downtrend. This does not rule out the propensity for a speculative frenzy if conditions become ripe.

Derivatives

Platinum futures are primarily traded in the United States on the COMEX division of the New York Mercantile Exchange (NYMEX), and on Japan's Tocom. Japan has the greater volume and open interest. This is partly due to the lack of promotion afforded platinum by the NYMEX, which is primarily interested in energy contracts. Both exchanges offer transparency with daily reporting of transaction volume and open interest (number of contracts between buyers and sellers).

Platinum also has a very active over-the-counter (OTC) market, which displays less transparency with high volumes and commitments. This market plays a pivotal role in price determination. Average speculators resort to futures because exchange markets are more accessible. Large traders tend to use OTC transactions for larger commitments. The OTC has less transparency and affords more subtle position accumulation.

I have raised the issue of speculative squeezes in many reports and studies. I believe investor-driven prices are a potent reality that the industry has yet to fully address. Laws about cornering physical markets are vague, at best. It is easy to do the math and determine that very little capital can control a huge position relative to available supplies. If strategically placed and held, a speculative position might drive platinum well over $1,000 per ounce. Of course, timing would be critical. At that price, platinum might crawl out of private storage and flood the market. But, unique to platinum and palladium (not to mention rhodium), the small total market value makes these metals ideal targets for manipulation across international lines. Even with the hoard, a modest amount of capital can absorb a huge chunk of annual platinum requirements. Do not be surprised to see just such a maneuver. If it comes, make sure you're in for the ride!

Total platinum demand has been growing steadily and will continue. As global industrialization moves forward, we can expect the slope of platinum's demand curve to steepen. From this perspective, platinum provides a comfortable fundamental foundation for those wishing to accumulate metal. Yes, lean-burn engine technology could shake the foundation. It is essential to be prepared for such a development. Also, the recoverable nature of platinum could slow demand at some stage. My assessment is that the world will still need to expand platinum output to accommodate needs through the twenty-first century. This assumes someone does not invent the perpetual motion machine!

SUPPLY

Most of the world's platinum comes from three major regions: South Africa, the CIS (Russia), and North America. By far the largest producer toward the beginning of the twenty-first century was South Africa with approximately 4.67 million ounces as of 2003. Next in line was Russia with less than one quarter of that amount at 1.05 million. North America accounted for approximately 295,000 ounces, with the rest of the world at just 225,000 ounces. A graphic representation appears in the pie chart of Figure 8.10.

This makes platinum supply easier to digest and assess, but far more vulnerable to massive disruption. Most importantly, the two largest sources have been highly susceptible to political and economic instability. This is the single most significant excitement factor. At any moment, a strike in South Africa or a mine closing can literally reduce new production to a trickle. Under such circumstances, prices can reach super impressive levels in incredibly short periods.

Both South Africa and the CIS were grappling with new political

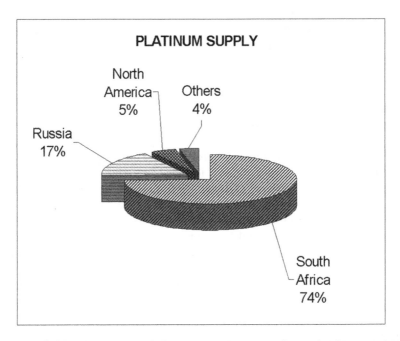

FIGURE 8.10 Platinum supply by region in 2003 reveals South Africa remained the production leader with almost three-fourths of total annual output. (*Source:* Johnson Matthey)

structures toward the close of the 1990s. South Africa's black majority rule had not changed mine ownership, which requires huge capital backing to remain operational and to expand. Nothing short of absolute cooperation will be required between labor and management into the twenty-first century if mine capacity is to grow. Clearly, platinum is an important income source. Mines provide jobs and revenues along with a measure of economic stability for the government. A small number of entities control most of South Africa's platinum properties. The Anglo Platinum operates the Amplats mines inclusive of Rustenburg, PPRust, and Lebowa. In 1996–1997, several capital expansion programs were under way to increase output between 10 percent and 15 percent. Steady platinum prices and improved technology were encouraging forces through the 1990s. By 2003, Anglo Platinum produced 2.3 million ounces of platinum, a 2 percent increase over the prior year. This represents more substantial growth than was projected in the late 1990s, but less than was expected for year-over-year results as of 2001.

Virtually all of South Africa's platinum producers have excellent growth potential. This is based on estimated reserves, new discoveries, improved recovery techniques, and modernization. Weak economics and a lack of increasing platinum values can be an impediment to expansion. Even with soaring platinum prices in U.S. dollars, the South African rand's appreciation paced enthusiasm. The result was a reduction in planned expansion. Thus, the obvious correlation does not always give the correct conclusion.

Platinum enthusiasts should keep their focus on developments among the South African producers. Aside from following daily news sources, the interim and annual reports from Johnson Matthey, PLC, give the most concise and reliable assessment of new developments. These reports are not limited to South Africa, but include all the important facts and figures for platinum and her sister metals. Key South African producers include Impala Platinum, Lonrho South Africa, Northam, and Anglovaal Limited. Keep in mind that relationships and corporate structures change. The trend toward multinational mining cooperatives was just under way in the late 1990s. Names, ownership, and entities can easily merge.

As the CIS adjusts to possible democracy and capitalism, platinum represents a solid economic base. Ownership issues within producing states are one facet of the total picture. As of this writing, the CIS was targeted for an international capital infusion free-for-all. Geological surveys indicate the CIS producing regions have the capacity to exceed South Africa to become the number-one supplier. In fact, expansion progress was under way from the mid-1980s forward with only a few glitches related to economic uncertainty in the early 1990s and a lack of capital for the Noril'sk Nickel mine, which produces substantial by-product platinum and palladium. My investigations in the late 1990s revealed Noril'sk was literally the source for the CIS. However, discussions with several informed groups led me to believe there were extensive and possibly exceptional properties looming for future development. Most notably, I was intrigued by geological surveys of alluvial formations located in the eastern region of Khabarovsk.

Alluvial deposits are formed when water flushes minerals out of rock and carries them downstream. Eventually, minerals precipitate out of the flow to form concentrations. These formations are also called placers as in the famous mining company Placer Dome. Within five years from my initial investigations, large platinum group concentrations were found in Khabarovsk and Kondyor. Additional deposits exist in the Urals and I feel it is more than likely large discoveries will be forthcoming over the next several decades. Forward momentum in these regions will be a function of price and politics. I would not be surprised to see CIS capacity double within a decade based on vast untapped potential.

The potency of CIS supplies was clearly demonstrated in the spring of 1997. From an equilibrium price of approximately $370 per ounce, disruption in Russian shipments quickly shot prices to almost $430. This 16 percent increase took place in only five weeks. Then, the resumption of Russian sales plunged prices back down in about half the time. Thus, as previously mentioned, supply is likely to play the dominant role in interim trends.

North American production was lifted from a static state with the development of the Stillwater mine in Montana, a joint venture between Chevron Resources and Engelhard Minerals. Stillwater is primarily a palladium mine. When falling palladium prices reached a low under $78 per ounce in 1989, the property became marginal. The partner corporations stalled the expansion project that would have allowed earlier development of the full potential. This same price decline forced a slowdown in South Africa and the CIS, too. However, palladium's price revival and strong demand potential rekindled interest in boosting Stillwater's capacity. Estimates suggest this single property will double production to yield a four-to-one ratio of palladium to platinum. This caught the eye of Russian interests, and a majority of the property was purchased by Noril'sk. After the announcement of this unusual acquisition, I raised the possibility that Russia was seeking a monopoly similar to OPEC's grip on oil. This was more the case for palladium as we review in the next chapter.

In Canada, the Ile de Lac region gave birth to Madeleine Mines, which subsequently became North American Palladium. This facility was just getting under way as a start-up in the late 1980s through the 1990s. After several troubled years, North American Palladium was finally reaching its stride in the mid-1990s. Like the Stillwater Mining Company in the United States, North American Palladium is primarily a palladium mine (as the name implies). Its financial success depends on strong palladium prices. Original revenue estimates called for profitable operations with palladium as low as $98 per ounce. Since then, North American has enjoyed far better profit margins. Hedging was viewed as an impediment to huge profitability, but a more dynamic approach to inventory management is capable of boosting the bottom line, as we will cover later.

Based on performance after 1989, there should be a sound basis for expanding palladium mines, which have the advantage of associated platinum production. Canada also enjoys significant nickel resources that produce excellent quantities of platinum group metals in addition to silver and gold. Inco operates the Sudbury mines and was on an expansion program that began in 1995 and should extend with good base metal price support.

As strange as it may sound, platinum resources have hardly been touched on a global scale. Aside from enormous by-product potential, new geological analysis in Indonesia, China, Australia, and regions north of South Africa including Zimbabwe, Zambia, and Zaire all show potential for developing platinum/palladium mines. Expansion of copper production in Chile and Peru will contribute to increasing platinum supplies.

Figure 8.11 illustrates supply trends from 1985 through 2003. It may not be evident from the graph, however, that advantages held by South Africa and the CIS could be challenged by other producing regions by 2015 to 2020. The number of new discoveries, and the speed within which mines can become operational, could increase the pace of world production more than tenfold, placing output of "Others" at more than 1.25 million ounces. Surely, South Africa and the CIS will not be standing still. Considering that within the United States, South Carolina went from zero to being the ninth largest gold producing state, anything is possible and probable.

Obviously, the trend is up. The question is whether the slope of the production line will begin to increase and when. This becomes a critical issue if we see a pronounced demand increase.

As is demonstrated in Figure 8.12, supply and demand were tightly matched for the years spanning 1985 through 2003. This clearly

PLATINUM SUPPLY BY REGION

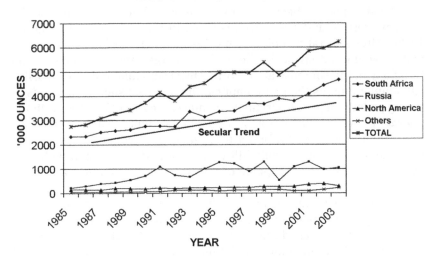

FIGURE 8.11 Platinum supplies from the two top producers, South Africa and Russia, have been steadily increasing. (*Source:* Johnson Matthey)

shows the reason why prices can become so volatile and news sensitive. As we see, we were fortunate that supply managed to keep up with demand until 1999. Thereafter, production ran at a deficit to consumption.

Figure 8.13 shows the deficit and surplus pattern for the period. Based on mounting deficits from 1999 forward, it is easy to see why platinum prices moved above $900 per ounce. The tendency for platinum demand to exceed supply is a characteristic that will remain as long as usage categories remain static—that is, there is no technological breakthrough substituting for platinum in major consumption categories like auto catalysts.

Investment accumulation can bring relief if it becomes supply; however, investors must overcome the desire to acquire on rising prices. As mentioned earlier, a very small speculative effort can swing the supply and demand balance. When graphically depicted, the picture becomes clear; profit potentials are truly exciting.

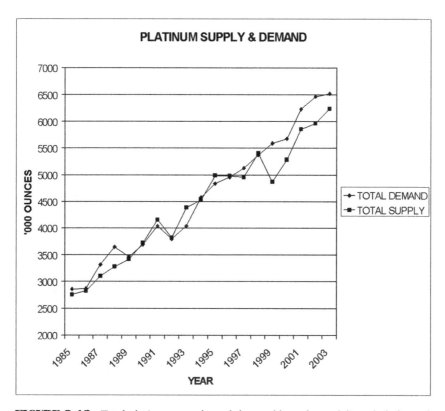

FIGURE 8.12 Total platinum supply and demand have been delicately balanced since 1985. The supply deficits beginning in 1999 culminated in significant price spikes from 2002 through 2004. (*Source:* Johnson Matthey)

CONCLUSION

Platinum has exceptional speculative potential with an extremely close and delicate supply and demand balance. The evolution of more stable economic and political environments within the two major producers (CIS and South Africa) could quell some of the speculative edge. If Latin America is any example, there will be several decades of uncertainty before the calm. Meanwhile, you should set your focus on selective fundamental trends. Technological challenge to platinum-based catalytic

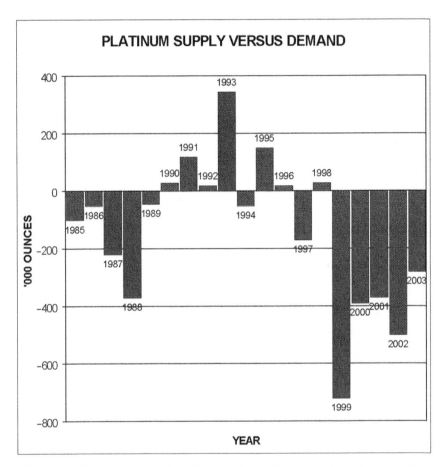

FIGURE 8.13 Twelve out of the 19 years from 1985 through 2003 show deficit production. (*Source:* Johnson Matthey)

converters is the main demand concern. Recycling is a starting point for tracking supplemental supplies. Labor, politics, and economic conditions are all part of the equation. Watch auto sales and remember that the average auto fleet life is approximately seven years. This gives an idea of recycling patterns. If a personality like Warren Buffett decides to have a platinum party, join his festivities!

CHAPTER 9

Palladium Fundamentals

Of all precious metals, palladium is the least known. Yet palladium may have the greatest profit potential. As a member of the platinum group, palladium shares many of platinum's characteristics, including hardness and a high melting point. Even palladium's applications parallel platinum's, including catalytic pollution control, chemical processing, electrical/electronics, and investment. Palladium has greater use in dental alloying, but far less in jewelry. Palladium's central long-term support comes from increasing encroachment on platinum. In the late 1980s, new palladium-based catalysts for cars and trucks were developed to reduce platinum requirements while targeting specific tailpipe emissions. This breakthrough established a greater industrial emphasis on palladium and opened the door for more consistent price appreciation.

DEMAND

The proven key to palladium's long-range potential rests with environmental concerns. As more of our world industrializes, palladium will be essential to keep air and water clean. Palladium is used to process industrial hydrogen peroxide, which has extensive applications in the paper industry. Traditional paper manufacturing bleaches pulp with toxic chlorine agents similar to products used for household cleaning and laundry.

Environmental regulations seek to reduce chlorine waste. Scandinavian paper mills have implemented highly effective bleaching systems using hydrogen peroxide that decomposes into oxygen and water. Computerized process control provides the same level of bleaching efficiency as chlorine. There is little doubt that hydrogen peroxide (H_2O_2) will find its way into global paper manufacturing. This will place a heavy demand on hydrogen peroxide production and palladium-based process systems.

On a smaller scale, hydrogen peroxide is used for cleaning sensitive electronic machinery and components. Because the electronics sector is expanding rapidly, it is a fair projection that associated demand for palladium will rise.

Palladium is also used in conjunction with platinum to manufacture purified terephthalic acid for the synthetic fiber industry. A number of advances in polyester fabrics and materials should have a positive impact on palladium consumption. Palladium is necessary for industrial as well as consumer fibers. Automotive, housing, aerospace, and boat manufacturing are using an increasing amount of synthetic materials that rely on terephthalic acid. Synthetic fibers are definitely a growth industry. The 2003 breakdown of palladium's primary uses is illustrated in Figure 9.1.

From 1996 through 2003, the majority of palladium consumption shifted from electronics into auto and truck catalysts. Thus, palladium

PALLADIUM DEMAND BY CATEGORY

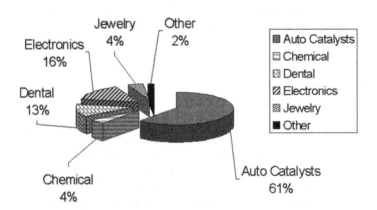

FIGURE 9.1 Palladium demand by category as of 2003 shows almost two-thirds allocated to auto catalysts. (*Source:* Johnson Matthey)

will share the same fate as platinum if new technology displaces auto and truck catalytic applications. The overall demand picture appears solid; however, advances in ceramic dental inlays, onlays, and crowns threatens to diminish dental alloying by as much as 5 percent to 8 percent from 2006 through 2009 as advanced technology spreads through Europe and Asia. Eventually, more than half of dental alloying will be replaced by synthetic materials.

The biggest speculative story affecting palladium began in March 1989 during a press conference at the University of Utah in Salt Lake City. Researchers Stanley B. Pons and Dr. Martin Fleischmann went public with their process for "fusion in a jar." Because their fusion took place at room temperature rather than at millions of degrees, their discovery was called "cold fusion." The cold fusion announcement came on the heels of Toyota's announcement of its intention to use palladium in catalytic converters for several car models. Palladium raced to more than $180 per ounce. Within a matter of weeks, the scientific community condemned cold fusion as junk science. According to conventional theory, such a process was impossible. Therefore, palladium quickly retreated from its lofty levels to lows below $80 per ounce in 1993.

The cold fusion debate never died; it simply went into hiding. Each year since the 1989 announcement, scientists from around the world gather to share experimental data at the annual Cold Fusion Conference. Several patents have been filed for cold fusion schemes, and it would not be surprising if cold fusion reemerges as a possibility by the time this book is widely circulated. I confess to being caught up in cold fusion intrigue to the extent of actually taking delivery on several hundred ounces of palladium that were minted in cold fusion medallions. From a speculative standpoint, a commercially feasible cold fusion process could easily propel palladium prices over $1,000 and even $5,000 an ounce. It seemed a reasonable gamble to hoard some of this metal—just in case.

I have followed cold fusion development since its inception. Even today, some form of energy-producing process seems to exist here. On the positive side, palladium appears to be the most efficient and consistent metal for generating a cold fusion reaction. On the negative side, several experiments seem to indicate that nickel can achieve the same type of positive energy production. Three approaches to cold fusion were touted as being of possible commercial scale in 2000. The first was the Pons/Fleischmann fusion in a jar using heavy water, a palladium cathode, and platinum wire. This device uses electrical current to begin the alleged fusion. Published results suggest that initial "reactors" will generate approximately 25 kilowatts, sufficient to power a home or small building.

Strangely, one of the problems associated with initial cold fusion devices is the power conversion technology. Cold fusion generates heat. The heat must be harnessed and converted into electrical power. Thermal conversion is not an easy process at low temperatures. Unless cold fusion generates sufficient heat to efficiently convert into mechanical energy (like a steam engine), equations for changing cold fusion into usable energy are extremely complex. Although some skeptics have turned the corner and accepted this unusual phenomenon or observation, the amount of positive energy has not opened the door to commercial feasibility. The palladium/platinum apparatus will require huge advancements before it finds its way into homes, vehicles, and power systems. Even if proven today (whenever today is), the lead time for commercial implementation would extend one to two decades.

A second energy prospect is called "sono-luminescence." You may be familiar with the unusual light that often appears in the wake of a powerboat at night. Sometimes the glow results from phosphorus algae. However, a blue hue associated with cavitation has been linked to a quasi-nuclear reaction that emits photons. Apparently, cavitation creates microscopic bubbles that collapse under extreme force. When these bubbles collapse, a photon is released as energy. There are experimental results that imply sono-luminescence can produce excess heat as a stand-alone process. When combined within a palladium shell or target, cavitation seems to stimulate a cold fusion reaction.

Still another approach is that of a Japanese group using palladium-based "energy generators" that rely on hydrogen. Their assumption is that palladium has a subatomic matrix capable of absorbing hydrogen atoms and compressing them to form helium in extremely small reactions. In the Pons/Fleischmann approach, heavy water is the vehicle for transporting hydrogen into the palladium matrix. In theory, a pure hydrogen process could be more efficient and controllable. Laboratories in Russia, India, France, England, Germany, Japan, and the United States all report positive cold fusion findings. Although there is no definitive explanation for the apparent process, data and observations are becoming increasingly difficult to deny.

Cold fusion has enormous economic and political implications. Investors should recognize that the energy sector has links to everything from transportation to environmental control (heating and air-conditioning) to all forms of manufacturing. Fossil fuels account for enormous industrial infrastructure that is responsible for massive employment, capital investment, and revenue. Cold fusion could be the single most destructive economic force ever known if its introduction dislocates the conventional energy sector.

In the past, most new technologies could be absorbed slowly. For example, nuclear energy has been gradually adopted because safety and cost issues have held back any formidable encroachment on the oil industry. Solar power does not share the same safety issues as conventional nuclear facilities, but efficiency and expense remained issues as of 2004. There are plans for wind farms, tidal generators, and even thermal power from volcanic activity. These new methods of powering society do not threaten to displace oil in a single sweep. In contrast, cold fusion could provide an immediate transition from oil, coal, and gas to limitless clean energy. Why would such a transition present a problem? After all, isn't a power source like cold fusion our ultimate goal?

The problem is not in the process, but in its implementation. Governments have been extremely reluctant to pursue cold fusion as a prospective science. The consensus is that cold fusion will come into use on its own *if it is real science.* There is no incentive to hurry its commercial introduction because disbanding the fossil fuel machine is a daunting task for the private and public sectors. The billions invested in power plants and electricity delivery systems would be laid idle. The massive employment in the energy and related sectors would be rendered obsolete. Cars, trucks, planes, and trains would all require reevaluation and redesign. In a word, *upheaval* best describes the economic consequence of rapidly deployed cold fusion technology. Even Hollywood has latched onto this reality with a number of films featuring cold fusion themes.

A preferred time line would be a slow move from experimental anomalies to small-scale laboratory curiosities. This appears to be the stage of cold fusion as of 2005. Thereafter, a modest commercial reactor might be tolerated if cold fusion exhibits no safety issues. This is the point of extreme investment interest. The moment a commercial cold fusion system is introduced, palladium could be the ultimate highflier. Assuming cold fusion continues relying on palladium rather than nickel or some other process, the investment potential becomes enormous. In fact, it may be impossible to obtain palladium once the rush begins.

Cold fusion is a trump card that may never be played. Even without this remarkable possibility, palladium has strong favorable fundamentals. Demand curves for auto catalysts, chemical processing, electronics/electrical, and even hoarding all look bright.

Auto Catalysts

Although palladium's catalytic properties have been known for decades, it was not until the mid-1980s that scientists noticed its potential for pollution control in cars and trucks. Several developments brought about palladium's success, including the move away from tetraethyl lead as an octane enhancer and improved refining to remove sulfur from gasoline and diesel fuel. Palladium is highly sensitive to lead and sulfur contamination. Until these components were substantially removed from fuels, it was virtually impossible to perfect a palladium device that could survive the required time for practical automotive and truck use.

Palladium is particularly effective in reducing unburned hydrocarbons. During cold starts, engines tend to burn rich fuel-to-air mixtures. By situating a palladium catalyst close to the initial exhaust, hydrocarbon emissions can be substantially decreased during the cold start phase and normal operation. As clean air becomes an increasing priority relative to population densities, the need for stricter tailpipe standards will intensify, as covered in Chapter 8. This should translate into greater palladium demand. Figure 9.2 displays progress in auto catalyst use of palladium from 1990 forward.

Until 1989, most of the palladium used in auto catalysts was complementary to platinum. Once the palladium technology was perfected, demand assumed an extreme slope. The huge price spike of 2000–2001 dramatically reduced palladium consumption through 2002, when platinum began to run up once more. Absent unusual price behavior, the slope

PALLADIUM AUTO CATALYSTS

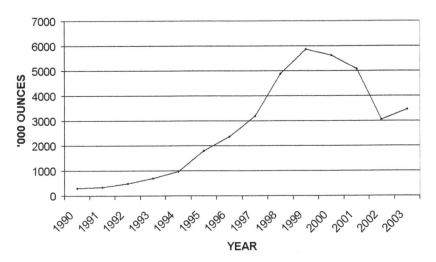

FIGURE 9.2 Palladium use in auto and truck catalysts from 1990 through 2003. (*Source:* Johnson Matthey)

should more directly correlate with auto production. The 10- and 15-year projections call for demand equilibrium because currently technology implies static expansion. This means that all car and truck models that can employ palladium eventually will. The intriguing aspect of palladium's auto catalyst growth curve was its potential to exceed supplies unless price forced more moderate usage. With approximately 6.8 million ounces mined in 1996, there was a projected possibility that auto catalysts would gobble up more than half the world's new annual supplies shortly into the twenty-first century. I pointed to this scenario in *The New Precious Metals Market,* completed in 1996. Indeed, by 1999, palladium use in automotive catalytic converters reached 5.88 million ounces while total supply was just over 8 million ounces. There was a shortfall of more than 1.3 million ounces. Prices responded accordingly.

Yet, this potential did not continue into the new millennium. Rather, the price spike of more than $1,000 per ounce in 2001 quickly pushed catalyst makers back to platinum. Our conclusion is that a price between $200 and $410 per ounce keeps palladium catalytic converters on a 4 percent to 7 percent growth path. Much depends on the rate of automobile growth in China, India, and other developing regions. The factors are almost identical to platinum with the exception of the ratio between gasoline- and diesel-fueled vehicles. As mentioned, diesel depends more heavily on platinum as of this writing.

Fuel processing will be a central focus because it is more difficult to rid diesel of sulfur. There are scrubbing processes that hold the promise of a cleaner diesel fuel and, in fact, some proposed methods use palladium as the cleaning element. There is always the obvious trade-off between the cost of purifying diesel and the benefits. To be clear, the purpose of clean diesel is not to implement palladium catalysts. The primary goal is simply to reduce sulfur dioxide, the ingredient of acid rain. Palladium catalysts happen to be beneficiaries, too. Clean diesel places palladium and platinum on near-even catalytic playing fields. At such a stage, other consumption categories will determine which holds the greater price premium.

One moderating factor in the demand equation might be palladium recovery. Like platinum, palladium is not consumed in auto catalysts. Unlike platinum, palladium does not release as much recoverable supplies when used elsewhere.

Electronic/Electrical

Palladium is extensively used in electronic components. Approximately 25 percent is for contacts, conductive pastes, specialized circuit components, and sensors. By far the largest electronic application is in manufacturing multilayer ceramic capacitors (MLCCs). Palladium has become an effective alternative to platinum-silver in MLCCs. These devices store electric charges like miniature batteries, discharging when needed. MLCCs are found in all forms of electronic components, from personal computers to mobile phones and extremely precise mechanisms in military hardware. The growth in palladium consumption for MLCCs is directly related to expanding global electronics applications. Through the 1990s, there was a trade-off between surging MLCC use and advancing miniaturization technology. Palladium consumption was balanced between MLCC usage and the decreasing size per average unit. Research trends indicate MLCC circuits are approaching practical limits in miniaturization. Virtually every long-range forecast calls for accelerating growth in production and sales of electronics. Aside from the obvious pattern in Japan, North America, and Western Europe, entirely new communications infrastructures are being developed in South America, China, the Pacific Rim, India, and former Eastern bloc countries.

In 1997, two communications technologies were under consideration for developing regions: wireless and fiber optics. Future wireless systems can consume more palladium because of the number of MLCCs needed in portable phones, beepers, and communications devices. However, my research indicates that hybrid systems are more probable and both fiber optics and wireless are evenly matched. Fiber-optic systems require couplers and repeaters that use MLCCs. Switches and logic circuits for fiber-optic systems use palladium plating and silver-palladium tracks on mission-critical printed circuit boards. Certainly, China's trend toward cellular and similar wireless communications systems give a more favorable palladium outlook because of the sheer number of handheld units likely to be placed into operation. Figure 9.3 shows a static growth curve that was adversely affected by palladium's price spike. Assuming stable prices, I believe we can expect the slope exhibited from 2001 to remain in place and possibly accelerate.

Like Moore's Law, it seems the ratio of palladium content in MLCCs is shrinking as the circuits themselves become smaller. This trend has offset the increase in overall circuit consumption. At some stage, there is a practical limit to the amount of shrinkage that can be accomplished. In my opinion, pronounced thrifting will diminish moving forward from 2006 and we should see acceleration in electronic consumption (absent any unforeseen interference).

Combining growth in electronics and auto catalysts, it is easy to project increasing supply pressures for palladium based on projected production. I do not foresee any immediate substitutes for palladium in either category. Much depends on the continuing balance between increasing

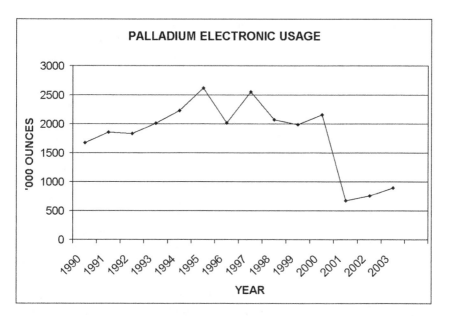

FIGURE 9.3 Electronic palladium usage dropped in conjunction with the burst in the high-tech bubble from 2000 into 2001. Any recovery will be directly related to an increase in the ratio of parts using palladium and a leveling in thrifting. (*Source:* Johnson Matthey)

demand and rising supplies. MLCCs, hybrid integrated circuits, printed circuit boards, couplers, switches, and a host of related components will rely on palladium and platinum. Even as prices fluctuate for these metals, better implementation has reduced required amounts in each component to a great extent. In my opinion, palladium's electronic/electrical future remains solid.

Dental

Like gold, palladium has enjoyed increasing popularity as dentistry moves away from silver-mercury amalgams. Palladium-gold alloys provide an excellent alternative to higher gold-content restorative materials in terms of price and durability. Restorative dentists point out that higher gold content is preferable when opposing surfaces involve a natural tooth against an inlay or onlay. However, if opposing surfaces are both restored material, the need for a kinder material is not as pressing. Palladium-gold material is harder and requires more careful margin preparation. In Germany, where restorations are considered an art as well as a medical procedure, palladium has made a more positive impression. (No pun intended for those dentists out there!) The United States saw a pronounced increase in palladium-gold use from 1993 forward as a direct result of lower insurance payments for restorative procedures.

This same sensitivity to insurance or government subsidy is experienced in Japan where palladium dental alloy (*kinpala*) has been subsidized by the government. As co-payment ratios rise, usage declines. Still, palladium alloys have been on a positive growth curve in Japan and other Pacific Rim countries.

Demographics are likely to play an important role in rising dental demand through the year 2020. The leading edge of the post–World War II generation did not receive the full benefits of fluoridated water. The population age curve in the United States, Western Europe, and Japan indicates increasing restorative dental requirements will occur from the years 2000 forward to approximately 2025. Further, as Third World countries develop, demand for dental care will increase. This can easily push the demand out beyond the year 2050.

There are a lot of teeth out there! However, earlier chapters mentioned the development of ceramics, polymers, and silicates that can be cast and implanted like their precious metal counterparts. If gold and palladium prices rise too high, there will be a push for nonmetal restorations. Like all sectors that consume palladium, the price spike of 1999–2001 took dentistry by surprise. We see a dramatic decline in dental alloying in Figure 9.4. In 1996, I predicted palladium's reaction to gold prices. That prediction was based on common sense and came to fruition.

Given the move to computer-aided design/computer-aided manufacturing (CAD/CAM) in dentistry, I am not as encouraged about the continuing use and growth of palladium dental demand. In all likelihood, this is a good thing. As requirements increase in other categories, it will be advantageous to see dentistry relinquish some of its demand.

Chemical

Figure 9.5 projects demand for chemical applications. I previously covered the mainstays of this sector encompassing synthetic fiber manufacturing and hydrogen peroxide production. Palladium demand for use in chemical processing enjoyed moderate growth after recovering from an industrial slump that ended in 1993. From 1998 forward, the chemical sector edged upward and flatlined in response to rising prices and the recession. Interestingly, this category was not as adversely impacted by the price spike from 1999 through 2001, indicating a lack of

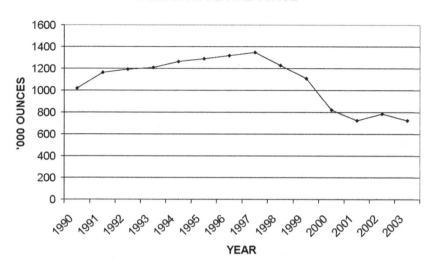

FIGURE 9.4 Palladium use in dentistry was modestly rising from 1990 through 1997 when rising prices began to interfere with palladium's price advantage. (*Source:* Johnson Matthey)

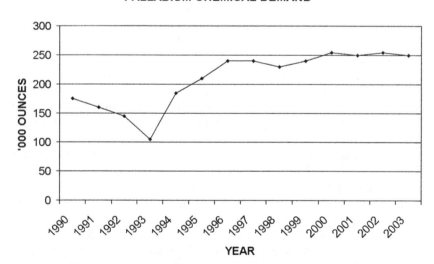

FIGURE 9.5 Chemical applications for palladium remained flat from 1996 through 2003. (*Source:* Johnson Matthey)

elasticity. Although Figure 9.5 may portray stalled demand, the trend toward increasing use in Asia and India for synthetic and vinyl paints a more positive picture moving forward. Much depends on palladium pricing; however, projected supplies coupled with a possible decline in dental alloying are capable of keeping an equilibrium. With a price below $300, we could see an accumulation. In particular, use in nitric acid production will experience opportunistic buying spurts based on favorable prices. Above $300 per ounce, alternative technologies become attractive. Investors can expect different methods for producing industrial hydrogen peroxide or alternative bleaching technologies in paper manufacturing. Palladium is also used to recover its platinum and rhodium sister metals. Systems using palladium "catch gauze" sacrifice palladium in return for platinum and, more specifically, rhodium.

The synthetic fiber industry and paper manufacturing industry are highly cost-sensitive. Both involve large volume and low selling prices. This means palladium use is likely to be more reactive to higher palladium prices. Based on the ratio of usage, I do not believe chemical applications will decisively swing toward palladium. Because it is only marginal, chemical consumption could sharpen a price movement based on changes in supply or auto catalyst and electronic sector consumption.

Analysis of the paper and fiber industries shows steady growth related to increasing global wealth and demand. There has been a sharp increase in paper shipments to the CIS and former Eastern bloc countries that has been attributed to more freedom of the press and rising print media advertising. Commercial enterprise in China is also increasing that nation's paper consumption. In fact, the United States is one of the largest importers of Chinese printing, which can be highly competitive even with additional shipping costs. Industrialized nations have been careful to impose a sense of environmental responsibility on emerging economies. This is why environmentally friendly paper bleaching is likely to be the process of choice.

Clothing is certainly a growth industry. Global capacity for natural fibers like cotton and wool is limited by the practical growing regions and cycles. This points to greater use of synthetic materials and, consequently, greater demand for palladium in the manufacturing of purified terephthalic acid.

There is a question whether the chemical demand category has been a catchall for increasing amounts of palladium used in cold fusion experimentation. Rumors for cold fusion reached as high as 50,000 ounces in 1996. This is a significant amount because it would account for nearly all the growth in the chemical sector from 1994 forward. However, industry representatives strongly refute any cold fusion use above "nominal levels" of a few thousand ounces.

Jewelry

Palladium was exclusively used for alloying platinum and gold. As a precious metal, palladium has gained popularity over nickel and other alloy metals used to create white gold and platinum blends. The trend toward using between 5 percent and 15 percent palladium content in platinum jewelry slowed during the late 1990s because most platinum jewelry was consumed in Japan where the status of "pure" platinum discouraged purchasing alloyed pieces. However, Italy began increasing palladium use for producing high-karat white gold. Palladium alloying produces a more workable product with better color than a nickel counterpart. The trade-off is the significantly higher price of palladium compared with nickel. Inexpensive gold chain rarely uses palladium. Some Middle East manufacturers have moved into platinum jewelry for export to Japan and some local consumption. Figure 9.6 graphs palladium consumption for jewelry from 1990 through 2003.

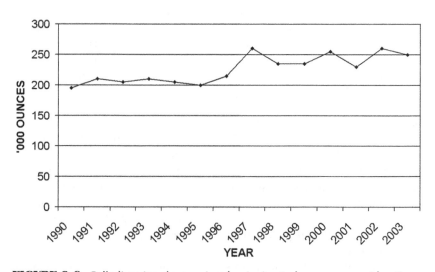

FIGURE 9.6 Palladium jewelry was just beginning to become a consideration in 2002. Prior to 2002, consumption was primarily for alloying with gold. Thus any projected growth for palladium jewelry is not indicated on the graph. (*Source:* Johnson Matthey)

As this graph illustrates, jewelry consumption is at approximately the same level and configuration as chemical usage. Together, these categories will probably be more price-sensitive than other uses because it is easier to substitute other metals for jewelry applications and change bleaching agents in paper mills.

The big story beginning in the new millennium was the introduction of all-palladium jewelry. The experiment did not make an impression on North American or Western European consumers, but popularity was seen in China and Japan. Initially, the huge palladium price swings discouraged manufacturers. Yet, aggressive Chinese marketing suggested the possibly of far more significant jewelry demand. Like catalyst demand, there may be real competition between platinum and palladium if prices equalize and palladium gains popularity. There has been a perception that platinum is the preferred metal *because is has been*. While it is a matter of personal preference, pure palladium has a distinctively rich color that takes on an appealing bluish-gray hue. When viewing palladium side-by-side against platinum and silver, consumers have actually *preferred* palladium's color. Unlike silver, palladium does not tarnish. Because it is a hard metal, palladium retains its luster without developing an excessive patina.

When platinum prices maintained extended lofty levels in 2003–2004, Chinese jewelry manufacturers began pushing palladium as an alternative. By 2005, consumers began viewing palladium as a choice rather than a substitute. Whether palladium jewelry can maintain appeal in China and extend to other regions is a critical question when considering the relative amount that might be allocated to the relatively new consumption category. Even if the trend remained unique to China, the huge population combined with a new and growing middle class could account for an additional 15 percent to 20 percent. This would make up more than any projected decline in dental alloying.

To establish palladium as a desirable fashion requires distinguishing the metal. As of this writing, palladium did not enjoy the same marketing organizations as the World Gold Council, Silver Institute, and Platinum Guild. Therefore, palladium was attaining its status on it own with very little formal help. Assuming jewelry demand heats up, I would not be surprised to see palladium represented by its own marketing organization. Having participated in palladium projects myself, I wouldn't mind being part of such an organization!

If you have an opportunity to see palladium jewelry, I encourage you to give it more than a casual glance. Compare its feel, color, and weight against silver, white gold, and platinum. I believe you will be pleasantly surprised to find palladium is a very attractive metal. In particular, hold palladium next to white gold. The contrast is striking!

Other Demand

Palladium's sensitivity to sulfur has generated applications for the metal as a scrubbing element whereby a palladium catalyst is used to remove trace amounts of sulfur from fuels like diesel and kerosene. Palladium is also used to reduce aromatics that form noxious fumes when burned. Like platinum and rhodium, palladium has properties that are suited for oxygen sensors. Palladium is used for anticorrosion plating in chemical process plants. Finally, a limited amount of palladium is used for investment bars, coins, and medallions.

Palladium hoarding has been too insignificant to justify its own usage category. However, this may change as the metal's popularity increases. The central problem with investing in physical palladium is its lack of supply. Although more wealthy individuals may afford delivery of a 100-ounce futures contract, this is beyond the means of the majority of investors. Aside from cost, housing 100-ounce bars represents a storage problem and risk.

The only official coin that had any notoriety was the Russian Ballerina that was briefly popular as a physical investment vehicle during the cold fusion frenzy. Other examples are medallions and bars produced by mines, like Stillwater's one-ounce .9995 fine round medallion and one-ounce ingot. Johnson Matthey produces one-ounce bars in small quantities, and it has become less difficult to find dealers with inventory.

Shortly after the March 1989 cold fusion press conference, a series of palladium medallions were marketed. The most common were the

One-ounce palladium medallions minted by the Stillwater Mining Company are an example of physical metal that can be accumulated for investment.

half-ounce and full-ounce cold fusion medallions sold by Benchmark Commemoratives from New Hampshire. These pieces had a higher purity of .9998 and were individually numbered for tracking. Various companies minted approximately 15,000 ounces, hoping to cash in on the cold fusion frenzy. The small quantity of medallions has made them more valuable as collectors' items than for metal content. More than 1,000 cold fusion medallions were purchased and melted down for experimentation because of their high purity.

Japanese hoarding was estimated at approximately 20,000 ounces in 1996 and rose to 60,000 ounces in 1999. Ford Motor Company attempted to hoard a large amount, as mentioned earlier. The attempt produced a $1 billion write-off when palladium prices collapsed in 2002. Overall, investment demand is a matter of education. As long as palladium is overshadowed by platinum and has very limited jewelry use, cash investment will be static.

The total demand picture appeared quite positive. The slope toward the end of the 1990s was rising, and most fundamental indications pointed to the same pattern through several decades into the new millennium. However, the 2000–2001 squeeze significantly set back palladium's momentum. Some analysts believe palladium's vulnerability to supply disruption creates too great an incentive to find more stable and less expensive alternatives moving forward.

As you will see from the discussion of supply, palladium has been on a hand-to-mouth basis for a long time. It is not easy to develop new palladium production. This metal is extremely rare and presents many challenges. Figure 9.7 plots all major use categories as a total.

SUPPLY

Palladium is a counterpart of platinum. Thus, most of the supply coverage for platinum applies to palladium as well. The largest producer has been Russia, followed by South Africa, North America, and others. Figure 9.8 shows producer positions as of 2003.

Russian mine output is the same as platinum with the majority coming as a by-product of Noril'sk Nickel. There have been some palladium-specific developments in some CIS regions. New properties are expected to add appreciable supplies well beyond the year 2020.

It seems Russia has a particular interest in palladium. While already the largest producer in 2003, Noril'sk Nickel finalized a deal to become majority shareholder in the U.S. Stillwater Mining Company. Some analysts were highly suspicious of the acquisition because it appeared as

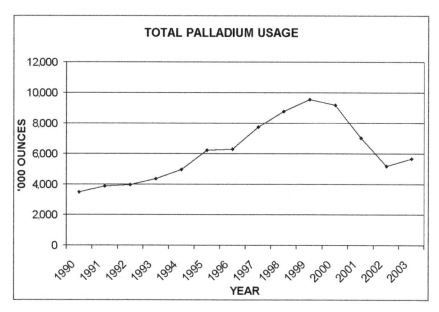

FIGURE 9.7 Total palladium consumption was rising until the price spike of 2000–2001 and the concurrent U.S. recession. (*Source:* Johnson Matthey)

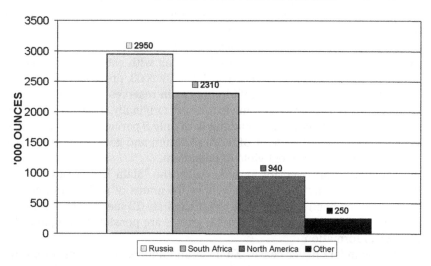

FIGURE 9.8 Although a 2003 snapshot, palladium production has been dominated by the same three regions since 1968, with Russia maintaining its lead. (*Source:* Johnson Matthey)

though Noril'sk wanted to control supplies across all markets. Having successfully manipulated palladium's price from 1999 through 2001, Russia may be honing its position as world price setter. Russia's President Vladimir Putin signed legislation to make platinum group metal statistics more accessible to industry. Whether this plays into a grand scheme or is a true attempt at creating transparency was yet to be seen at the end of 2004. Firm prices with good prospects encouraged the rebuilding and capacity expansion for the Stillwater mine in Nevada as long as it is not stalled by the new majority shareholder.

We do know Noril'sk used Stillwater to market several thousand ounces of palladium in 2004, and it seemed the primary purpose was to establish a North American marketing arm. As we cover in the chapter on stock investing, the combination of Stillwater and Noril'sk may represent a unique and exceptional investment opportunity because it provides a U.S. vehicle for participation in Russian palladium production and marketing.

If there were attempts to purchase interests in other palladium mines throughout the world, I would move into some speculative positions. Palladium is a very important metal. Global dominance could become a real problem for users and a source of wild speculation!

South African supplies will track the same course as platinum with almost identical mine development. Although some areas have more palladium-rich ore, expect the emphasis to remain with platinum and gold unless palladium morphs into a dominant industrial role. Two regions with the most potential for boosting palladium supplies were North America and Indonesia. Both Canada and the United States had significant palladium mine developments, as mentioned in Chapter 8. North American Palladium in Canada represented a beginning with estimated annual capacity of 2,400 tons of ore per day in 1997. By 2003, processing exceeded 15,000 tons per day. Several million ounces in reserves are located in the Ile de Lac region where the mine is located. Originally, analysis indicated that ore yielded 95 percent palladium with only 5 percent in other metals. Ratios have changed in favor of more platinum and gold with only about an 85 percent to 15 percent yield of palladium.

Prospects improved for an area called the "Main High Grade Zone," which the company represented to have 6.6 grams of palladium per ton. This zone has been measured at approximately 12 meters thick and extends several hundred meters. Similar grades are possible throughout the geological formation.

Will wonders never cease? Kalimantan, Indonesia, may represent the most impressive new gold and mineral fields ever discovered. Along with gold reserves that may range from 50 to 150 million ounces, ore analysis reveals potential for palladium production exceeding 1 million ounces per year. Depending on the speed of development, full capacity should be available by 2010. Of course, we cannot be sure about the scope of "full capacity." During the 1950s, geologists believed South African accessible reserves would be depleted within 10 years. . . . "Fooled ya!"

The Pacific Rim represents vast unexplored geological riches. I believe investors can easily see a 400 percent increase in palladium supplies by 2020 and a 10 percent increase each decade thereafter. Figure 9.9 breaks out production from 1990 through 2003.

As with any analysis based on shifting sands, Figure 9.9 does not paint a realistic picture moving forward from 2003 because it fails to consider explosive growth potential in the "other" regions and the possibility that Russia holds far more capacity than has been revealed. Australia, Indonesia, China, Chile, Peru, and a host of other promising regions combine to make this category as impressive as North America and, eventually, South Africa. One projection based on properties cataloged toward the end of 2000 provides the forecast for new-region production illustrated in Figure 9.10.

The bounce in Russian supplies and, hence, total 2004 supplies suggests a resumption of the former trend and output. The combined picture extrapolates total supplies reaching above 10 million ounces within the first decade of the new millennium.

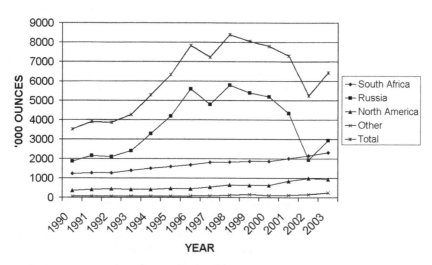

FIGURE 9.9 Palladium production by region shows the dominance of Russia in determining total supplies. Russian restrictions are clearly shown beginning in 1999 through 2001. (*Source:* Johnson Matthey)

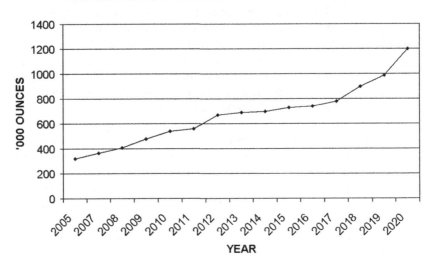

PROJECTION FOR OTHER PALLADIUM PRODUCTION

FIGURE 9.10 Projected palladium production for regions other than South Africa, Russia, and North America shows a potential to reach 1.2 million ounces by 2020. (*Sources:* Johnson Matthey and EQUIDEX, Inc.)

As the chart reveals, new regions are forecast to rival South Africa. If history is our guide, this projection is understated. In the late 1980s, gold production was thought to be at a peak. Not long ago, the earth was believed to be flat!

Scrap recovery is a particularly important supply dimension because palladium auto catalysts were new in the 1980s and 1990s. Since the average fleet life in the United States has been estimated to be seven years, the recovery cycle was timed to significantly increase approximately seven years from 1993. I used this same logic when forecasting platinum recovery. In both instances, the pragmatic prediction is reflected by the data. As seen in Figure 9.11, palladium recovery began accelerating by 1996. Notice the increasing slope from 1999 forward. This trend is destined to continue based on the former and continuing growth in palladium auto catalysts.

Figure 9.12 plots supply and demand and provides a perspective from 1990 forward. Like platinum, the balance is almost uncanny, with a near match from 1990 through 1995. Interestingly, projections for both supply and demand show the same close proximity for each curve. This is extremely important for the price dynamic. As with platinum, any supply disruption can immediately send palladium spiraling to new highs. This was

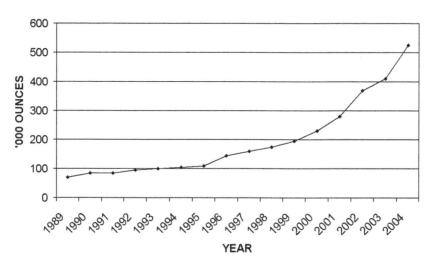

FIGURE 9.11 Palladium recover will grow to be an increasing source of supply as indicated by the rapidly accelerating trend. (*Source:* Johnson Matthey)

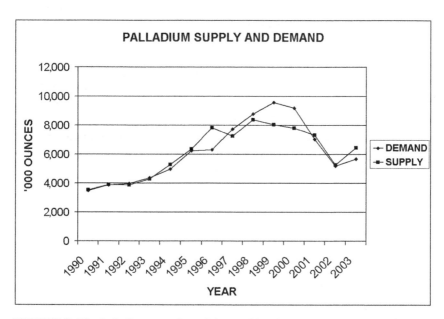

FIGURE 9.12 Palladium supply and demand has been extremely tight. This is why palladium remains vulnerable to extreme volatility. (*Source:* Johnson Matthey)

the case in 1997 when Russia suddenly stopped palladium and platinum shipments and again in 1999–2001 with palladium. As previously mentioned in Chapter 8, prices immediately reacted higher. Palladium touched $210 per ounce from its interim consolidation near $150 in 1997 and rocketed above $1,050 an ounce in 2001. These spectacular movements prove how exciting and potentially rewarding palladium trading can be!

CONCLUSION

It should be apparent that platinum-group metals offer excellent long-term potential for price appreciation. Although computerized vehicle pollution control systems threaten to obviate auto catalysts to an extent, I do not foresee a significant decline in the use of converters well into the twenty-first century. The mandate for zero emissions in California and New York will turn attention to alternative transportation, which may include commercially feasible electric cars and trucks. Again, such prospects extend well into the twenty-first century.

Unlike silver, platinum-group metals have a strong industrial foundation because available amounts are substantially smaller and technological alternatives less prominent. Digital photography can easily assume the premier role for snapshots and newsprint pictures, sharply decreasing demand for silver. No such decline in palladium use looms close on the horizon as of this writing.

Palladium also offers unique opportunities for the stock investor because there are publicly traded primary palladium mines like North American Palladium (on the Nasdaq Small Cap Market)) and Stillwater Mining. I expect to see more palladium companies as the popularity and necessity of this metal continues to grow. Palladium may not have gold's appeal and long-standing reverence. However, in a modern industrial society palladium can perform better than gold, as we have seen!

CHAPTER 10

Investing
in Stocks

A lthough a less direct means of acquiring precious metals, one of the most popular ways to participate is through stocks of producing companies. It is not the purpose of this book to recommend specific stocks by naming particular companies that are good buys. By the time any book goes to press and is digested, corporate structures can change, as can the economic environment. However, certain fundamentals should remain in place as long as precious metals markets remain open and free. Efficient producers will have good equity performance. The evaluation of precious metals companies requires the same attention as does an examination of a food, computer, or drug producer. What is the product? Does the company exclusively produce gold, silver, or platinum-group metals? Are precious metals coincidental to the production of other base metals? How is the product positioned? Who manages the company, and what is his or her management style? What are costs relative to revenues? What are prospects for profit margins?

Because most of this book is dedicated to evaluating metals as products, there is no need for repetition. However, there are subtle areas worth exploring. For example, how are gold, silver, platinum, and palladium marketed? We have identified various uses, but are there active efforts to sell precious metals? Then we should touch on cost structures. Can we define cost for an ounce of gold or silver? Finally, we should look at capital structures that reveal the price of entering the precious metals business and the attractiveness of mergers and acquisitions. Will investors see a trend toward new mining companies or a move to consolidate? Through the 1990s, several large mining companies went into "merger mania." The economics of mining forced alliances between former competitors. Politics played an increasing role in securing mineral rights in foreign territories. All these developments influence stock performance.

MARKETING

Precious metals are promoted by trade groups, retailers, and governments more than by individual producing companies. It is rare to see an advertisement by a mining company touting virtues of gold, silver, or platinum-group metals. Instead, ads and marketing campaigns are placed by the World Gold Council, the Silver Institute, the United States Treasury, government mints, coin and bullion dealers, and jewelry manufacturers. Producing companies may conduct image campaigns to promote stock values; however, the product is not the focal point. Investors should examine marketing efforts as a whole against specific corporate positions to determine whether a stock represents a good value.

Throughout the years, various trade groups have marketed precious metals based on traditional perceptions. If you read research reports from these institutions, you will see a heavy bias toward projecting higher prices. Regardless of reality, trade groups are supposed to be optimistic. In the precious metals area, "up" is an essential attitude. The World Gold Council and similar organizations receive funding from members who are producers. Marketing strategies center around "telling the story" of why precious metals are good investments. When economic environments favor metals, there is a tendency to see more advertising and marketing. Spokespeople frequently appear on television and radio programs to paint positive pictures. As an adjunct activity, public relations efforts reach out to the stock brokerage community to make sure precious metals companies are properly represented.

Monitoring these marketing activities is important. There is a correlation between efforts made by trade groups and the acceptance of their members' stock offerings. When the senior metals analyst of Prudential Bache is convinced that silver is a good investment, customers flock to futures, options, individual stocks, and precious metals mutual funds. This additional demand can translate into better near-term performance. By the same logic, if perception is negative, investors will seek alternatives more aggressively. Most prospective investors have seen advertising for silver, gold, and platinum. Small ads appear in the *Wall Street Journal* and *Investor's Business Daily* offering one-ounce coins and even five-pound blocks of silver. This marketing helps maintain a steady interest in metal at the retail investment level. Jewelry marketing is equally important for promoting retail sales volume. Consider the amount of metal consumed by the jewelry sector. The more popular jewelry with high metal content becomes, the better prices will be supported.

Investors do not always make the connection between a Rolex watch advertisement and gold or platinum values. Yet a strong influence exists. Ads for solid 18-karat gold Rolex watches market large quantities of gold. Kmart/Sears, J. C. Penney, Wal-Mart, Consumers Distributors, and hosts of other chain stores can move significant quantities of gold chain, pendants, earrings, rings, bracelets, bangles, lockets, silver jewelry, and watches. When these retail giants run jewelry specials they become marketing arms for mining companies.

Occasionally, the World Gold Council or Silver Institute will run advertising. However, these trade associations provide more fundamental marketing in the form of brochures, informative pamphlets, and research reports. In fact, this book contains information derived from these excellent data sources. During inflationary periods, trade associations and groups help to keep precious metals in the limelight. During times of monetary stability, the concentration is on maintaining awareness about the virtues of precious metals.

The truly exemplary performance of gold mining stocks and mutual funds during most of the 1990s changed some marketing philosophies. Companies realized the investment trend was too strongly entrenched in paper asset accumulation. This made it practical to market the precious metals business as much as the products. Many mining companies hired public relations firms to address issues like environmental concerns, job growth, economic contributions to communities, and profitability. The mining community seized the opportunity to market its business and attract investors, fund managers, and financial consultants.

COST STRUCTURES

A curious phenomenon took place from 1987 forward. Just after the October 1987 "Black Monday" crash, gold stocks began leading industry performances. Yet, interest in gold itself was static moving through the 1990s. Why would gold stocks move higher while gold was unable to break out of a moderate trading range? A combination of excellent marketing and increasing operational efficiency provides the answer. The average world price for extracting an ounce of gold was declining. Figure 10.1 provides a graph of estimated extraction costs in U.S. dollars through the year 2000.

The representation provides a view of overall efficiency; however,

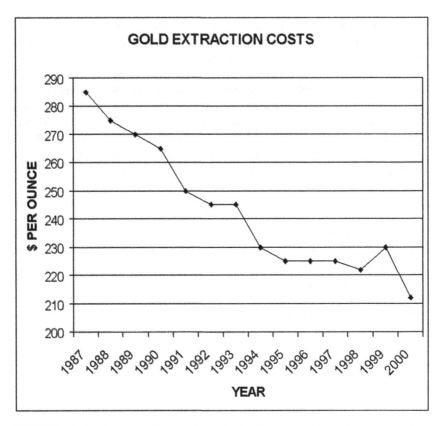

FIGURE 10.1 The cost of extracting gold has been steadily declining since the 1980s despite inflation. (*Source:* U.S. Bureau of Mines, MacKay School of Mines, Newmont Mining)

some variation is due to changes in dollar parity and very low interest rates from 2000 through 2004. Although there is a practical limit to the near-term decline in extraction costs, we cannot know what new technologies may yield in efficiency and cost reduction.

The slope of the cost curve decline is likely to flatten, and may even begin rising over the next few decades. Yet, the decline in costs helps explain how a gold company can perform well even as prices decline; the decrease in costs was so dramatic that it actually offset any price weakness. This same situation held true for silver and, to a lesser extent, the platinum-group metals. In the case of platinum and palladium, recovery from old catalysts and components accounted for a decrease in average prices while mining costs remained relatively firm. Silver production was estimated to cost between $0.50 per ounce and approximately $5 per ounce. The Mackay School of Mines, University of Nevada, released a 1995 report entitled "The U.S. Gold Industry 1994," which analyzed 1994 cash costs for U.S. gold mines in terms of:

Extraction	$107
Processing	84
Administration	18
Royalties	4
Taxes	9
Total	$232 per ounce

This was an average estimate and carried projections for reductions in extraction costs because of increasing efficiency. A trend toward lower cost was aided by lower interest rates and computerized administrative operations. In 1994, 11 mines had estimated operating costs below $200 per ounce, whereas 38 mines were at less than $300 per ounce. Compare these costs to an average price that exceeded $360 per ounce.

As long as technology pushes the efficiency envelope forward, we should expect healthy stock performance. Gold stocks, in particular, offer a double-edged protection and appreciation incentive. First, gold production is profitable. Then, the product offers the ultimate hedge against a monetary meltdown. This combination makes gold stocks and mutual funds fundamentally attractive. Because other precious metals are associated with gold production, there is some participation for silver and the platinum group. However, most of the stock emphasis has been on gold. It is important to recognize that costs for gold are not always directly correlated with silver, platinum, and palladium. Precious metals that come from primary copper, nickel, lead, tin, and zinc have significantly different cost allocations.

Suppose you are considering investing in stocks. When you conduct your research, try to determine how costs are allocated. What is the cost per ounce, and how does it compare with alternatives? As previously mentioned, there are many types of mines. From deep-shaft properties that have dominated in South Africa to surface mines like those in South Carolina, costs will be substantially different. If you are inclined to maintain a dynamic portfolio to seek maximum performance, then monitoring cost structures will be extremely important. Keep track of each property acquisition and type. It is also important to associate base and precious metal production. Make sure you evaluate nickel, copper, and other mines in conjunction with companies that are exclusively focused on gold, silver, or the platinum group.

It is often difficult to determine which metals lead profit margins. For example, when copper has a cost of $0.50 per pound and a selling price of $1.20, it is easy to understand why by-product silver might be sacrificed. If silver is at $30 per ounce, copper might become secondary to extracting precious metals. Demand stability for base metals' prospective growth indicates precious metals will remain the by-product through the foreseeable future. Therefore, you should concentrate on overall efficiency rather than allocations for precious metals. Keep an eye on political changes that might affect royalty rates and taxes. Never forget that governments are always the partner in any business, especially mining.

Not all annual reports specify cost per ounce for gold, silver, platinum, or palladium. As reviewed, some companies may actually list a negative cost of production depending on the primary material being mined and the cost allocation used. A careful examination of the balance sheet and notes can give a reasonable perspective. It is frequently a good idea to review analysis provided by brokerage firms that follow specific companies. I say this cautiously since many investors have a distrust for brokerage research because New York Attorney General Eliot Spitzer revealed corruption in research departments of major firms. The scandal was concentrated in the telecom area, but the tarnish remains, nonetheless.

Certainly, mutual fund managers are involved in cost analysis for the precious and base metals industries. This makes mutual fund investment efficient and, perhaps, less risky. There are hundreds of cost factors to consider when evaluating individual stocks. For most of us, there is neither enough time nor sufficient resources to conduct as complete a research job as do professional managers. Still, the exercise is often fun and worth the effort for those inclined to go it alone.

CAPITAL STRUCTURE

Mining is generally an expensive business. Capital investment has been a barrier to new entries in modern mining companies. However, there have been exciting discoveries and stock issues that prove there is still room for new players. Two categories warrant special attention. Established companies with proven reserves and track records make up the industry's foundation. Small exploration and development companies provide a second tier.

Nothing illustrates market potential and danger as well as the 1995–1996 introduction of Bre-X. This Canadian upstart managed to hype a property with initial estimated reserves exceeding 70 million ounces of gold. Politics and capital structure forced Bre-X into a joint venture with Freeport-McMoRan. With more intrigue than a spy thriller or adventure movie, Bre-X unfolded into one of the greatest scams in recent stock market history. Once the alignment with Freeport-McMoRan took place, new surveys revealed almost no gold on the Bre-X property. Millions in stock value instantly evaporated.

When the Bre-X "find" was initially announced in 1996, I appeared on CNBC to comment on its potential impact on gold prices. In my five-minute appearance, I concentrated on two points. First, I was skeptical about the huge reserve estimates because my research indicated that several reputable mining companies had been exploring the area with far less spectacular results. Caution was in order. Then, I said gold prices would not be significantly affected because production would take time to develop. I was correct on both counts.

You may have drawn the same conclusion. A small amount of research showed the Bre-X situation was questionable. Frankly, I was at a loss to understand how so many experts bought into the Bre-X story.

Small start-up companies can give investors an exciting ride, but you must always be careful. Be wary of sensational stories about discoveries and gold-laden properties. For example, my own investigations suggest some of the projections for various new companies have been overstated. That's marketing! If it were so easy to find gold, the metal would be worthless, or certainly worth less! However, new companies can yield exceptional profits if they are in the right place at the right time with the correct incentives and ethics. Investing in the stock of small start-up companies is serious business. All too often, we take promotional literature at face value. Here is a checklist to follow if you are solicited for such an investment:

- Take the time and make the effort to check with authorities about the company being offered and the brokerage firm making the offer. Never commit to an investment by telephone unless you have had an opportunity to review facts and verify sources.
- Consider the nature of the offering. Where is the company located? Is it incorporated in the United States, Canada, or within a member nation of the European Union? If it is a South American or African company, make sure it is properly registered with authorities. Ask for geological surveys and assessments. If none are available, that is a red flag!
- New discoveries are likely to be in undeveloped regions. Consider political environments. Is the government stable? Is the company well connected?

- Be practical in your commitment. Never overextend and always view investments in small or start-up companies as speculative. Never put day-to-day living capital on the line; invest only your risk capital.

If you follow these four guidelines, you should eliminate some of the exposure associated with new companies and stock issues. No checklist is perfect. Even well-established companies stumble and fall.

I simply urge investors to be extra careful of the so-called great deals. Low-priced stocks can present opportunities, as was the case for Royal Gold, Inc., of Colorado. But we see examples like Capital Hill Gold, Inc. (CHGI), which was touted as having a significant property named the "Mexican Hat." Like Bre-X, the company received notoriety when Placer Dome allegedly released impressive surveys covering the property's potential. However, the measurements were not in accordance with industry standards. The stock experienced wild swings. All the while, the company was being admonished by the British Columbia Securities Commission in Canada. The company was heavily promoted on the Internet by sites like Undervalued.com.

Toward the end of the 1990s there was a series of mergers and acquisitions among the large mining companies. Most notable was the four-way "Pac-Man" involving Barrick Gold, Placer Dome, Homestake, and Santa Fe Pacific Gold. This marked the continuation of a powerful industry trend toward capital consolidation. Whether this extends or dissipates remains a question for the future. But no company is beyond merging or being acquired. Such consolidations represent enormous profit opportunities. Properties, technology, and capital can combine to double and triple values, or even multiply them by greater amounts. In 1996 I recommended a portfolio consisting of highly diversified entities. In the United States there were:

Newmont Mining
Freeport-McMoRan
Santa Fe Pacific Gold
Royal Gold (small cap)

In Canada the firms were:

Barrick Gold Corporation
Placer Dome, Inc.
Noranda, Inc.
Lac Minerals, Ltd.
BP Minerals Limited

In South Africa I recommended:

Anglo American, PLC

GFSA (Gold Fields of South Africa merged with Gencor, Ltd.)

JCI (Johannesburg Consolidated Investment Company, Ltd.)

Randgold Resources Limited

In Australia, the following were recommended:

Normandy Poseidon Limited

North Limited

Gold Fields Limited

Plutonic Resources Limited

These were primarily gold-producing companies. This group performed well compared to other equity sectors. In the eight years since my initial recommendations, some names merged along with operations. Other names disappeared entirely. My prediction that mergers and acquisitions would continue came to fruition. The dynamic nature of precious metals mining represents a healthy environment. Unlike industries where consolidations represent weakness, mining achieves economies of scale with size and financial prowess.

Thus, regardless of precious metals' prices, the facts clearly showed a new precious metals bonanza was on the horizon through the 1980s and 1990s into the new millennium. Profitability expanded along with incentives to improve technology and increase properties. The trend remains strong for virtually all precious metals except, perhaps, primary silver mining. This is not to say prospects for silver have discouraged production; it is simply that primary silver mining is limited to countries like Chile, Mexico, and Peru.

Although we have not examined copper, lead, tin, zinc, and other base metal mining operations, these metals have exhibited exhilarating trends of their own. Volatility in base metals can translate into good or bad stock performances. Generally, metals are considered economically sensitive. A booming consumer economy demands greater amounts of base metals. Weak economies slow consumption in housing, transportation, electronics, and packaging. Just as recycling impacts platinum and palladium, it can take a toll on metals like aluminum and tin. Recycled aluminum from cans costs a fraction of the virgin metal. The efficiency of collecting and recycling placed the entire industry into near crisis because prices could not support primary production.

Thus, the metals industry is extremely dynamic and interwoven. This suggests any approach to equity investment should follow basic rules that apply to all industry groups. I believe an expanding world economy translates into profit potential. While there are bound to be bumps in the road, metal is here to stay. Mining, processing, and marketing companies should perform well in stock portfolios.

Since the publication of *The New Precious Metals Market*, I have received hundreds of letters, e-mails, and phone calls from investors about various companies. I receive tout sheets from new as well as established companies about project development and income potential. What has been striking is the superficial nature of investor inquiries. More frequently than not, the discussion begins with, "I received this tip about . . . " The tip might consist of some new property being developed or some new "more efficient" extraction process. When I ask about the corporate structure, balance sheet, property rights, long-term plans, and projections, there is usually silence at the other end of the phone, e-mail, chat, or whatever.

Even when I attend investment symposiums and seminars, the discussions are the same. It is not just true of precious metals concerns. I have had the same discussions about agricultural and energy investments. Whether it is oil and gas, a gold mine, or an alleged cold fusion breakthrough, it seems the sizzle is what gets our attention, whereas the steak always remains in the kitchen. For this reason, I would like to review the who, what, when, where, and why (the five Ws) as they relate to real-world examples.

Newmont Mining, "The Gold Company" (New York Stock Exchange symbol ASX), is (by its own admission) the world's largest gold producer. Right away, you have some important information. As the largest gold producer, Newmont is clearly not an object of speculation. This is an established company with properties on five continents and a highly diversified metals business. When you inquire about Newmont, there is an entire book of information available for download from its web site. This *Information Handbook* spans more than 200 pages and is far more comprehensive than even the content of this book. It is really a primer in how a gold mine operates.

The advantage of doing business with Newmont is its operational transparency. The company provides all the vital information that permits you to make an educated decision about the value of Newmont stock. In addition, a company like Newmont is like an insatiable giant that must constantly find new sources of food—hence, new properties. Future success requires constant exploration and partnering. This brings up an interesting adjunct. Companies like Newmont frequently partner with other companies that may be small or large. These relationships can represent separate and distinct investment opportunities. If you are looking for that penny stock with true appreciation potential, examine low-cap stocks that have partner or royalty deals with a company like Newmont, Freeport-Mc-MoRan, Noranda, and the like.

When you examine the properties under development, you can identify the major new gold-producing regions with the highest potentials. Hence, if there are stakeholders within the regions being pursued by Newmont, they may offer investment opportunities. Of course, a great deal of secrecy remains when it comes to new discoveries. Still, a company like Newmont is not likely to risk its entire reputation by releasing questionable surveys or sensational projections.

This is not to say that a large and well-respected company will never become involved in a scam. Recall Bre-X. They were being examined by the copper and gold giant, Freeport-McMoRan. The twist was that initial core samples were reported by the Bre-X geologists. Once Freeport became more closely involved, the story quickly unraveled. Thus, the involvement of a reputable name in the beginning should not be taken as a sign of security. Always make sure that there is more than just an interest by a large concern. If the deal is not done, doubt remains.

As of 2004, Newmont reported equity interests in Nevada; Ontario, Canada; and Sonora, Mexico. These North American properties represented 39 percent of Newmont's global production and reserves. The projection was for the sale of 2.8 million ounces of gold at $280 per ounce. In two sentences, investors gain a sense of operational depth. Each of Newmont's operations can be researched in detail. In contrast, look at some of the small-cap issues that promise to bring huge returns based on a single find. These are speculations. Consider the huge capital costs associated with developing a mining property. If you are examining a small company, pay *very careful attention* to the capital structure, balance sheet, and financial backing. If there is a partner, make sure it is a *real* partner with substantial financial and capital resources.

One of the least understood aspects of precious metals mining is the implementation of hedges and forward contracts. Unfortunately, there is an automatic tendency to assume that higher gold prices will lead to higher earnings. However, mining companies do not speculate with their production. If projected production is hedged, it means that the gold, silver, platinum, or palladium has been sold in advance of production at the then prevailing price. Thus, if the price moves higher, the company *does not benefit*. The hedge generates a loss against inventory.

As an example, suppose gold is selling at $450 per ounce. The mining company has a cost of production of $225 to produce a net margin of $225 per ounce. If the company sells futures against production at $450 per ounce and the price goes to $500, there is a $50 loss on the futures position. At the same time, the company has a $50 gain on its inventory that can either be delivered against the futures position or sold for cash as the futures contract is covered (closed out). If gold drops from $450 to $400, the *short* futures gain $50 while the inventory experiences a $50 decline. The effect is to *lock in* $450 as the selling price.

The purpose of a hedge is to insure a known price. The company does not want to speculate on the price of gold moving forward. However, hedging limits upside potential in a bull market. For this reason, the hedge policy of any company—large or small—is critical to its bottom-line performance. To be sure, companies do make educated assumptions about the general direction of their products. When gold is in a cyclical or secular uptrend, savvy management reduces forward selling and hedging. When hedging is reduced in a rising market, the bottom line does, indeed, gain. However, if a hedge is not in place during a falling market, the bottom line can suffer. When there is extreme volatility, even the most nimble hedge manager can get caught. Admittedly, some of my income is derived from consulting services I provide regarding price forecasting and trading strategies.

With an understanding of hedge policy, it is easy to see why a company's performance may lag rising prices. In fact, if a company is over-hedged, it can lose its competitive position and significantly decline relative to industry peers. If you look at the hedge and forward commitments, you can determine when earnings might break out. Precious metals represent one of the few industries where the price does not impact production costs.

While Newmont is the largest gold producer, Freeport-McMoRan Copper & Gold, Inc. (symbol FCX) is one of the largest copper producers in the world. As a consequence of Freeport's significant copper mining operations, it is, as its name states, a large gold producer. One advantage associated with Freeport is the diversity over two major metals that respond to different fundamentals. As such, Freeport can enjoy bull markets in copper or gold or both. Recall my earlier discussion of the potential inverse relationship between base metal and by-product production. Reviewing, it is possible for surging copper prices to encourage expanding copper capacity. As a consequence, gold output will proportionately grow. If gold fundamentals are weak, the increased gold capacity could have a price-dampening effect despite copper's strength.

A company producing only gold cannot benefit from strength in copper or other base metals associated with ancillary gold production. Assume China's growth accelerates and we see a significant demand increase for copper, lead, zinc, and nickel. Prices inflate for these base metals and the rush is on to create more capacity. In the meantime, demand for gold has waned. (Remember, this is hypothetical. Don't panic!) Under such circumstances, the base metal stock is likely to outperform a gold-only stock. This is why Freeport may be a good addition to a diversi-fied precious metals stock portfolio.

Another advantage held by Freeport is its political relationship with Indonesia. As mentioned, this is a region that holds impressive precious metals potential. Whenever a company deals with multinational mineral rights, a strong political position is extremely important. Freeport has been able to advantageously negotiate everything from compensation funds for local populations to government work contracts.

Freeport boasted the "lowest production costs" for copper at about 8 cents per pound in 2002. However, this cost is based on applying precious metal credits against operating costs for copper. Recall that it is possible for a company to post negative costs when allocating by-product income toward cost reduction.

Extending our examples of gold mining companies, Barrick Gold (stock symbol ABX) is another giant that offered unique advantages as of 2004. Key features included excellent property diversification mov-ing forward with projects in Peru, Australia, Argentina, and Chile. Bar-rick also boasted solid properties in the United States, Canada, and Tanzania. In 2003, the company produced 5.5 million ounces of gold at a $189 per ounce cash cost. In addition, it estimated reasonably accessi-ble reserves of 86 million ounces at the end of 2003. On top of these en-ticing features, Barrick had zero net debt and approximately $1 billion in cash.

Understand that this is a snapshot as of 2003–2004. *No company re-mains static!* The purpose of this review is to illustrate that Barrick has important characteristics:

- Excellent properties moving forward.
- Powerful cash position to facilitate acquisitions, exploration, capital equipment upgrades, leveraging, and derivatives trading.
- Diversity over several regions.
- Low per-ounce cash cost.
- Large estimated reserves.

These are excellent ingredients when evaluating any stock, which brings us to the sixth largest gold mining company as of the end of 2004. Placer Dome dates back to 1910. Like Barrick, Placer maintained a strong bal-ance sheet with almost $7 billion in assets at the end of 2004. Although one might consider Placer to be a replication of Barrick, there was a new emphasis on copper and silver moving forward from 2000. Thus, Placer was between Freeport and Barrick. In 2004, Placer was expecting to pro-duce 400 million pounds of copper and approximately 3.6 million ounces of gold.

However, one of the challenges facing Placer was the development of its South Deep mine located on the Witwatersrand Basin in South Africa. Recall my comments about labor and the potential impact of the AIDS pandemic. A significant percentage of the available labor force was affected by AIDS, which presented two problems. The most obvious is the diminishing workforce. The second is the economic burden of sustaining those already infected and unable to work. This problem extends to all African properties inclusive of Placer's North Mara mine in Tanzania.

A balancing wheel existed in the larger Canadian and United States holdings. Placer had a 60 percent ownership interest in the U.S. Cortez mine that had 3.2 million ounces in estimated gold reserves at the end of 2004. Additional properties boosted reserves to the point where healthy operations could be sustained in areas with more stable, albeit more expensive, labor.

Noranda (stock symbol NRD) is an example of a more fully diversified mining company that is one of the major producers of zinc, nickel, copper, lead, aluminum, and consequently gold, silver, platinum, and palladium. Like Freeport, the major advantage of owning a stock like Noranda is its wide product diversity. Not only is there potential when gold and silver move, there is even greater potential during global expansion because demand for base metals is directly linked to such growth. But herein is the vulnerability. Traditionally, a stock like Noranda has been linked to the cyclical stocks. This means that the stock is supposed to correlate to economic cycles of boom and bust. The stock is presumed to do well in a boom and poorly during a recession.

This raises an interesting question as the third millennium progresses. Throughout the ages we have seen structural economic changes that have permanently altered relationships and rules. Globalization is just such a structural change that may have diminished the cyclical correlation associated with raw material companies, and particularly mining companies. The classic boom/bust cycle attributed to capitalism ran into some theoretical anomalies beginning with the Nixon-era stagflation. The assumed relationship between high inflation and high economic activity was contradicted by energy sector inflation. Suddenly, it was possible to experience high prices and low employment. This phenomenon was cataloged, but never fully dissected.

The 1980s displayed another contradiction when U.S. Federal Reserve Chairman Paul Volcker used high interest rates to combat high inflation. Although that strategy was generally accepted and understood, the assumption was that real estate would suffer along with other interest-rate-sensitive sectors. However, the extremely high interest rates produced windfall profits for fixed income investors and kick-started a financial boom. Real estate did not take the expected hit because of passive pass-through expense rules and positive tax benefits. Capital equipment did not falter as expected because a 20 percent investment tax credit offset the high-interest-rate carrying costs. Of course, when the rules were changed, we saw negative consequences as equipment leasing companies shriveled and sinking real estate values jeopardized the savings and loan industry.

The Clinton era brought about another anomaly of high employment and near zero inflation. This was partly attributed to a shift away from military budgeting toward domestic budgeting as the Cold War came to an end. For the first time in decades, the U.S. experienced a true peacetime economy. More importantly, the Cold War's end marked the beginning of a new movement toward capitalism in the Eastern bloc and China. Herein is the possible root of cyclical change.

With a global move toward capitalist structure, raw materials might achieve a minimum steady state that preserves mining company operating margins. Yes, there will still be periods of greater and lesser demand. But bottom-line performance may not be subject to the same severity during expansions and recessions. Further, the length of recessions may be shortened, benefiting a company like Noranda.

Every single metal in Noranda's portfolio is hugely important for global economic growth. This places Noranda in a powerful position as long as management remains diligent and sound.

Many years ago, I became acquainted with Royal Gold, Inc., a Colorado-based precious metals royalty company (stock symbol RDLG). At the time, Royal Gold had promising properties, but lacked the capital to develop without major assistance. Rather than bet the farm of a single-handed venture, Royal Gold developed royalty relationships that provided participation in the properties without the lead time and risk associated with self-development. The result has been a unique structure and philosophy that takes advantage of precious metals value while remaining highly mobile to develop royalty deals between property owners and mining companies.

I must admit that I found the company intriguing enough to add to my own portfolio. Although I have divested my holdings, I illustrate this company because it brings another approach to the table and presents a different risk profile when designing a diversified mining stock portfolio. As of this writing, the majority of Royal Gold's royalty properties were located in Nevada. There was a particularly interesting royalty with Coeur d'Alene Mines Corporation's (stock symbol CDE) Martha Silver Mine in the Santa Cruz province of Argentina. As of 2004, Coeur was the largest primary silver mine and was seeking to move beyond silver to diversify its base.

Coeur represented an aggressive company that promoted a quasi-speculative stance by *not hedging*. One reason for adopting this strategy was Coeur's projected lower silver production costs. As of 2004, Coeur's cash costs were approximately $3.81 per ounce of silver. Without a hedge, the company could take full advantage of silver's appreciation during 2003–2004 and, presumably, moving forward. I emphasize that these company profiles are snapshots that illustrate an analytical approach and do not represent investment recommendations or advice.

The higher the profit margin, the greater the royalty. This means that the benefits of Coeur accrue to Royal Gold. Royal Gold does not have the same direct exposure related to nonhedged positions. As of this writing, Royal Gold had exploration projects in Greece and Bulgaria in addition to Argentina.

In 2004, Coeur stock was trading between $3.00 and $7.70. For investors who believe in the "greater upside" principle, the lower stock price alone represents an attraction. However, the 2004 ride was generally in the downward direction based on negative net earnings. Price volatility and timing resulted in less than ideal selling prices, while capital and property development ate into earnings.

The company projected a 40 percent increase in silver production from 2004 levels and a 75 percent increase in gold by 2006. By the time this book is widely read, these numbers will have been tested. Coeur's eventual success is grounded in two essential components: first and foremost, the relative price of silver and gold to production costs, and second, property development. The balance between developing properties and earning positive cash flow is not so easy. In addition, there was the potential for hard times as silver makes a transition away from photography and into new consumption trends.

For investors interested in Coeur's position as the largest operator of primary silver mines, there was no other choice as of 2004–2005. With the no-hedge policy in mind, Coeur represents a more powerful link between precious metals prices and stock performance. However, the buffer between declining metal prices and stock value is found in production volume. As long as Coeur maintains a strong growth curve and low cost structures, increasing output can offset falling prices and, thus, create a positive stock performance despite a declining silver or gold market.

A Canadian company I mentioned that began as Madeleine Mines became North American Palladium. I must admit to personal ownership since the company's original offerings dating back to when palladium was selling for less than $100 per ounce! This is one of my own "hot tip" stories and illustrates the process of evaluating, deciding, encountering pitfalls, and experiencing resurrection.

I received a call from a fellow named Wynn Wozobski who worked in Merrill Lynch's Private Client Group out of the Tulsa, Oklahoma, office. One of his clients was Kaiser-Francis Oil Company, a large independent oil and gas producer out of his area who was heavily involved in a start-up called Madeleine Mines. Wynn heard of me because I was working with Merrill Lynch's managed commodity funds department on a relationship that never materialized. Nonetheless, Wynn described Madeleine's operations and explained that the stock was available on the Toronto Stock Exchange, priced in Canadian dollars. The exchange rate was favorable and I could participate at an opportune time, in his opinion.

At the time, Wynn had a few things going for him. Most important was his position at Merrill Lynch. Mind you, this was way before New York's attorney general, Eliot Spitzer, justifiably cast aspersion on the research and sales departments of the large investment firms! Wynn also gave me access to the corporate insiders—not for inside information (heaven forbid), but for a solid look at the company's operations, philosophy, and plans for moving ahead.

Coincidentally, I was already involved in trading palladium, which I concluded was underpriced. (That's another story about how I almost went broke buying palladium futures as the price dropped from $98 to below $70.) After investigating Madeleine's backers and the Lac des Iles stake in northwestern Ontario, I decided to take the plunge. The stock was under $1 U.S. if I recall correctly. My reasoning was partly my misguided futures speculation that eventually proved correct and positive feedback about the Lac des Iles mineral deposits. Besides, the most I could lose if the company went bust was $1 a share. I was not a big player, so my exposure was limited.

Without going into all the details (which would, themselves, fill a book), some friends joined me in my venture and the stock did have a nice run. My buddies took profits and I stayed in—only to watch my gains dissipate into a loss. The company became entangled in complex litigation and some foreign properties. Things did not look good. Again I emphasize that my exposure was limited to a moderate position. Admittedly, my broker on the transaction was not Wynn because Merrill Lynch was not keen on a potential fund manager having an open stock account with its Private Client Group. So I used a relative. When the stock appeared to tank, he laughed, "You should have bailed!" Ah, 20/20 hindsight.

Cutting to the chase, Madeleine became North American Palladium, litigation was settled, and the main property revealed more potential than originally accessed. After a long holding period, the stock finally came into its own.

By 2004–2005, North American Palladium was a stronger company with 2.9 to 3.4 million ounces in estimated palladium reserves and complementary amounts of gold and platinum. The main objective was cost reduction and increasing volume. The company experienced ongoing capital equipment problems that continuously frustrated shareholders who anxiously awaited the big breakout. I am sure management was equally if not more frustrated.

Leaving my personal story behind, anyone evaluating North American Palladium needs to consider:

- Current debt structure.
- Plans for further development of a new underground mine.
- Hedging policy.
- Prospects for palladium and platinum prices.
- Possibility of a merger.
- Outlook beyond current reserves.

If North American Palladium is to have staying power, the obvious question is, "What happens when reserves are exhausted?" This projects to 2015 unless there are significant new finds. Like many properties, the Lac des Iles geology supports an assumption that there is more metal within the area held or prospected by the company.

A shot of profitability could come from a more aggressive hedging policy that appeared to be indicated in the 2003 annual report implying no new hedges were being placed in anticipation of average spot prices above the lowered production costs. However, the 2005 palladium outlook released by Johnson Matthey on November 16, 2004, anticipated an expanded palladium surplus exceeding 1 million ounces with a lower price boundary of $150 per ounce. This raised a question about profits because the 2003 annual report boasted cost reductions from $264 per ounce in 2002 to $175 in 2003. Although the 33.7 percent year-over-year cost reduction was impressive, a decline to $150 per ounce still puts spot palladium below cost by $25!

Depending on exploration and efficiency, the company could be targeted by a larger concern and the associated stock play could be exciting and profitable. The company has been recognized by Johnson Matthey as a major North American producer. With the purchase of a majority interest in the Stillwater Mining Company in Montana by Russia's Noril'sk Nickel, North American Palladium stood alone as an independent company as of 2004.

Examining palladium fundamentals in the previous chapter, we know the supply and demand balance remained extremely delicate. The possibility of another Russian squeeze, coupled with North American

Palladium's attempt to limit hedging, could result in spectacular performance. Many shareholders were supremely disappointed when the stock failed to skyrocket as palladium prices soared above $1,000 per ounce. Hedges can be a limiting factor. Imagine if there are no hedges in a huge bull market!

As briefly mentioned in Chapter 9, the second largest palladium producer in North America as of 2004 was the Stillwater Mining Company in Stillwater, Montana. Before North American Palladium, Stillwater was the *only* palladium mine in the region.

Interest in Stillwater reached a peak when a joint venture between Chevron Resources and Engelhard Minerals promised more infrastructure investment. At long last, it seemed Stillwater would reach its full potential. However, palladium prices faded and the economic feasibility of expanding operations fizzled.

Timing has not been ideal because there is a long lead time for developing mine capacity. Just when Stillwater had the right price environment, prices seemed to collapse. The purchase of a majority interest by Noril'sk presents an interesting hybrid ownership that could represent the better of two worlds, so to speak. While Russia was making the transition toward capitalism, political instability represented excessive risk for mainstream investors. First, the ruble was not widely traded in currency markets. Second, Russian companies lacked financial transparency and trustworthy accounting standards.

This foreclosed confidently participating in Russia's stock market at the beginning of the twenty-first century. However, Stillwater represents a unique blend of Russia and the United States. The stock is priced in U.S. dollars, eliminating the risk of an unhedged ruble position. Since Stillwater is a U.S. company, investors have the confidence of domestic accounting standards and transparency. Yet, Noril'sk will be providing the ability to participate in a global palladium mining and marketing entity.

When considering that Noril'sk is the number-one producer and Stillwater is the only U.S. palladium facility as of this writing, it is an easy leap to the conclusion that Stillwater has significant appreciation possibilities. Even if the full potential of the mine is not realized, the marketing operations might yield handsome returns if supplied with Noril'sk production. In addition, Noril'sk's backing makes Stillwater a very stable candidate for a diversified precious metals stock portfolio.

Of course, we should not overlook Stillwater's properties. According to the company web site, its 28-mile-long JM Reef in Montana is the highest-grade ore body containing platinum-group metals. In 2003 the company projected platinum-group production to total approximately 615,000 ounces—450,000 from the Stillwater mine and 165,00 ounces from the East Boulder, Colorado, mine. During 2003, production was approximately 428,000 ounces of palladium and platinum, compared to approximately 492,000 ounces in 2002 and approximately 504,000 ounces in 2001.

Stillwater has impressive mineral reserve estimates that have been verified by several core samples and the realized yields for each ton of ore. With more than 35 million ounces held in the ground, the mine has staying power based on its own properties without considering Russian supplementation.

The Stillwater Mining Company's total cash costs were $262 per ounce in 2003 compared to $263 per ounce and $264 per ounce in 2002 and 2001, respectively. These figures were high in comparison to North American Palladium and represented exposure to a decline in palladium spot prices. However, management identified cost cutting as a priority. Investors should watch the cost trends carefully to determine the stability of earnings.

Stillwater also had the most aggressive marketing plan when I reviewed operations. The company was involved in promoting physical metal sales through its adjunct web site and encouraged palladium use in jewelry. Company representatives were even sporting palladium watches to tout the metal's aesthetics.

EXPANDING GLOBAL MARKETS

One striking observation when reviewing various companies is the global nature of precious metals mining. Some of the largest and most profitable mines are located in South Africa, which had the highest platinum and gold reserves as of this writing. Therefore, investors inclined toward stocks must consider the global picture when developing a diversified portfolio. Keep in mind that every region has its own unique cost structures based on labor, ore quality, internal interest rates, currency parity, and political stability.

When you pick up any report on platinum-group metals, you will see names like Anglo Platinum, Impala Platinum, Lonmin, Northam Platinum, Aquarius Platinum, Southern Platinum, Noril'sk Nickel, and more. Of course, as this book ages the names will probably change with mergers, new entries, and expirations. A review of every platinum-group company around the globe is an extensive exercise. The Internet is one of your best resources.

We have reviewed the implied problems of AIDS and the African labor force. AIDS could have a negative impact in Indonesia, Malaysia, and even China and Russia. The flip side is the differential between North American labor in Canada and the United States versus South American labor in

Chile, Peru and Argentina—or labor in Russia, China, Indonesia, and Africa. In 2004, the developed nations had higher labor costs and consequently a disadvantage in controlling overall costs. But as time progresses, other labor markets are bound to tighten, unionize, and move up the wage scale. This is a longer-term process, but some portfolios are, indeed, longer-term.

A critical consideration is the pricing of stocks in the currency of origin. Consider that North American Palladium might double in value in Canadian dollars but decline in U.S. dollars if the Canadian currency slips against the greenback. Thus, foreign companies carry a currency risk. When considering the euro's range against the U.S. dollar, it is not difficult to comprehend the magnitude of this exposure!

MUTUAL FUNDS AND EXCHANGE-TRADED FUNDS

The average investor may not have the time or resources to properly investigate and evaluate each individual stock. I have reviewed a few companies to provide a background for the process rather than the companies. As I have emphasized, any review is a snapshot in time. Company dynamics are just that—*dynamic.* Any number of events can positively or adversely influence company performance and, hence, stock value.

Mutual funds offer an alternative to picking and choosing. There are several metals funds that provide portfolio diversification and professional management. However, investment policies can widely vary between funds and it is extremely important to fully understand the differences and significance. Most notably, many funds invest in physical metal as well as company stocks. There are eight major policy criteria worth examining:

1. Is there diversity? What type of companies make up the fund? Is it an international perspective? If international, is there any currency risk associated with holdings? Is the fund a fund of funds, meaning it invests in other mutual funds or exchange-traded funds (ETFs)?

2. Does the fund invest in physical metal? If so, is it stored in certified depositories that can deliver against futures contracts? Does the company loan metal? If so, how does it determine the loan rate?

3. Does the fund use futures to speculate or hedge? What are the percentages, and how high is the leverage? Where are the futures traded? That is, what exchanges and who are the brokerage firms through which trading is conducted?

4. Does the fund use options on futures or physical metal? If so, what is the objective—hedging or yield enhancement? Does the company write covered calls or buy puts for inventory protection?

5. Does the fund use options on stocks? If so, is it selling options for performance enhancement or buying options for protection?

6. Does the fund sell stocks short for speculation or hedging? What is the leverage policy, and what is the interest rate?

7. Does the fund permit borrowing to create leverage or cover cash shortages?

8. What are the overheads? How is the fund manager compensated?

This is a basic checklist that helps determine a fund's risk profile. You are the ultimate judge of what fits your needs. However, if the purpose of investing in a fund is to participate in the business of producing and selling metal in contrast to owning physical bullion, then you do not want to invest in a fund that allows physical holdings, futures trading, or options on futures trading.

You can find lists of top gold funds in Eaglewing's *Guide to Gold Funds*, which is regularly updated and available on the Internet. The guide's stated purpose is to provide information about gold funds, but not to promote gold as an investment. There are many services that help investors sort out the best fund fit.

Exchange-traded funds are composite stocks representing a group of stocks within an index or a group of sector investments. The advantage of an ETF over a mutual fund is that ETFs trade like stocks; they are shares rather than interests. They trade all day in sessions on various exchanges. Like traditional mutual funds, ETFs must be evaluated based on the eight criteria just listed.

CONCLUSION

Equity participation in precious metals represents an *investment* approach. As mentioned, metals are not really investments because they do not have a yield or dividend. Although I have described how physical metal can earn income through the sale of covered options, the traditional view of investing does not accommodate bullion or coins.

Companies that produce precious metals are like any other companies that manufacture and sell products. The unique aspect is the underlying product's intrinsic value. Recall, nothing else is "as good as gold"—unless it's soaring platinum, palladium, or silver. The advantage to metals stocks is the two-tiered nature of the investment. First, the stocks do well if the company has good performance. Second, the stocks *tend* to do well if precious metals prices are rising.

Stocks and mutual funds have their own risk components that include management, politics, and other factors mentioned. The decision to buy equities in lieu of metals is not necessarily *the* decision, since you can do both. As I have said, the purpose of owning physical metal is in the event of a paper crisis—a confidence meltdown. Like diamonds smuggled during World War II, you might need a hard asset if financial markets become irrational. Under such a scenario, even stocks in precious metals companies can falter.

Thus, stocks and metal are two totally different "investments." Owning physical gold, silver, platinum, and palladium is the ultimate insurance policy against disaster. Owning equities is simply participation in the mining business.

CHAPTER 11

The
Physical Market

S trange as it may sound, even investors who have purchased physical
precious metals as bars, coins, or medallions are not always familiar
with the marketplace that deals in this medium. We might respond
to an ad offering a commemorative medallion struck in silver, gold, or platinum. We may purchase a numismatic coin for its metal content and its rarity as a coin. Less frequently, we buy investment bars in half-ounce and
one-ounce weights. Even less frequently, we might accumulate kilo bars
and multikilo bars. As size and financial commitment increases, the number of experienced investors decreases.

Aside from the casual ownership of a few coins or bars, most investors are not inclined to keep large quantities of metal in their homes
where it is susceptible to loss or theft. Many a stamp, coin, and bullion collection has been lost to fire and other unforeseen personal disasters. Thus,
when considering physical ownership, there are several alternatives. First,
you can lease a safe-deposit box. The immediate drawback is the size of
the box versus the quantity of metal. Yes, gold is dense, and a small safe-
deposit box can house a sizable value when gold is trading above $400 per
ounce or platinum is above $600. Generally, a safe-deposit box is not suffi-
cient for any quantity of silver. Other drawbacks include convenience, security when transferring metal, and appropriation upon death. When you
take physical possession, there is a question of authenticity. When transferred, the metal must usually be assayed for a fee.

Another way to own metal is through a depository or custodian. Your
bullion or coins are stored with the depository or custodian and you receive account statements that verify the amount allocated to you and any

associated charges. Usually, there are fees for storage and insurance. More often than not, the custodian company will be in the precious metals business. For example, FideliTrade Incorporated, located in Wilmington, Delaware, offers a variety of services for investors dealing with physical metal:

- Trading services: buying and selling precious metals bullion.
- Custodial services:

  Commercial omnibus account.

  Commercial custody accounts with subaccounts.

  Investor custody accounts with power of attorney.

  Investor custody accounts without power of attorney.
- Transportation services:

  Deliveries to customers or third parties.

  Federal Express—insured.

  U.S. Postal Service—registered mail, insured, receipts.

  Armored car.

  Personal pickup.

  Receipts from customers or third parties.
- Support services:

  Customer support for tradespeople.

  Private-label telephone services.

  Marketing support.
- Operational support:

  Use of company staffing.

  Report generating.

  Data downloading.

As the list illustrates, FideliTrade offers more than accounts for everyday investors. The majority of the services cater to other companies in the precious metals business. Still, an individual trader can open an account and purchase, store, or trade metal. In fact, my infamous palladium transaction was conducted through a FideliTrade account.

The full range of customer services allowed me to pack up my palladium medallions and ship them directly to FideliTrade via U.S. Postal Service registered mail. The inventory was received, assayed, and sold on my behalf. When the transaction was completed, I asked for payment and receive a check. In reverse, I could have purchased palladium, platinum, silver, or gold bullion. The metal would have been shipped to me via the transport I requested. I would have funds on deposit with FideliTrade and my account would be debited for the transaction.

FideliTrade is a certified depository. There are several types of certification, however; some companies can act as warehouse to commodity exchanges. This is an extra facility that permits an investor to take or make delivery against a futures position. Recall my description of covered option writing. If you own metal on deposit or in the custody of a certified warehouse, it facilitates going into and out of metal when futures contracts expire.

When I was speculating in palladium, I actually took delivery of several hundred ounces by allowing my futures position to expire. I deposited the full contract value with my broker who, in turn, wired the funds to the depository. I provided transportation instruction to the depository for the metal to be shipped to the mint. Everything is checked and double-checked. Dealing in physical metal is very serious. Reputation is all anyone has to go buy. One slipup and a company can be ruined.

Once my account was established, I also used it to purchase U.S. Silver Liberty dollars. Every so often, I would give silver dollars as premiums for my subscription services or as Christmas and Hanukkah presents. The very same silver dollars that were advertised in newspapers and magazines for $29.95 with case were available from FideliTrade at a modest premium over the spot silver price. If I recall correctly, I purchased when silver was under $5 per ounce. They made great gifts and a great impression. Anyone can give $5, $10, or $20 as a Christmas tip, but a silver dollar has the ability to appreciate in value. It may actually be *less expensive* (depending on the spot price), but considered *more valuable*!

When considering a depository, there are credentials worth checking. I mentioned North American Coin and Currency of Phoenix, Arizona, which went out of business when the owner absconded with all the assets! Take the time to determine the following:

- Is the company registered with any regulatory agencies like the National Futures Association, Commodity Futures Trading Commission, state banking authority, or state licensing authority?
- How much insurance coverage does the company have relative to assets held? Is there carrier-independent insurance for shipping and receiving?
- Is the company certified or approved by any commodity exchanges like the COMEX Division of the New York Mercantile Exchange, Chicago Board of Trade, or foreign exchanges?

- Are there any professional association affiliations like the Silver Institute, Gold Institute, and Retailers Association?
- Is there any outstanding litigation, arbitration, or reparations?
- Who are the principals? What is their background?
- What is the privacy policy? Will your name be shared with any other firms?

A company like FideliTrade is more likely to deal with larger investors, traders, wholesalers, and retailers. It is a full-spectrum firm as opposed to the local retail store or even the mail order firms that advertise in newspapers and magazines. You may not know it, but many retailers actually transact their businesses through the facilities of companies like FideliTrade, Moccatta Metals Corporation, and others. They carry corporate accounts and simply request drop shipping from the depository. Given insurance costs and the dangers associated with carrying physical inventories, many retail dealers carry only small display quantities of inventory.

When buying bulk quantities of 100 pieces (coins) or more, I have found cost advantages when dealing with firms like FideliTrade. The spreads are more favorable and there were no extra charges, nor markups on shipping. When testing two identical transactions, I discovered the handling charges could be relatively high.

On the off chance that some readers may be interested in becoming dealers, you will find that the process can be remarkably easy if your custodian is full-service and professional. When precious metals are in the news, or even when there are new issues, wholesale and retail dealing can be exciting, fun, and very profitable. Just check the number of dealers on the Internet! You will want to establish a corporate account. Make sure you can rely on the credentials of your custodian. Some features to shop for include:

- Diversified inventory. There are many different coins of the realm minted in gold, silver, and platinum. You want access to a wide variety so you can fill most customer orders. There are also many different investment bars, bullion, and medallions.
- Telephonic and electronic order processing.
- No-surcharge funds transfer facilities.
- Private labeling and private drop shipping.
- Confidentiality policy.

If you intend to conduct newspaper advertising, check with your newspaper first! Many newspapers as well as television and radio stations will not accept advertising for precious metals because there have been many scams. Find out if you can get an endorsement that will allow you to advertise.

HALLMARK BULLION

Coin of the realm is relatively easy to identify. However, bullion bars that make up those enticing pictures in gold investment brochures come in all sizes from many different regions, mines, and processors. Investment bullion is generally associated with a hallmark emblem that represents the origin. Hallmark bars are uniquely numbered and can be tracked.

A major deficiency in the bullion trade appears to be the lack of a single international hallmark that would streamline physical transactions moving forward. The most powerful argument in favor of a universal hallmark is obvious—it converts physical gold back into a form of exchange. The strongest argument against a universal hallmark and tracking system for physical gold is also obvious—many investors don't want a traceable transaction.

Hallmarking is a very important part of the bullion trade because it is a measure of quality, origin, and authenticity. Some hallmarks carry more credibility than others. There are old or traditional hallmarks and more modern names. Lists of all recognized hallmarks are available through the Internet and trade organizations like the World Gold Council, Silver Institute, and Platinum Guild.

GOLD BULLION SECURITIES

An emerging concept in a world of growing uncertainty is the "bullion security." This is a securitized certificate of deposit whereby your security or stock is represented by deliverable physical metal. The advantages are that you do not store metal, you have liquidity, there is easy market access, you can buy through your regular investment account, metal is fractionalized in quantities as small as one-tenth of an ounce, and as a security gold can be easily included in fiduciary accounts like IRAs and other retirement plans. Disadvantages are the usual fears about not having physical possession in a time of extreme crisis, commission charges on transactions, corporate risk if your brokerage firm experiences financial problems, and the possibility of spreads based on premiums and discounts when bullion is bought or sold. Tax laws have viewed gold as a collectible and may apply unfavorable capital gains treatment to gold-backed securities.

As you may have surmised, gold bullion securities are the equivalent of exchange-traded funds, whereby the underlying value is physical gold. In fact, the World Gold Council introduced such securities, appropriately called Gold Bullion Securities, which were available in Australia and the United Kingdom. StreetTrack Gold Trust securities were recently introduced in the United States. The bullion used to back these securities is allocated. This means it is specifically held in trust for the shareholders. Allocated bullion may not be loaned, swapped, or hypothecated. The metal is segregated from unallocated bullion and is not associated with the custodian's inventory. No derivatives are written against allocated metal, and all bars are uniquely identifiable.

This form of gold is consistent with a subcategory or supercategory of metal-backed currency that floats against world currencies. In effect, the securities are priced in accordance with the fluctuating value of the underlying metal. Thus, it becomes extremely easy to include the equivalent of physical gold in a stock portfolio by simply acquiring gold ETFs. If your total investment portfolio is $250,000 and you want to allocate 10 percent to physical gold, you do not need to open a futures account, establish a depository account, buy coins, bars, or medallions. You simply buy the appropriate amount of Gold Bullion Securities. Of course, the purpose is to participate in gold's price fluctuation. There are no dividends and no earnings—just the price, whether up or down. This is why the initial public offering of StreetTrack Gold Trust did not have any impact on share prices. Any appreciation must be derived from gold.

I must congratulate the World Gold Council on its initiative in introducing the first liquid gold-backed ETFs. In a phrase, "It's about time." Earlier in this book, I discuss the decline of precious metals, and particularly gold, as economic indicators and/or financial benchmarks. Regardless of gold's performance or popularity, there should be facilities for carrying this former and perhaps future monetary standard as an asset. I believe gold-backed ETFs will add considerable overall strength to the market.

While I believe ETFs in other metals will emerge, I was not aware of any as I was researching this material. There were suggestions that a silver-backed ETF was appropriate based on the same principles applying to gold. This begs the question, "Why not platinum and palladium?" Based on the size of investor participation and historical balance between supply and demand, I sense that the platinum-group metals are not as prone to the ETF construct. ETFs require industry support. The platinum-group industry is not inclined to encourage overspeculation.

We see the results of minor supply dislocations. Palladium can reach above $1,000, as can platinum.

GOLD ACCOUNTS

Some banks and institutions offer gold accounts whereby the bank acts as custodian for physical metal. These accounts can draw upon allocated gold, as previously described, or unallocated gold. The more popular accounts use unallocated gold because it provides flexibility for the custodian and investor.

Unlike physical holdings and ETFs, gold accounts frequently offer leveraged holdings whereby the investor only puts a margin deposit down for the gold. Granted, an ETF can be purchased on margin, but the margin pertains to all holdings within the brokerage account. Gold accounts can have many different fee and interest rate schedules. Unallocated gold can be loaned, hypothecated, and leveraged. This adds a level of risk to these accounts. Institutions offering such accounts maintain that the added risk is hypothetical because of investment policies and the balance sheet behind the firms. I caution that anything can happen. If the purpose of owning gold is as a hedge against crisis, what would be the condition of the custodian during such a crisis? Further, unallocated gold is lumped in with all assets. This could be a concern for the highly conservative investor.

PLATINUM AND PALLADIUM

Like gold and silver, platinum and palladium are minted as coins of the realm. Palladium does not have the diversity of the other metals because investor interest has not been as strong. However, there are some palladium coins like the Russian Ballerina and Portuguese 100 Escudos palladium proof coin. Platinum and palladium coins, medallions, and bars are the most popular methods of participating in physical metal.

I touch upon the cold fusion theme once again to make the point for owning physical platinum or palladium. As described, they are very unusual metals with unique and even strange properties. In all probability, we have hardly scratched the surface of their full potential. If some groundbreaking, world-shaking discovery were to be made, it might be impossible to participate in the enormous profit potentials unless you already have some physical inventory.

CONCLUSION

There are very sound reasons for investing in physical metal, as described in this chapter. In the beginning pages of this book, I mentioned the most fundamental incentive for having real honest-to-goodness gold, silver, platinum, and palladium. Putting financial appreciation potential aside, it just looks good and feels great. Again, I urge all who have not had a personal encounter with the real thing to do so!

CHAPTER 12

Projections

Any long-term forecast is simply a conjuration of best guesses based on current facts. If there is anything constant about precious metals markets, it is their propensity for dramatic and fundamental change. Precious metals are emotional investments. Value is based on a dual standard rooted in rarity and utility. This book has attempted to separate fact from desire to provide an objective view of the four most popular investment metals. This is an important endeavor because of the tendency to romanticize these markets and lose reasonable objectivity. My personal experience spans the prohibition of U.S. gold ownership only through its emancipation in 1975. I am not a product of the Great Depression nor have I had the pleasure of gold coinage in my pocket (yet). My exposure to the first half of the twentieth century is based on discussions with those who were there and my review of associated documentation. For whatever their value, I became aware of precious metals during the transition from asset-backed currency to floating exchange. Having seen how the structure of precious metals markets can change, I must be cautious about offering predictions.

Indeed, the historical perspective on which investors might rely is brief. Gold and silver have only recently become commodities without monetary ties. Platinum and palladium were just coming of age in the late 1970s. Everything from how people use precious metals to investors' very perception has been challenged. Production technology has advanced as well as exploration techniques. Vast new territories are opening. New government structures are forming. Global communication is expanding, and wealth accumulation is no longer restricted to post–World War II industrialized nations.

All these changes are bound to impact precious metals. The ultimate question is, "How?" As bold as any prediction might seem, I believe there is a pattern. The pivotal event that converted gold into money was supply expansion during the mercantile period. When sufficient gold could be circulated, it assumed a place along with silver as nations' monetary foundations. Once world economies expanded more rapidly than gold and silver supplies, the monetary link had to be broken.

Humanity has endured the Stone Age, Bronze Age, Middle Ages, mercantilism, the industrial revolution, rapid transit, the communication age, the electronic revolution, and the information age. Each represented a structural change that broke old rules and formed new guidelines. With the information age, there is a global awareness of modern society, politics, products, and services. It is as easy for a student in China to observe the latest toys in the Sharper Image catalog as it is for the customer in New York City or Chicago. The Internet takes us well beyond the communication age represented by the telephone, television, and radio. We are exchanging and processing information, conducting transactions, and monitoring the world. At the same time, technology is altering living standards almost daily.

Although I have discouraged the idea of returning to a gold standard, I offer these snippet observations to provide a ray of hope to die-hard gold and silver bugs. It's possible we will return to some form of hard-asset monetary standard. Consider trends toward consolidation. We see consolidation of currencies and markets. We see consolidation through corporate mergers and acquisitions. We see political consolidation. At some stage, the easiest way to consolidate monetary systems is to pick a standard. The standard will be defined by a world community consisting of government organizations subject to human tendencies. While the "Group of 5" or "Group of 7" or "Group of 20" may have dictated monetary relationships, such control has historically been temporary. What is the possibility the world will return to gold or silver to establish values and parity?

CHANCES OF PRECIOUS METALS AS FUTURE RESERVES

If the rate of silver and gold production begins to substantially exceed consumption, I believe there may be strong incentives to return to fixed standards. There will be issues of trust as the Third World industrializes, China capitalizes, and Russia democratizes. There will be concerns about cyber transactions and computerized bank accounts. Although there are predictions for a violent return to gold and silver in the form of a paper crash, I am not sure this must be the form of transition. The amazing tool for disseminating information over the Internet and by television can be used to reintroduce silver coinage and gold-backed transactions. Just as the closing of the gold window did not bring disaster, the reopening of negotiated gold or silver instruments should not upset the system. The process may already be under way in the form of gold securities or ETFs as we have reviewed.

Why would we return to gold or silver? In the absence of monetary panic, a metals standard must be convenient. If gold and silver become cheap, they can be as convenient as alternative metals and paper currencies. If inventories can be logged and tracked electronically, hard assets offer a measure of security that becomes convenient because fear is not healthy for active world markets.

Trends in supply and demand reviewed in this book suggest silver and gold are on track for the same expansion seen during the original Gold Rush. Massive amounts of new metal may become available and a market must be developed if the industry is to survive. The most stable market is monetary absorption. Demographics allow alternatives. There is always a chance cultural demand from China, India, and the Pacific Rim will match supply. If this develops, monetary applications may be held in check.

Without new demand, I do not see effective ways to offset the progress of digital photography against silver halide film or the sizable expansion in world gold output. Even with outside projections for electronics, thermal and reflective treatments, chemical processes, and other industrial applications, the equations do not assure bull markets.

If metals are monetized, speculative roles will diminish. However, mining stocks can become as solid as utilities. Once value parity is properly established, producers will have assured markets with absolute profit margins. Thereafter, volume and efficiency will distinguish between the better and less desirable companies. Systems for storing and tracking metal will be needed. Where there is a need, there is an investment opportunity. All businesses related to precious metals will derive some benefit from the stability of monetary roles. This means that there will still be opportunities for gain. The approach will be different.

It is difficult to predict whether nations will see central banks divest before any new standard is established or whether reserve assets will be held as an insurance policy. International agreements point to eventual divestiture. As long as there are treasury hoards, there will be a monetary relationship with the stored metal. Sometimes you have to temporarily give up a relationship to save a marriage. Perhaps this will be the next chapter in the dynamic life of silver and gold.

Certainly, the formation of unified markets in Europe, the Americas, and the Far East began a process of gold divestiture marked by central bank sales from Portugal and Belgium to Australia. The 1997 price depression that overwhelmed gold and silver was aided by pronouncements that metal was being converted into money. Both the sale of Australian gold and the potential of revaluing German reserves as a monetary ploy demonstrated the continuation of gold's role as a monetary instrument.

I would not be surprised if a massive reallocation of central bank reserves takes place before hints of a new monetary role surface. Money must circulate. When gold is in central bank vaults, it cannot act as money. With metal discoveries in virtually every corner on earth, I am optimistic that we can reestablish bonds with precious metals without economic dislocation. In other words, nations that have in-ground reserves will not necessarily dominate as economic powerhouses. Instead, we will see a smooth flow of new metal to market in conjunction with diversified exchanges of previously existing supplies.

FUTURE USES IN INDUSTRY

Platinum and palladium are likely to march to different drummers. Prospects for expanding industrial applications seem encouraging. Even if there is a move away from auto catalysts, there appear to be enough new applications to fill any consumption void over time. I like to dream. The possibility of platinum fuel cells or palladium energy anomalies is sufficient incentive for me to accumulate some of these metals. No, I am not inclined to bet the farm. It is not necessarily a good idea to store a thousand ounces under your bed or even in an expensive safe-deposit box. A small collection can ride the wave if exciting new technologies develop.

The electronic explosion will be a massive force driving the demand side of precious metals. I cannot speak about the next developments in electro-polymers and any potential to encroach on silver, gold, platinum, or palladium. By 2005, there were still no viable replacements for metals in electronic components. I believe there is a consensus that electronics are a growth sector that will take precious metals along for a strong demand ride. Demographics suggest untapped demand is enormous. Wealth patterns confirm demographics.

So there may never be a return to metal as a monetary standard, but it may never matter. Gold, silver, platinum, and palladium are still on a technological fast track for industrial usage. From an investment standpoint, the more the speculative opportunity without monetary linkage, the better!

A true follower of precious metals must study geology, technology, geography, demographic patterns, politics, economics, and history. Gold, silver, platinum, and palladium can take you down fascinating roads. Read about cutting-edge science and all four metals are there. Pick up any electronic device and most will be within the components. Observe the open Middle East markets—gold is there. People's lives have been, and will continue to be, surrounded and influenced by precious metals. I encourage you to read more, study more—and perhaps buy more, just in case. However, always try to be objective and avoid the spell precious metals can often cast!

Periodic Table of Elements

As elements progress in atomic weight they frequently become more rare. Each of the precious metals has unique characteristics that add to its individual value. The Periodic Table helps to describe these characteristics and certain chemistry aspects associated with each element.

Rh (#45)   Rhodium
Pd (#46)   Palladium
Ag (#47)   Silver
Pt (#78)   Platinum
Au (#79)   Gold

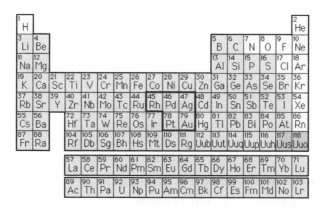

Weights and Measures

1 ounce avoirdupois =	437.5 grains
	28.3495 grams
	0.91146 ounces troy
	0.06250 pounds avoirdupois
	0.02835 kilograms
1 pound avoirdupois =	453.592 grams
	16 ounces avoirdupois
	14.5833 ounces troy
	1.21528 pounds troy
	0.4536 kilograms
1 ounce troy =	480 grains
	31.1035 grams
	1.0971 ounces avoirdupois
	20 pennyweights
	0.08333 pounds troy
	0.06857 pounds avoirdupois
1 pound troy =	5,760 grains
	373.242 grams
	12 ounces troy
	0.82286 pounds avoirdupois
	0.37324 kilograms

1 ordinary ounce = 0.9155 troy ounces

1 ordinary pound = 14.58 troy ounces

Avoirdupois Weights and Conversions

$27^{11}/_{32}$ grains = 1 dram

16 drams = 1 ounce

16 ounces = 1 pound

1 pound = 7,000 grains

14 pounds = 1 stone (U.K.)

100 pounds = 1 hundredweight (U.S.)

112 pounds = 8 stone = 1 short ton (U.S.)

2,240 pounds = 1 long ton (U.K.)

160 stone = 1 long ton

20 hundredweight = 1 ton

1 pound = 0.4536 kilograms

1 hundredweight = 45.359 kilograms

1 short ton = 907.18 kilograms

1 long ton = 1,016.05 kilograms

Metric Weights

1,000 grams = 1 kilogram

100 kilograms = 1 quintal

1 tonne = 1,000 kilograms = 10 quintals

1 kilogram = 2.240622 pounds

1 quintal = 220.462 pounds

1 tonne = 2,204.6 pounds

1 tonne = 1.102 short tons

1 tonne = 0.9842 long ton

Karat

Karat = gold purity in parts per 24

100 percent pure = 24 karat = 1,000 fine

91.7 percent pure = 22 karat = 917 fine

75 percent pure = 18 karat = 750 fine

58.5 percent pure = 14 karat = 585 fine

41.6 percent pure = 10 karat = 416 fine

Index

Printed and bound by CPI Group (UK) Ltd, Croydon, CR0 4YY

16/04/2025

14658501-0004